So Farewell Then

The Untold Life of Peter Cook

So Farewell Then

The Untold Life of Peter Cook

Wendy E. Cook

HarperCollins*Entertainment*
An Imprint of HarperCollins*Publishers*

This book is dedicated to our daughters,
Lucy and Daisy.
Also to Peter's sisters Sarah and Elizabeth.

HarperCollins*Entertainment*
An Imprint of HarperCollins*Publishers*
77–85 Fulham Palace Road,
Hammersmith, London W6 8JB

www.harpercollins.co.uk

Published by HarperCollins*Entertainment* 2006
1

A catalogue record for this book is
available from the British Library

ISBN-10 0-00-722893-7
ISBN-13 978-0-00-722893-5

Set in Sabon by
Rowland Phototypesetting Ltd,
Bury St Edmunds, Suffolk

Printed and bound in Great Britain by
Clays Ltd, St Ives plc

Contents

Acknowledgements

It is with deep gratitude that I would like to thank all those friends who made themselves available to relive bygone times spent with Peter and me. It has been such a real pleasure and a cathartic journey as well.

Thanks then to: Elizabeth Cook, Peter's sister, Elizabeth Luard, the late Harry Thompson, who despite his serious illness insisted on doing our interview, even in hospital – his biography of Peter has been a great help; to Simon Gough, who encouraged me to write many years ago; to Bruce Copp, manager of The Establishment, who came to meet me in Mallorca and filled our days with vivid memories of that extraordinary time; to old Cambridge friends, Christopher Booker, Colin Bell, Jack Altman, Glenys Roberts, Peter and Melanie Rouse, Roger Law, Rosemary Myers, Annie (Watt) Wingfield, Helen Nichol and to Peter's schoolfriend from Radley, Michael Bawtree, and to the friend and neighbour of the teenage Peter, Dr Jenifer Elton-Williams (née Platt); to *Beyond the Fringe* colleagues Sir Jonathan Miller and Alan Bennett and to John Bassett, who talent-scouted The Four Fringers; to Dudley's first wife, Suzy Kendall, and to Establishment friends, Eleanor Bron, Roddy Maude-Roxby, Christopher Logue, Jean Hart, Paul McCartney, Adrian and Celia Mitchell, Venetia Parkes (née Mooreshead), Anneke Gough, Nick Garland and Harriet

Garland, Gaye Brown, Barbara and Terry Downes; to Gay Gottleib and to Nathan Silver, who 'gave me away' at my wedding in New York, and Caroline Silver, his ex, who accompanied me to the divorce court! To Laura Eastwood, friend from Mallorca, and to my children's nanny, Sue Newling-Ward.

To Lucy, my daughter, who braved the cobwebs in the loft and emerged with an amazing trawl of photos and letters and ephemera that I didn't know I still had. (To Daisy, my daughter, to say that our children are our real teachers.)

For help with providing photos, John Bulmer, Lewis Morley, Christopher Angeloglou, Ian Fleming, Peter Goodliffe and to Mike Alexander for scanning. For their strategic aid and technical skills, to John Elliott and John Platt and, certainly not least, to Susan Hannis, who painstakingly and efficiently typed up and polished my original handwritten manuscript.

To Vanessa Thorpe, who somehow brought this project about and who has collaborated with me through the duration, patiently editing my 50-odd interviews and judiciously incorporating them into my narrative. Always cheerful and positive, it has been a real pleasure to work with her.

Finally then, to Ben Dunn, who saw the potential in my synopsis and signed me up and to Monica Chakraverty, who then took over the project to midwife its ultimate birth.

Preface by Elizabeth Luard

YSTRAD MEURIG, Cardigan, 2006

(In 1963 the food writer and columnist Elizabeth Luard, author of European Peasant Cookery *(1986) and* Family Life: Birth, Death and the Whole Damn Thing *(1997), married Nicholas Luard, co-proprietor with Peter Cook of The Establishment Club.)*

Memory is like flypaper – things stick to it, refusing to be dislodged – so I haven't looked to others for confirmation of what I remember of those days when I knew Peter Cook. Then again, so many people have told the tale of how *Private Eye* began – how it was first published, a scrappy yellow rag, the bastard son of *Parsons' Pleasure*, an undergraduate jape – but after that, well, memories diverge.

I went to work for *Private Eye* soon after the first issues appeared. For a young woman of that time – the late 1950s and early 1960s – there were few options other than marriage as a means to gain her freedom. Mine was to move out of my allotted circle – young men who bought their way into Lloyd's and the debutantes they married – and head for more dangerous waters. I took employment at the *Eye* as stamp-licker, typist, bookkeeper, dogsbody – nothing intellectual. This brought me into the orbit of the stars of that time, Peter Cook and Nicholas Luard, owners and begetters of The Establishment, a Soho theatre club which took its subversive lead from the Berlin nightclubs of the 1930s. Wendy married Peter, I married Nicholas.

I should explain how it was. There were three underclasses in that post-war world: the young, the workers and the women. The young sang protest songs, the workers went on strike, the women . . . well, we had the vote and we (eventually) had the Pill, but we hadn't yet got the message. Women of my generation took our status from our men – husband, father, employer. We were born into a paternalistic society locked into its own certainties. We grew into adulthood liberated, as we were, by the Pill, but not yet certain that sexual freedom could be translated into something more valuable – political and economic power. We couldn't open bank accounts, take out mortgages or claim passports unless some man (husband, father, legal guardian – take your pick) agreed to act as guarantor. The changes which took place in the sixties – political and social – were not particularly designed to be of use to women. For that we had to find a voice. We found it in sisterhood, in the writings of Germaine Greer, Kate Millett and all the other women who spoke for us, the underclass. We're not there yet, but we're heading in the right direction: our daughters, happily, don't know how hard we had to fight to get as far as we've come.

Our mothers – most of them anyway – found freedoms during wartime of which we daughters of the brave new world could only dream. And if hadn't been for the men we married, we'd still be dreaming. The *Zeitgeist* was on our side. Earthquakes happen where there is pressure along a fault line. And we, the young women of that time, needed something seismic to happen. Fortunately for us there were young men of our generation, our brothers – our own or other people's – who knew the world must change. Small things came first: jokes, comedy talk, a thousand people on a march to ban the bomb. And when small things change, everything changes. For many of us, uneducated by design (marriageable girls didn't talk back), the cracks through which we glimpsed the daylight were fashioned by the men we loved or married.

Matrimonially, some of us were more fortunate (or stubborn) than others. Wendy, married to Peter a year or two before I married Nicholas, made the choice to leave her marriage – not easily, with two young daughters to bring to adulthood. I stayed the course – forty years and some – though with four children and an unreliable income that wasn't straightforward either. Dangerous men are never easy, but most of all they're a danger to themselves.

Introduction

DARTINGTON, Devon: 2006

The idea of writing about my life with Peter remained, despite offers from publishers, no more than an idea for some time. Life was too full and the project too difficult, even painful in parts. I did not particularly want to rake over the coals for the sake of family and friends, because it was not all a laugh, I have to say.

However, over the years several one-sided and, to my mind, erroneous portrayals of my ex-husband have appeared in the press and media, and recently on television and on stage too, spurring me into reconsidering the challenge. Representations of the working relationship between Peter and Dudley Moore, in particular, are often quite unrecognisable.

My time with Peter constituted an extraordinary period in my life, set as it was in the context of the social and political upheaval of the late 1950s and 1960s. We met as students at Cambridge, married and spent twelve years together, during which time Peter's career as satirist/writer/performer reached its zenith. We had two beautiful daughters and lived through a time when many taboos were destroyed – a process which, once begun, knew no bounds. Peter Cook was in the front line. What were the conditions that allowed this young man, himself a 'son of Empire', to stand up in front of a packed theatre audience, including the Prime Minister of the day, Harold Macmillan, and have the temerity to stray from the prepared script into lengthy, unflattering pastiches of Macmillan, trapped in his seat before him? Peter's co-stars suffered apoplexy. Few young people today would appreciate just how outrageous this was then. Tony Blair has to put up with a lack of deference all the time, but Peter was the first.

My memories were still vivid, so I agreed to meet Harper-Collins editor Ben Dunne and journalist Vanessa Thorpe, who had recently interviewed me. We had lunch at the White Hart in Dartington, Devon, where I live, and we seemed to be in agreement over the treatment of such a memoir, placed firmly in the context of those years of expansion and upheaval. As we walked in Dartington's beautiful gardens Vanessa's mobile rang; there followed a somewhat enigmatic conversation. When it ended, Vanessa, looking a little bemused, said, 'That was Rainbow George. He only rings me about once a year.' Rainbow George had been Peter's neighbour and drinking buddy, with whom he had emptied many a bottle while tape-recording their extravagant and drunken flights of fantasy. I thought: 'Funny!', as Dudley might have said.

Having agreed to write the book, it was clear I would need to look up some of our old friends and colleagues. So many of them had gone, but we tracked down a fair number, finding them only too happy to recall some really splendid accounts of the magical times we shared, often around our dinner table in Hampstead.

The journey began with Bruce Copp, the manager of The Establishment club, a great character now in his eighties and living in Barcelona, but still with a flinty memory of startling and amusing clarity. Others too have kindly met up with me to restoke the fires of memory: Jonathan Miller, Alan Bennett,

Eleanor Bron, Christopher Logue, Elizabeth Luard, Christopher Booker, Paul McCartney and Suzy Kendall (Dudley's first wife). One morning I found myself standing once again on the doorstep in Duncan Terrace, Islington, of Jay and Fran Landesman, watching Jay (well into his eighties) driving away in his ancient white Bentley to sell it that very day. I had crossed this threshold on many occasions with Peter; we spent one evening there with Christine Keeler and another with Barbra Streisand. Jay and Fran were an extrovert couple of American club owners and songwriters who really hit the London scene running with their 'hip' language and publicly open marriage. Now Fran's eyesight has deteriorated but her memory is brimful with colourful people, Lenny Bruce, Mort Sahl, John Lennon among them. These were real celebrities, real icons who found fame and notoriety because they were extraordinary, not through some clever packaging.

And so it began, a wonderful, interesting and cathartic pilgrimage, retracing steps and mining hilarious memories – magic evenings long ago, but remembered by so many people with relish, during which we had shared wine, food and wit. There are also many friends out there who I have not been able to find my way to, but they live on in my memory. All these voices have contributed a measure to my story, for which I am extremely grateful.

Some of the sides of Peter that I reveal may not be recognized, but then again I do not altogether recognize some of the descriptions that others come up with. It only goes to show that nobody is a fixed entity; the enigmatic Peter Cook is less fixed than most. My perception is that we are all like musical instruments – some more in tune than others – and that the music we bring out of each other is unique to that particular constellating pair or group. So it was with Peter and Wendy: great symphonies sometimes and junk-band sounds at others.

I think that most people should be given the opportunity to put their past into perspective and to see their youth through the mellow eyes of their autumn years. My work has included training in giving biographical workshops, which has been invaluable for viewing my own biography. I so often hear (usually from young people) the defiant cry 'It's my life', and yet, when it comes to removing layers to find out who one might have been if one hadn't met such and such a person, we realize that the very fabric of our lives is fashioned from our relationships with others.

What would my life have been if I had not met Peter? What would his life have been if he had not met me? Difficult to say. One thing is certain: we would not have had Lucy and Daisy Cook and that would have been a great shame!

A 'Child of Empire' in Devon

Opening the scuffed cover of an old copy of the authorised version of the Apocrypha one afternoon, I discovered I was somehow in possession of Peter's schoolboy edition. As I flicked through, layer upon layer of thoughts about his early life began to take shape in my head. On the inside flap I saw the price paid, 4s 6d, and underneath was written, like a strange code from another age, 'also available in superior binding, French morocco, gilt edges, 10s 6d'. Spelled out in ink on the flyleaf was the name 'P. E. Cook'. It was a child's handwriting, not yet the illegible scrawl it was to become. The book had clearly been used, the pages certainly well turned. I tried to picture the young boy with a super-fertile imagination reading in church, or in RE lessons:

> Esdras 11: Then saw I a dream and behold, there came up from the sea an eagle which had twelve feathered wings and three heads.
> And behold, she spread her wings over all the earth and all the winds of the air blew upon her . . .

All the ingredients for future wordplay! These were the epic images forged in that young soul, later to emerge, metamorphosed, channelled by his inimitable comic personas.

I remembered how Peter and Dudley had us all convulsed one Christmas in New York as they listed the ludicrous contents of their version of the Dead Sea Scrolls and I could well imagine when the seeds for these jokes had been planted. The same kind of religious imagery had been part of my own childhood too, but I took it a lot more seriously. What, I wondered, had made this clever boy so entertainingly irreverent? Certainly, his background was very different from mine.

The arrival of Margaret Cook's first baby, weighing eight and three-quarter pounds, on 17 November 1937, was as uplifting an event as any mother could hope for. Margaret noted in a letter at the time that he was, from the beginning, a remarkable little boy. 'He has quantities of mouse-coloured hair, lovely deep blue eyes – set quite far apart, quite long eyelashes and the beginnings of eyebrows, which he lifts rather cynically at the world.'

But the joy felt by this doting mother, secure in her home by the sea in Devon, must already have been tinged with a dark sense of the sacrifices that lay ahead. The mewling Peter Edward Cook might well be adorable, but when he reached the age of just seven months he was to be left in the care of others. Margaret would, she knew, be expected to join her husband in Africa. Out in Nigeria, serving as the District Officer in the Calabar region, Alec Cook was eagerly awaiting the return of his wife – but without their new baby son. Nigeria was not thought a suitable place for an infant to be brought up. It seems strangely cruel now – probably it seemed so even then – but the accepted practice in the colonial middle classes was for a young wife to put duty to her husband before her bond with a new child.

So in the summer of 1938, at the end of Alec's four-month leave in England, the couple set out for West Africa together and the infant Peter was handed over to his maternal grandmother. In Torquay Granny Mayo, as she was known, organized the care of her grandson, with the help of other female relatives and professional nannies. Alec and Margaret Cook did not see Peter for another year.

Although Margaret's dutiful action – this leaving of her tiny child – seems extraordinary to me now, and tempts one to put many of her son's later problems with relationships neatly down to this, I do have to acknowledge that Margaret managed to keep her family together. In fact, she created a very strong, almost adamantine, wall of mutual loyalty around them that survives to this day – twelve years after her own death, never mind that of her famous son.

Margaret's own parents' marriage had been unhappy and Elizabeth Cook, Peter's youngest sister, still suspects this was a big factor in her mother's decision to leave her new baby. 'I think she was very torn as her parents hadn't had a good marriage.' She had simply wanted to give her life with Peter's father the best chance she could. Margaret, academically gifted as a child, was the daughter of an Eastbourne solicitor and had worked on the Continent as a governess before she married. A frustrated intellectual in many ways, she was an impressive woman. When Jonathan Miller was introduced to her years later, just as he and Peter were poised on the edge of fame, he says she reminded him of Margaret Dumont, the actress who played the straight role in the Marx Brothers' films. Like many respectable women of her era, her style of dress was redoubtable.

Alan Bennett also remembers Mrs Cook as an imposing figure. 'I was rather terrified of her,' he recalled.

Elizabeth describes her mother as 'a real Christian'. Although not a deeply religious woman, Margaret prayed every night, on her knees. She also had a creative urge, but 'didn't know quite where to put it, necessarily', and reached out for methods of self-expression. Elizabeth's fondest memories of her mother are of long walks together in Devon when the family had returned to Britain for a while. 'Mum was a great walker. There was a lovely five-mile walk we used to do to pick up clotted cream. She used to introduce me to wild flowers along the way.'

In spite of the fact that Elizabeth, the youngest of three, was the only Cook sibling to enjoy her parents' physical presence for most of her childhood, she recalls now that even she used to be hungry for their attention and quite jealous of any competition. 'I used to go on walks with one or the other of them, rather than together,' she says. 'Maybe I was rather a possessive child, so I would like having each of them to myself.'

Peter met his father, Alec, for the first time when he was three months old and this set the pattern for their relationship. They didn't really see each other regularly until Peter was old enough to join his parents abroad during school holidays.

Alec was, according to Elizabeth, a 'very modest man' with a strong sense of order. 'His bedroom was always very ship-shape. He didn't have many possessions. There was always a little pile of handkerchiefs folded to look like sandwiches in the drawer. He didn't own very much and nor did he want to own very much.' But his doting youngest daughter also remembers a funny man, with 'a sort of whimsical sense of humour'. 'He liked making up silly rhymes and funny dances,' she says.

Alec also was an enthusiastic home-movie maker and some of his domestic footage, shot in Devon, gives a good idea of the emerging personality of his little son. I watched a sequence of this film recently with our daughters, Lucy and Daisy. It was filmed on one of Alec's rare visits and Peter is seen trailing behind the gardener with his own little trowel, turning over earth to examine worms or centipedes, and watching grasshoppers. Insects and small creatures fascinated him: newts, or tadpoles fattening into frogs. Minutiae, the tiny details, were always important in the way he thought and wrote.

Seven years after Peter's birth, Alec and Margaret's second child, Sarah, was born. Margaret travelled back to England to have the baby. A hard-working employee of the Humanitarian Society for many years, as well as a talented singer, Sarah has an unusual, clever mind and an admirable philanthropic passion. All the Cook children were remarkable, I feel, although perhaps it would have been hard to spot it from the conventional external appearance of the family. People who know Elizabeth today regard her as unorthodox and charismatic, quite aside from any interest they may have in who her brother was. An established poet, she is also the acclaimed author of an unusual piece of fiction, *Achilles*, which revolves around the legendary Greek hero. Venetia Parkes, a former *Private Eye* employee and a friend I share with Elizabeth, puts it well: 'There is that calm thing to her that is very attractive. Elizabeth is one of the most intriguing people I have ever met. There is a magnetism to her.' Alan Bennett, who knows her work, is also a fan. 'I loved her book on Achilles. It was a wonderful book. A poetic book.'

Perhaps the individual talents of the children were inspired by what Elizabeth characterizes as the 'intellectual confidence' of their father. There was also the lurking influence of a sad secret in the family's history, as there is in so many families. Alec's father, Edward Cook, had committed suicide, shooting himself with a revolver one May evening in 1914. Nobody quite knew why he did it. Elizabeth has been told that a promotion at work (he was a manager with the Malayan railways) had led to attacks of anxiety, but, as she points out, 'There is no clear evidence that this was the reason. It might have been that he was finding it hard to be away from his wife and children. I don't think it was just his job.' His sibling, Peter's aunt, was badly affected by the secrecy, if not the death. 'Looking back, I think they unconsciously knew about it in some way, although they were never told how their father had died. There was a great shame about suicide in those days and the shock waves go on reverberating.' Every family has its skeleton in the cupboard, but I think the cultivation of secrets was something the young Peter learned to use as a shield.

Nevertheless, the colonial life, and the strong sense of responsibility that goes with it at its best, provided the framework for Alec Cook's way of living too. His job in Nigeria was not just a job: it defined him and, as his wife, Margaret must have understood that. Elizabeth thinks that 'guilt' is too modern a word to describe how her mother coped with leaving her first-born back in England. 'I think "real sadness" would have been her words, and "regret",' she says. 'It was more like a deep sorrow which she and Peter shared and which was ineradicable.' Her mother 'just adored' Peter, Elizabeth recalls. 'It was a dreadful thing for her, but it was very much batten down the hatches and do what you should do. She really felt she had to.'

If there was a hidden emotional legacy for Peter, the effects of the split showed themselves plainly in Margaret's lifelong dislike of Nigeria. 'Because there was so little for her in Nigeria it must have been particularly hard,' Elizabeth thinks. 'And because of the way Mum was, bright and bookish – to have so little to feed those sides of her must have been difficult. What she really hated about Nigeria, though, was the separation it caused her from her children.'

In an attempt to exorcise some of these family demons Elizabeth told me she went out to Nigeria herself in the early nineties. She stayed with friends and found the Cook family home. During her stay, however, back in England her mother remained 'absolutely terrified' and suddenly became quite ill.

Peter managed to reach his little sister on her travels by telephone and suggested she came back, just in case. 'Mother had thought it was a very unsafe place for me to go on my own. It was irrational, I mean it really wasn't a very safe place actually, so there was some reason for her fears, but there was also a feeling that this was the country that had gobbled up her children, so she was scared. I think she was frightened by it because she was so unfree there, so unautonomous and so trapped. She just felt she was in the wrong place for so much of the time. Dad was out working all day and there she was with very little to do.'

The separation from his mother had a lasting impact on Peter, of that Elizabeth is fairly certain. There are hints of this continual feeling of 'something missing' in elements of his comedy; in the ludicrous but melancholy phrase 'I was an only twin', for instance.

Elizabeth believes her brother felt incomplete: 'I think a lot of children have this feeling of a missing other half, but I also think Peter did suffer very much from the separation as a child. It wasn't the simple key to him; he was heartbroken though.'

Peter could lampoon the mores of the gentry with ease, but, although his own family background somewhat daunted me, it was actually upper middle class, or even middle middle class, in truth. There was a gentility, respectability and even style, but there was no real financial security.

Elizabeth and I share a telling memory of her parents tearing up their breakfast toast rather than buttering it whole. This, she thinks, was an aspirational tick among well-to-do folk who effectively wanted to show they didn't need to stake ownership on a complete slice.

'It has gone down in history that we were rather a grand family,' Elizabeth complains. 'We weren't. We had never been a wealthy family. Dad had no money at all. His mum really struggled because she was bringing up two children. I don't know how she did it. I don't think there was any pension from her late husband. She took in lodgers. Dad was brought up largely by friends and he needed to earn money. He inherited nothing and when he died there was no money for anyone else to inherit. So he needed a job and it says something for his altruism that he chose something with a fairly modest income. A lot of contemporaries of his made more money by going into the City.'

Following his first stint in Nigeria, Alec Cook was posted to Gibraltar where he briefly took up the position of Financial Secretary to the colony. Unimpressed by pomp, Alec was some-one who appeared, at least to his children, to be interested only in helping things run smoothly. He took no personal pride in the idea of British international power. 'Empire' was for him not a good thing in and of itself, according to Elizabeth. 'He came to visit me when I was working in Leeds and he met a friend of mine, a Singaporean Chinese who specialized in post-colonial literature. They got on well and he would al-ways say to her, "When I was out in Nigeria propping up the Empire . . ." in an ironic way.'

She remembers attacking British imperialism when she was a 'stroppy adolescent' and in reaction he would be defensive about the colonial enterprise. 'I did not understand Dad's impulse to do this work, which I think now was genuinely idealistic and the equivalent of what Voluntary Service Over-seas work might be today.' Something of this idealism had taken seed in Peter too and it was this that drew me to him at Cambridge. Anyway, Elizabeth says, alongside his noble motivations, her father had actually shared some of her own doubts about the general impact of British involvement in Africa.

'He was torn between wondering whether it would have

been better, for instance, in Nigeria if the British presence had been a longer one, and gone on after independence, or whether it had been interference in the first place,' she says. Her trip to Nigeria as an adult was an attempt to find out what her father's work had been about.

'Dad didn't regard himself as an imperialist. He felt he was involved in local government. He was sorting out horrible things like twin murders, common there then because twins were thought to be inauspicious. He was a very conscientious man and he agonized over wanting to get things right. I remember in Nigeria there was a village fête and Dad had given me ten shillings, which was a lot of money in those days, and I lost it. Awful. I told him about it and he just gave me another. How wonderful! I had expected him to be cross and instead he was generous. He overheard me saying this later and said later he thought to himself, "Oh, I did the right thing." This was very much a quality of Dad, that he wanted to get it right and be just.'

That trait earned Alec the family nickname 'the sea-green incorruptible', once applied to Robespierre, and Peter was to fall foul of his father's scrupulous honesty on his last holiday visit to Gibraltar. He told me that when the family were leaving their home and driving back in the car, he secreted his most treasured belonging inside a teapot. It was a small turtle and he cradled the pot in his lap until they reached the border. Customs carried out a thorough search of the car and would have waved it through if it hadn't been for the incorruptible Alec, who gave the game away. The turtle was confiscated and Peter was bereft and inconsolable for some time. Elizabeth still remembers her father's integrity with pride. 'I rather liked his high standards. It makes life a lot clearer.'

By this time Peter was coping on his own at a prep school

in Eastbourne. St Bede's, a cliff-top cluster of buildings close to Beachy Head, was not far away from Grandfather Mayo's home, but the new boy got no comfort from this and apparently burst into tears at the railway station at the start of his first term. He eventually learned to cope with the bullying he suffered at St Bede's with the judicious use of sarcasm and by playing a lot of football, gaining quite a reputation as a sportsman. An obsession with football would remain with him.

Growing with the Brussels Sprouts

Among my mother's belongings is a yellowing letter, slipped inside the covers of the family Bible. It is in my father's unmistakable hand. A civil servant, just posted to Oxford, he was writing to my mother back in Manchester – the city where they had both been raised and had their first matrimonial home together. The letter was dated 1 September 1939. My mother would have been four months pregnant with me.

> Things look grave now, dear, and we'd better plan quickly.
> If war actually breaks out you must come down at the earliest possible moment. I'll look around for rooms, furnished, of course, to begin with, until we can make arrangements about the furniture.
>   . . . Please could you also send my laundry and socks and shoes now to this address but please, dear, do not get upset and don't try to do too much and put a strain on yourself, darling. Take your time . . . as I say, don't try to do too much at once, take things in a leisurely way. I hope that there is still a chance for peace, but it seems a faint chance. However if trouble comes we will not mind if we are together.
>
> All my love, Bill.

This was written on the day Hitler invaded Poland. Chamberlain's piece of paper promising peace was suddenly worthless. Two days later the whole country tuned in to hear the Prime Minister's announcement that, as there had been no reply to Britain's ultimatum, we were at war with Germany. 'Now may God Bless you all. May He defend the right.' These words were followed by the National Anthem. The mood was sombre; memories of the First World War had not yet faded. The threat of bombing and the possible use of poison gas prompted the distribution of millions of gas masks. More than three and a half million people relocated within a couple of months as it was thought imperative to move women and children out of the largest cities. There were half a million mothers with children under school age at the time and more than ten thousand expectant mothers, my mother being one of them.

My parents were accommodated at first in the leafy suburbs of Oxford, in the house where my father lodged. Most people with large houses were pressed into sharing them with evacuees. My parents, 'foreigners' from 'the North', were lucky to find good hosts, but those last months of pregnancy must still have been fraught. The winter was severe. Blackout descended and food was scarce. When war was declared Britain had but a month's supply of wheat and sugar. We were importing much of our food from our colonies, but German U-boats put a speedy end to this.

I was born on 19 January 1940 in Oxford's Radcliffe Infirmary. My mother's waters had broken over a week before, but no contractions came. When they did begin that night in the blackout, a threatened air raid meant medical staff were at a minimum. My mother had only a gas and oxygen mask as company. I think I must have been reluctant to be born into a world at war. When I eventually emerged I had jaundice. My mother, looking on the bright side, said I looked 'like a little peach, all yellow and pink!' I was named Wendy after J. M. Barrie's character in *Peter and Wendy*, for whom he created the name.

The winter continued to be fierce. My mother had to melt ice in order to get water to wash my nappies because the pipes were frozen. But my parents were young and still in love, it seems, and most people were experiencing the same difficulties. Their time together with a new baby did not last long as my father was posted to Hitchin, a small town in Hertfordshire. I don't think he had much choice. He mostly hated being a civil servant, yet was meticulous, usually bringing work home. He was a good cartoonist and would have liked to have been an artist, but he had known the Depression of the 1930s and the Jarrow hunger march, and was terrified of unemployment. So he took a secure job and clung to it.

My mother, with a four-month-old baby in her arms, now walked the streets of Hitchin finding us lodgings. We were billeted with the Hawkes family and were there for nearly four years. 'Auntie' Betty, a bosomy, generous woman, and 'Uncle' Bill, smaller than his wife, and their two children, Jack and Jane, took us into their family, so I had the equivalent of a new brother and sister. I remember a large garden with a swing and a sandpit. The two families pooled their ration books and shared the cooking and the childminding. We pulled together despite all the privations, the disturbing wail of the sirens and the constant fear of impending attacks.

I was a slightly built child, with dark hazel eyes and straight auburn hair, worn either in plaits or 'paintbrushes' and always festooned with crisp ribbons; a child who would stand and stare into the distance, trying to work things out. My mother was petite, but with a wonderful figure, blue-eyed and dark-haired. She looked very pretty when she found the time to dress up. She always wore lipstick and was quick in her movements.

Wendy as a four-year-old

When I was four my mother became pregnant again and my father was called to work in London. Once again my mother took to the task of knocking on doors. This time she wanted a place of her own. Her search led her to the little riverside village of Langford in Bedfordshire, only fifteen miles from the Hawkes's bustling home in Hitchin. Our new house had no bathroom or inside loo. There was a large copper boiler to heat the water and a black-leaded fireplace and range dominated the living room. Once part of a farm, it had many outbuildings and an acre of garden and an orchard which proved a saving grace; a place to grow our own food and for me to explore.

My mother was now alone with me and pregnant in a strange place, her husband sixty miles away in London at the most dangerous time of the war. He was charged with assessing families whose homes had been damaged or destroyed during bombing raids. A compassionate man, he often reached into his own pocket to help others, but these magnanimous gestures made it more difficult still for my mother, who was trying to manage on my father's meagre wages. It led to regular quarrels about our lack of funds. Thank God my mother was capable and creative. She made our clothes, knitted sweaters in complicated Fair Isle and cable stitch, ran up gossamer party dresses out of scraps of fabric, all embroidered with flowers. She had an immense gift for gardening too, a miracle considering she had been reared in the sooty suburbs of Manchester. (She was ninety when I asked her what her first memory was. She replied that as a child she had germinated an apple seed and had grown a little tree from it.)

Mother decorated the house and made the dank cottage bright. On regular visits to the market she would spot colourful fabric remnants which would be turned into cheerful looking curtains and cushions on her treadle sewing machine. Of course, with the blackout blinds in place these domestic details could not be seen from outside. I was routinely sent out to check that no chink of light was visible at night. Our trusty copper was continually on the boil, steaming up the windows upon which I amused myself by practising my drawing skills. My mother was not so amused, however, at having to clean them afterwards: the water was needed for washing clothes and for the weekly bath, when a tin tub would be placed before the fire. I would stay in there, splashing and watching the fire goblins, until I was hauled out and tucked into bed so that the adults could have their turn. I never, ever, saw my parents naked – something of a feat on their part, considering the enforced intimacy of our conditions.

Many people in the village did not have bathrooms, so there

was no social stigma, but having home-made clothes was something that I was made to feel bad about several times. The first and most memorable occasion was when my mother recycled an old, worn Union Jack into a pair of knickers. She considered this a patriotic act and I too was proud of them, although they were a bit itchy. I made the mistake of asking some visitors whether they would like to see them, exposing the knickers as I spoke, and they burst out laughing. I found this utterly humiliating and rushed out of the room in tears. I was four and clearly a sensitive soul.

The radio proved a great comfort during those long blackouts. I was allowed to stay up to keep my mother company. The gloom was lightened by Tommy Handley's radio broadcast *Itma* – 'It's That Man Again'. This was my introduction to satire. The show's irreverent humour sniped at officialdom and was incredibly popular. The 'Office of Twerps' working in the 'Ministry of Aggravation' resonated with a population constantly being cajoled to make more and more sacrifices to support the war effort. The dialogue of the legendary Mrs Mopp with her 'Can I do you now, Sir?' was peppered with sexual innuendo. When my father was around I would watch him become quite apoplectic with laughter. He appreciated the sending up of the kind of pompous and bumbling officials he encountered in the civil service.

Across the nation, ingenious efforts were being made to fox the enemy. Signposts and street names were removed in the countryside and didn't reappear for a long time. The *Beyond the Fringe* sketch about this, years later, captured the absurdity of it all and, until researching the period today, I hadn't realized the joke was so firmly based on fact. Britain's greatest domestic weapon, however, was the Home Guard, of which my father was a member, though thank heaven he never had to set forth with a rifle in his hand.

Women were showing they were capable of doing jobs that had been considered a man's prerogative and certainly my mother could do many things that a man might do. She had to. My father was in London, only returning at weekends. He put a brave face on it, but must have been traumatized by what he encountered after the various bombing raids. Every Saturday morning we would go to the bus stop to meet him. After a particularly dreadful air raid we would not know if he would be on the bus or not. We had no telephone and one's heart missed a beat at the sight of a telegram.

I do remember learning to skip on the way to the bus stop. Thrilled at the feeling of levity, I couldn't wait to show my dad. Seeing him get off the bus was such a joy and relief. He was a handsome man, slender, with reddish hair: a man who took great pride in being well turned out, with polished shoes, tweed suit and a felt trilby, which he always raised to greet ladies. Then we would all go down to the village shop to get the sweet ration. I'd watch transfixed as the shop scales shivered from side to side. 'Go on, put another one in,' I'd silently plead. Sometimes the assistant would notice and pop in an extra aniseed ball. Daddy would cut up the jelly babies and a Mars Bar into razor-thin slices and create a garden on a plate. I was careful not to disturb this wonderful mosaic too hurriedly, thereby beginning to practise the art of delayed gratification.

Daddy always told me a bedtime story when he was home. One of my favourites was the Princess and the Pea, the story of the princess who, despite mountains of mattresses and feather eiderdowns on her bed, could always detect the presence of a pea beneath them, placed there by her stepmother to test her sensitivity. For me this story has always served as a metaphor for detecting the untruths in life, beneath all the seduction of comfort and luxury. Fairy stories were an important part of my early childhood since I spent a fair amount of it in bed. The common childhood illnesses – measles, chicken pox, tonsillitis, mumps, whooping cough – would all be accompanied by raging fevers and often hallucinations too, where the wallpaper would turn into dragons and horrible goblins. I still remember the taste of quinine and other dreadful remedies. Coughing badly, especially in the winter, I suffered grim visits to Victorian, Dettol-drenched hospitals to have clanging X-rays taken, as the operator abandoned one for the safety of a protective screen. The X-rays showed up small TB patches on my lung. That meant more horrible medicine and confinement to barracks.

I was so thin as a result of all this that my mother found it distressing to bathe me. I was 'as skinny as a rabbit', she told me later when the danger had passed. To flesh me out, my anxious parents pooled the family protein ration to give me a portion of fish: a small and lonely piece of cod. The sacrifice placed in front of me, the tension was too much. I could not accept this piece of piety and sat there for what seemed like hours, full of resentment and stubbornness. In desperation, they sent me to my room.

Rationing and anxiety about food were to be an undercurrent throughout my childhood. I envisaged juggling those precious coupons in adult life and, in fact, ration books were still in use until I was fourteen. Government special supplies for children and pregnant women consisted of concentrated orange juice and cod-liver oil, which we had to hold our noses to take. Virol, a malt syrup, was given as a reward afterwards.

Often, if I was ill, supper would be a bowl of onions boiled in milk, a folk cure for fevers. Tripe and onions was a North Country favourite of my mother's. Sometimes we would dig up a few new potatoes and have a plate of vegetables with mint, or a slice of bread and dripping. Thank God for my mother's garden. There were plum trees, apple trees and a wonderful espalier pear tree, whose golden fruit, individually wrapped in tissue or old newspaper and stored in a great chest of drawers, would supply summer sweetness through the winter. There were blackcurrant and redcurrant bushes too. I loved making earrings by dangling these jewels over my ears. There were gooseberry bushes, fat marrows, peas and beans, lettuces, tomatoes, radishes and onions. It was a miracle to me, and still is today, that from a few packets of seeds you could grow a whole garden of wonderful produce. Harvesting and bottling would occupy a special time at the end of summer. I was already keen to get into the kitchen.

Next door was our landlady, Mrs Street, an elderly widow who lived with her bachelor brother, Mr King. Since Mrs Street was increasingly infirm my mother used to take her her supper every night and put her to bed. I imagine this kindness must have stemmed from my mother's northern upbringing, where community survival was dependent on neighbourliness. I used to help Mrs Street with her washing-up. We would gather all the tiny scraps of leftover soap together and place them in a special long-handled wire basket which you then agitated to produce foam. I would lose myself playing with those bubbles, whose fragile surfaces reflected rainbows. Mrs Street's house was full of untold numbers of Victorian knick-knacks which she allowed me to play with: a carnival glass, jars of coloured sand from Woburn Sands, a musical box and an articulated wind-up monkey. One day her brother came round to tell us a wounded swan had found its way to their garden from the river. His intention was to dispatch it – no mean feat considering he was an elderly gentleman – and he asked my mother whether she would be prepared to cook it. This would be a crime since swans, injured or not, we understood, belonged to His Majesty. Meat was at a premium, however, and so my mother agreed to undertake the cooking if he would pluck and gut the bird. These deliberations were conducted *sotto voce* so that I would not hear, but I fancied something was up. Complex manoeuvres to get the creature into the oven resulted in something rather grey being served in slices. It tasted unmistakably muddy and, given my fastidious palate at that time, I rejected it. The others soldiered on. They must have felt obliged to do so after all that effort. The remnants had to be buried for fear of reprisals. An experiment not to be repeated.

As sickly children do, I played on my own and developed my imagination in the garden. My cooking career began with mud pies, studded with dandelions and cowslips. I ran a post office in the bicycle shed, had a tea shop in the big barn where a snowy owl lived and my dolls had a hospital in another shed when they needed expert medical care. All of this kept me very busy. I did see nature spirits too; they were a total reality for me. They appeared in those numinous moments of silence and showed themselves as part of a throbbing, pulsating network of colour and movement of which I was an integral part. Such moments comforted and sustained me.

At night, in the darkness of the blackout, there would be sirens and unseen threats sending me scurrying into a dark cupboard under the stairs with my little stool, alone and wearing a Mickey Mouse gas mask that smelled revolting and promised to suffocate me with no help from the Germans. For my mother, now six months pregnant, it must have been pretty frightening too. She coped well, chopping wood, bringing in coal, doing the washing and putting it through the mangle. She had that acre of garden to look after as well. At the weekend she played the piano exquisitely. She and my father, both of whom had been members of an operatic society in Manchester, would get together and sing their favourites. Their lives had been full of activities before the war; as well as attending art and music classes, they belonged to tennis and rambling clubs.

My father even had his own car, a beautiful Daimler. All that gone, it must have been depressing for my parents to find themselves surrounded by cabbage fields and 'people with the mentality of Brussels sprouts', as my father condescendingly described the locals. My father complained, but my mother made the best of it.

The Americans joined the war in 1941 and the summer of 1944 saw the decisive D-Day invasion of Normandy. This marked the high noon of what sometimes felt like the American occupation of Britain. Across the Atlantic, the anti-British lobby in the US was asking why America should be protecting and sustaining that anachronism the British Empire. In Langford, as Christmas approached, there was little money with which to celebrate. Toys were only for the rich, but my resourceful mother wouldn't let that be an obstacle. She had begged a sturdy orange crate from the greengrocers and for many nights after I had gone to bed she busily turned it into the most wonderful doll's house. She melted old wax gramophone records to make little saucepans, made bowls of shiny fruit from glitterwax, chests of drawers from matchboxes and knitted pipe-cleaner dolls. Our house was decorated with holly and ivy and fir branches sprayed with silver and I wore a new dress made by my mother for Christmas Day. A chicken had been exacted from our neighbours in exchange for sewing work and after lunch my parents even had a bottle of port. Then I was allowed to open my large and mysterious present. Nothing before or since has afforded me so many hours of amusement as that doll's house.

What could we expect of the new year? At the end of March 1945 my sister Celia Patricia (to be known as Patsy) was born. I waited outside the nursing home and my first glimpse of my new sister was as a white bundle held up to the window of the first floor. I had rather mixed feelings about the newcomer.

The attention focused exclusively on me for five years now shifted drastically. This blonde, curly-haired, accident-prone but apparently divinely lovable baby quickly became the apple of my mother's eye. She was more robust and extrovert than me, but was given to eating worms and poking glass beads up her nostrils.

On 8 May Victory in Europe was proclaimed and I remember being taken on my father's shoulders to a huge celebration in Biggleswade, our nearest town. Everybody had flags and waved them energetically, and the town band played. The clamour was deafening. Winston Churchill had made sure there was plenty of beer, so Britain became one grand street party. Before long, however, the reality of the post-war Britain sank in. Four million homes had been destroyed and eighteen million tons of shipping. The American GIs certainly had left their mark on the British way of life too. Showers of candy, cigarettes, chewing gum and nylons had been strewn around as bait in the search for 'beer and broads'. Not only single girls, but mothers with small children, whose husbands were away in the services, often fell prey, seduced by the luxury gifts. People did not know whether they would see each other again, so long-held taboos about pre-marital sex were frequently thrown to the winds. GIs were issued with condoms and discarded ones started to appear in the countryside. The first one I ever saw was festooning a hedge.

The American way of life already had the British in its thrall, partly through the influence of Hollywood movies showing affluent car-owning families with refrigerators. It was true that without the belated intervention of the US we would never have won the war, but there was still national pride, an idea that our country was endowed with unique imperial values on which the sun never set. Unlike the First World War, this had been a war in which women had been widely recruited to do men's jobs and had handled them with skill and determination. New strategies in negotiating male and female roles would have to be worked out and I was going to be in the thick of it.

Our 'battle for civilization' had required sacrifices from everyone and the working classes now demanded acknowledgement. Under the leadership of Clement Atlee the Labour government had the task of initiating social reforms. An ardent socialist, my father was committed to the ideas of the welfare state. After the terrible hardships he had seen in Manchester and London during the war, he longed for a more just world. He listened to the radio and read avidly, following political developments.

In the September of that year of landmarks for me – the birth of my sister, the end of the war – I found myself at another threshold. I was to go to the local primary school and take the first big step out of my make-believe world. The school was about a half-mile walk from home so I was placed in the care of the butcher's somewhat older daughters, Eileen and Audrey, whose chubby, rosy features hinted at a nutritional advantage, or so my mother grudgingly suspected.

Each classroom exuded the unmistakable smell, a bouillabaisse of chalk, Plasticine, gouache, empty milk bottles and children's well-worn plimsolls. I found my fellow pupils rather rough and frightening. Apart from Eileen and Audrey, I knew only Michael Dear, the coal merchant's son who lived near me and whom I might have hoped would feel a little protective towards me. Soon after I arrived, however, he chose an appropriate moment to humiliate me. 'Wendy Snowden's parents are so poor that her mother has to make her clothes!', he cried. Immediately my exotic, custom-made wardrobe appeared abhorrent compared to the smart wear of the children of those who had made some money on the black market. I can still feel the dart in my heart.

I wanted to learn, though, and I liked the headmistress, Miss Elizabeth Bowen, a spinster in her late fifties. Slim and elegant, she wore her grey hair in a chignon and had a necklace of toffee-coloured amber beads. She had a soft spot for me too. One day when I was six I was called upon to perform the honoured task of making tea for the headmistress and staff. I poured the boiling water into the great enamelled teapot and then sprinkled the allotted amount of tea leaves on top. This was the wrong way round, of course, and a soggy mat of tea leaves sat on the surface. Tea was still rationed and precious and, although I don't remember being told off, the domestic perfectionist beginning to emerge suffered a great deal of anguish over this failing.

Then came a day when we received one of those calamitous telegrams. It was for my mother and her face went pale. Her own mother had become seriously ill. 'We must go quickly!' she said. Father saw us on to the steam train to Manchester. For me it was exciting to go the big city and to travel on a tram out to the suburbs. I saw black people for the first time and mother had to pinch me and tell me not to stare. I saw a Sikh wearing a turban and thought he was Ali Baba. The city looked so huge and ugly, with many bombed-out buildings.

Grannie Green was a shadowy figure to me. We seldom saw her. She wore long black dresses and lace shawls and was known as a 'seer': people came from all over to consult her. She now lay in her room, her long white hands motionless on the counterpane, her breath uneven, her eyes closed. She was like a bird, shrunken to occupy hardly any space in the great Victorian matrimonial bed. She finally died a few days into our stay, as I lay in a little bed in the room next door, watching flickering gaslight throwing ghostly shadows on the thickly carved furniture. I was frightened, but also sad: I still believe I saw the bright light of an angel as she died.

On the train back to Bedfordshire the carriages and corridors were full of demobbed American GIs, smoking and laughing. My mother was still pretty and she chatted with them. I was frozen with embarrassment, being a reserved child, and I remember asking her later, 'How can you bear to talk to those strange men, Mummy, when you didn't know them?' It was anathema to me that anyone could speak to strangers like that.

My mother inherited a little money from Grandmother and, keen on good education, took me out of the village school, away from those 'rough farm labourers' children' with their Bedfordshire accents. I was sent to the Sacred Heart Convent in Hitchin. No matter that we weren't Catholics, it was a school with a good reputation and, what was more, Jane, the daughter of our old wartime companions Mr and Mrs Hawkes, was already there. A thrilling series of visits to the school outfitters followed in order that I could acquire a brown gymslip, cream shirts, brown blazer with school badge and a brown broad-brimmed hat with a yellow striped ribbon: the pupils looked like little honey bees.

At the convent I found an atmosphere more suited to my temperament. I loved the prayers and the incense and the saints' days, when we were given a holiday or were shown some grainy film on a squeaky projector. The food was terrible, although the nuns fed themselves on roast chicken and other unheard-of delicacies. Somehow they managed to get hold of a consignment of American emergency rations: tins of barley sugar, Horlicks tablets and chewing gum. Sweets were still rationed, so these nuns were on to a good thing. They were very entrepreneurial: we could bet our pocket money on a roulette wheel to win some of this treasured booty as a prize. Sometimes we were sent to do a 'penance walk' around the playground several times or say fifty Hail Marys if we had committed some sin. This was a little bewildering, but I got the hang of it and developed a deep affection for Mary. We were taught deportment in the gym classes, learning to walk with books on our heads and to keep our tails well in. The net result was an inhibiting of any kind of natural sway in the walk. One day I remember overhearing, with some surprise, the gym teacher asking another member of staff, 'Who is that girl with the beautiful auburn hair?' Could that be me? I'd always felt somewhat invisible. I was a shy child, and this moment was significant. At last somebody had noticed me – or was it just my hair?

My favourite teacher was Sister Veronica, who smelled of roses. She was French and had a beautiful face. Her black gown rustled as she walked and I used to wonder what she might look like without her coif. I'd heard that nuns were made to shave their heads when they took orders and had to bathe fully clothed, but I never dared ask anyone about these matters. It is Sister Veronica I have to thank for my handwriting. I was left-handed and in those days it was thought this should be changed. (As a schoolboy Peter too, I later learned, was a natural left-hander who was forced to change. The resulting script was one of the most illegible I've seen.) But Sister Veronica persevered with me, teaching the flowing copperplate that is often the stamp of French handwriting. I am grateful to her to this day.

One incident from this period continued to haunt me for some time. One day I noticed that one of my classmates was not on the bus as usual. She didn't come the next day either. I heard some whispers, but I couldn't make out what was going on. Then it was in the newspapers: her father, an RAF pilot, had returned home from service to find her mother with another man. He had gone berserk, taken out a revolver and shot his wife and the two children and then himself. Although this was one of the most shocking affairs in the area, it was not unheard of in the country as a whole. Such men, who had endured so much during the war and then discovered their wives had taken up with someone else, were driven to distraction. This is the unexpected legacy of war. I used to have nightmares about my dead classmate calling to me to help her.

The educational ethic at the Sacred Heart was good. We were mostly girls with a sprinkling of boys and I spent three important years there. There were ballet classes too, which my mother had organized in a room above the local pub; she played the piano and engaged a ballet teacher. I loved dancing. All of this was to change, however, when my parents realized I would not be able to get a scholarship from a private school to the newly planned local grammar school. The money just wouldn't stretch to cover another seven years or so of private fees.

So, at eight and a half years old, I returned to the village school. This time round the local kids were merciless. My accent was now markedly different and I was targeted by the bullies. I tried to keep my head down and applied myself to study: the dreaded Eleven Plus was already hanging like the sword of Damocles over my future. I stuck close to a new friend, Anne Dunbar, who came from a huge family (even poorer than us) and with whom I attended the Salvation Army Sunbeams (a pre-Girl Guide Salvation Army Youth group). She too wanted desperately to get a scholarship to grammar school so we made a pact to look out for each other. Inside, all the same, I often felt distressed and vulnerable.

Bouts of bronchitis erupted, landing me in bed for weeks. Below my bedroom I would hear my parents quarrelling. Since the end of the war these rows had become a feature. My mother had become accustomed to doing things to her own rhythm and now that my father was back he expected to assume the dominant role in the home once more. He also expected his conjugal rights to be reinstated, but since the birth of Patsy my mother had taken the toddler into her bed and insisted that my father have a separate bedroom. She claimed he snored. Only much later did I come to understand that much of the tension in the home was due to my father's unreciprocated sexual overtures and not altogether about lack of money. (I never saw my parents in bed together and had no idea how babies were made.) My father went to the pub whenever he could for a beer and to chat up the pretty barmaids, often returning late for meals. As children we didn't know what caused these undercurrents and outbursts. Divorce was not an option, but one day I overheard Mother saying with such force that I've never forgotten it: 'I am NOT going to be your doormat!' Her cry was to resonate with me down the years.

It wasn't all strife. There were many jolly times too. With their northern roots my parents prided themselves on 'calling a brush a brush', which wasn't the way among our Bedfordshire neighbours. Claire and Bill Snowden, I now see, were also frustrated artistic types with creative talents. On birthdays my father would blow up balloons, put on a red nose and invent wonderful games. My mother would put on a great feast with shiny fruit jellies, wobbly blancmanges, trifles decorated with glacé cherries and angelica and always a special, themed birthday cake.

It was unfortunate that Patsy, five years younger, was always at a different stage of development from me. She seemed bent on destruction much of the time. While I was meticulous and careful, setting up my dollies' tea parties with everything in an allotted place, this ordered universe was not appreciated by the ebullient Patsy. Short of tipping her out of her pram (which I once did) my strategy was to lose myself in nature. I loved roaming in the countryside. It seemed reliable. In a world where adults fought and caused unhappiness, healing came with the sight of spring's budding bushes, full of sap, blossom and the blue of a clutch of blackbird's eggs – so small, so perfect; then the ripening of fruits, pink-gilled field mushrooms, blackberries, rosehips and crab apples from which to make jelly. This constant theatre, the ever-changing colour, smell and texture, provided me with a sense of order that I was to call upon again in adult life. And behind the visible world of fragile spider webs, the lichens that crumbled rocks, the ants that bored away with their formic acid, reducing old tree trunks to a powder – behind all this was the teeming world of the suprahuman: the twitching grasses of shape-changing beings. Who could not be enthralled?

I also found escape attending the local Methodist Sunday school. I missed the religious rituals of the convent, so Sunday school, with its hymn singing and friendly people, was a good substitute. I also fell in love for the first time at Sunday school with a boy who shared my love of nature. The river and the common were the focus of our lengthy explorations. Sometimes we wouldn't come back until dusk and once nearly drowned ourselves in a flimsy cockleshell of a craft he called a boat.

After this episode I stayed on the riverbank and took up fishing. Armed with a bamboo cane, a thread, a bent pin and a worm I landed perch and tench. This caused the boys at school to view me in a different light and to solicit my participation in their games. I thought their play more interesting anyway, but discovered my role was to be limited to gangster's moll or cook. Having been christened Wendy after J. M. Barrie's creation, I seemed to grow into this role of 'den mother' and have looked after numerous 'lost boys' all my life.

The 1950s were a time of anticipation and impatience for the young. Selective secondary education saw 82 per cent of the nation's eleven-year-olds go into the new modern schools. I was to be no exception. My parents had drummed it into their daughters that education was the only way out of the poverty trap. So I worked hard, sat the Eleven Plus and got a scholarship to the new local Stratton Grammar School in Biggleswade. I was a star for a meteoric moment. Unfortunately, at home I was never provided with what is now called a 'consistent mirroring' of my personality. I was either the worst, laziest, cheekiest girl ever, or the most brilliant, talented, destined-for-great-things person in the whole world. No matter how flawed one's parents, we seek their approbation. In getting a place at grammar school at least I had made them proud.

Chalk and Greasepaint

If Cambridge University was to turn out to be the launching pad for Peter's precocious show-business career, then the five years he spent before 'going up', as a boarder at one of England's more respected public schools, was the workshop in which his unusual talents and very self-contained personality seem to have been put together. Having endured the heartache of being sent off alone to his draughty prep school in Eastbourne, the schoolboy emerged at the age of fourteen with a keen sense of how to avoid bullies and gain popularity through a combination of wit and determined bouts of silliness.

Alec and Margaret Cook had enrolled their son at St Peter's College, Radley, and at this rambling Georgian mansion near Abingdon, in Oxfordshire, a fresh circle of school friends soon started to defer to his improvisational comic style. It was here too that Peter first felt the pleasure and excitement, largely unsuspected until then, of entertaining large groups of people.

He arrived at Radley in 1951 and had to fall in quickly with the kind of invented hierarchy set up in such schools to train the boys how to respect 'their betters'. There was a strict system of pretty arbitrary privileges at Radley. First-year boys, for instance, had to keep all their jacket buttons done up, while second-year boys were allowed to loosen just one. Prefects were the only ones permitted to close the door when they

visited the lavatories. I have heard anecdotes of several different initiation rites inflicted on new boys – all of them cruel –
but the only one Peter told me about involved forcing a
newcomer to climb naked over hot water pipes while being
whipped with wet towels. Possibly Peter was exaggerating to
horrify me, but while his old school friends say they do not
remember being made to do this, they do consider it typical of
the things that went on there.

I certainly remember him telling me how desperate his
asthma had made him. On some lonely nights he used to bang
his head against the wall because he could not breathe and had
no one to turn to. As a fellow sufferer from breathing difficulties throughout my childhood, I felt so sorry that he had to
go through this far away from his relatives. It brought out the
maternal instinct in me.

Part of the appeal of sending Peter away to Radley for the
Cooks must have been its reputation for producing linguists
who would be useful in the modern world. The emphasis at
the school was on French and German rather than on classical
languages and this was designed to shape pupils for future
service abroad. Making the most of these strengths, Peter won
prizes in his last year for German. All the same, his sister
Elizabeth is not convinced that a career in the colonial service,
following in their father's footsteps, was what their parents
had in mind for her big brother. They were happy, she claims,
to let him find his own path and, according to her, Radley was
not part of some grand plan.

'It has become a bit of a myth that Peter was being groomed
for the Foreign Office. There may have been a conversation
at some time in which Mum and Dad said they thought it
could be a possible direction, but there was certainly no sense
of grooming going on. I don't think that was part of the
agenda.'

Although Alec's working life had been devoted to the smooth running of colonial outposts, Elizabeth says there was no long historical line of Cook men toiling overseas as 'sons of Empire'.

'There is this idea that generations had gone out to serve the Empire,' she says, 'but there is no evidence that was so. My father's father was in Kuala Lumpur, but he was not exactly serving the Empire. He was working for the railways. It was just two generations really, and each doing quite different things.'

What Radley actually did for Peter was to introduce him to the thrill of writing for the stage. He had some early successes acting in school productions, notably in drag as Doll Common in a staging of *The Alchemist* in 1954, but he really hit the big time in schoolboy terms with the musical show *Black and White Blues*, which he wrote in 1956 with his friend Michael Bawtree, who went on to become a writer, actor and theatre director in Canada.

Michael remembers spotting Peter as a new boy cadet being drilled on the school parade ground, but, since they were in different houses – or 'Socials', as Radley styled them – it took some time for the two to become friends. The schoolboy Peter was, Michael still believes, the funniest person he has ever met, but by the time they were collaborating on their musical adventure Michael himself was something of an all-round star of the school too. He, like Peter, was a prefect and won several prizes, in his case for music.

Produced by the Radley's Marionette Society, *Black and White Blues* was about an evangelist called Mr Slump who was sent out with a jazz band to convert the natives in Africa. It was written by Peter in rhyming couplets, while Michael composed the music, and such was the success of the show, peppered as it was with coded in-jokes about Radley's teaching staff, that a record was eventually cut in Oxford. It sold a few hundred copies among boys and their families.

Elizabeth remembers her parents going to see the musical at the school, while she had to make do with listening to the record. Looking back, Michael puts Peter's burgeoning wit down to the fact that he simply 'found people terribly funny'. 'He was able to share his amusement with us,' he says. 'He was a very good mimic, so he was able to do all the teachers.'

While all the boys often mimicked the masters, Peter apparently did so with more absurdist flair than the others. Most famously, he began regularly to imitate one of the waiters, or table butlers, who served the prefects at High Table, named Mr Boylett. This impersonation would metamorphose into Peter's comic character Mr Grole and finally into the guise of E. L. Wisty, the inconsequential man in the hat and old mac who sits around on park benches and whose droning voice Peter turned into a national comic institution.

'Mr Boylett was dressed in stripy trousers like an old-fashioned waiter and Peter was able to pick up things he said,' Michael remembers. 'But Peter's point about the character was that he had absolutely no personality at all. He would quote Warden Wyndham Milligan, the headmaster at Radley, who used to say, "Mr Boylett is such an incredible character. A terrific personality." But Peter would point out that Mr Boylett actually had no character at all. He would start to tell a story as if it was a big thing and it always came to nothing. This is where it all came from. Everything Boylett said was totally boring.'

Although the school obviously gave Peter great opportunities and took him on to Cambridge, because of the terrible deprivation of family life that is imposed on young children at such boarding schools I now feel strongly that public school was also the place that forged aspects of Peter's personality that were to cause so much sorrow for me and ultimately, I think, for him. It was true that he had already survived the abandonment of his mother as a tiny infant, being 'raised by goats' as he later elliptically joked – in other words, being raised by nanny goats, or nannies – but being moved away again from everything that had become familiar must have had a hardening effect on his emotions.

Nick Duffell, who calls himself a 'boarding school survivor' and runs workshops for other 'survivors', believes that young children can only get through this kind of separation from the things they have relied upon by cauterizing their feelings. In his book *The Making of Them: The British Attitude to Children and the Boarding School System*, he writes, 'The first lesson I learned about boarding school life is that if you want to survive being deprived of your parents' affection then you have to persuade yourself that you did not need it in the first place. Herein lies the great flaw in the public school system. In many ways prep schools are idyllic places. They are usually in the country. You can play football and cricket and make huts in the woods. But what you cannot do is love. You can't love your parents because it hurts too much. And you most certainly can't love your fellow-pupils because there is an overriding taboo against any hint of homosexuality. So, after a while, you just get out of the habit of loving. As I dare to say many of those Boarding School Survivors – not to mention their wives – will testify, getting back into the habit can be a very difficult task.'

Michael Bawtree, who had at least enjoyed some happy home life with his parents before he too was sent away, believes that 'abandonment, or a sense of it, is a very important consideration' for all boarders. 'A lot of public school boys do grow up and get married and have children, but I don't know how sexual they are. I think a school like that could make you a homosexual, but not necessarily. There is no question but that at boys' schools you do get strong affections and passions. It is bound to happen. I don't think it is a good idea.'

I don't know if Peter had homosexual experiences at Radley. I think it very likely, but they were never divulged to me. Perhaps he kept alive his interest in the other sex by closely perusing the naturist magazines he once told me he used to receive by post in a brown-paper envelopes during his time at the school. (*Health and Efficiency*, and other such publications, was no doubt an influence on his performance as the Minister for Nudism in the sketch 'Peace Through Nudism': 'Good evening. This is the Ministry of Nudism. Take off your clothes and begin to dance about.')

In his 1929 autobiography, *Goodbye to All That*, Robert Graves, a writer who was later, strangely, at the centre of a pivotal moment in my life, appears to have had no doubts about the disruptive effect of the British public school on the erotic hard-wiring of their pupils. A Charterhouse old boy, he wrote:

English preparatory and public school romance is necessarily homosexual. The opposite sex is despised and treated as something obscene. Many boys never recover from this perversion. For every one born homosexual, at least ten permanent pseudo-homosexuals are made by the public school system. Nine of these ten were as honourably chaste and sentimental as I was.

Whether or not sexuality is influenced forever, it seems that an attempt to inhibit emotions was – and for all I know still is – on the agenda at such public schools. Systemised flogging, though now thankfully outmoded, was the clearest signal of this in Peter's day. In his study of corporal punishment in education, Robert McCole Wilson wrote, 'To bear discomfort and pain without flinching was a necessary mark of a gentleman. To show distress when being caned was to suffer the contempt not only of the master, but also of one's peers.' 'Softness' of any sort was the enemy.

When Peter made it to the position of prefect, he and his associates started to reform some of the more barbaric traditions of the school. Senior boys were given quite a bit of power in the classic model of the British public school and in the 1950s things were starting to change. The writer Christopher Booker, who attended Shrewsbury with a group of boys – Richard Ingrams and the late Willie Rushton and Paul Foot – who were all to go on to be an important part of the 'satire boom', says he saw the old structures beginning to fall down while he was still in school uniform:

'I arrived at Shrewsbury in 1951 and it was a very tradition-bound school, with lots of discipline, and beatings and an intense sense of hierarchy and privileges, all the things associated with the traditional public school. But during the five years we were there you could feel all that beginning to crack up and crumble.'

What was at work here was a widespread questioning of the old order. Christopher believes that the values of discipline and authority, the masculine values that had been important in the war, were now being discarded because Britain's place in the world was weakening: 'We had believed we were part of something pretty important. London was the biggest city in the world and the port of London was the biggest port in the world. That was the world that we had grown up into. Those were our assumptions and obviously in the ten years after the war it was quite obvious we weren't any longer a big world power. We started to give away all of Africa in the 1950s. We had all had, like Peter had, relatives, lots of members of our family, who were part of all this.'

Defending her parents' choice of such a cold bastion of tradition for their eldest son, Peter's sister Elizabeth argues that her family was a strong and warm one simply trying to do the right thing. She emphasizes that the decision to send all three Cook children to boarding schools stemmed from Alec and Margaret's conviction that it would offer the best start.

'We all felt they were very loving parents,' she says. 'They did very much believe in education and thought this was a good education.' She denies the truth of the idea I have that her family were a little distant with each other. 'They were affectionate. They hugged us too. They wouldn't canoodle on the sofa, in fact, they had separate rooms, partly because Dad snored. I am sure there were nocturnal visits, though.'

At this stage in Peter's school life there was at last the comfort of a parental family home on these shores for Peter to return to in the holidays. The Cooks were now living at a house called Knollside in Uplyme, near Lyme Regis and on the Devon and Dorset border, and Peter's old friend and neighbour down there, Jenifer Elton, or Platt as she was then, remembers spotting him at the end of one trip back home. Here was a potential beau who, on closer inspection, was less promising than she had hoped.

'The first memory I have of Peter is quite definite. I know it was on a bus and we were, I think, coming back from Lyme Regis. I saw this moody, very good-looking, beautiful-profiled boy, which of course I was very interested to see, being a pubescent fifteen-year-old. He was leaning gloomily against the glass of the window up ahead of me. Then I noticed he had lots of spots and immediately was put off. We got off at the same place and realized rather embarrassedly that we were both walking up the same bit of road.'

If Peter failed to entrance Jenifer, who was living with her parents in a bungalow opposite the Cook's home in Uplyme, his parents certainly did appeal. While I was often mystified by their upper-middle-class Englishness, Jenifer found them glamorous and sophisticated and loved their pretty black-and-white house.

'There was a mimosa tree. I have a mimosa tree outside my kitchen window now. It was the Cooks who gave me the idea. It was my dream of a white house. I loved going over to see the Cooks and so I would do anything for them – babysitting and playing with baby Elizabeth. What I loved was corridors with books.

'Every space, as I remember it, had books in it. In the bathroom, everywhere. It was all rather what would now be called "shabby chic". Lots of shabby furniture, comfortable but old and good.' While I was often surprised at the unimaginative gifts Peter's mother gave on special occasions, for Jenifer this kind of thing was a welcome sign of Margaret Cook's aloof style and otherworldliness.

'For me, that was rather the thing that I liked in her, compared to my mother, who I saw as materialistic and obsessed with nice things. It was this unostentatious, middle-class thing. Margaret seemed to me to be benevolent. I admired her. I thought she was a sort of perfect, calm Englishwoman.'

Every so often Jenifer and Peter were thrust together by their parents' friendship and found they got on well. 'What we had in common, though I didn't particularly think about it at the time – I took it for granted – was that we were both boarding-school people. We both had colonial parents who had lived abroad and we had been sent to school in England. I didn't see my parents at all for four years between the age of seven and eleven.'

The two met up in school holidays and even went off to a village hop together. 'We didn't plan it. I think our parents must have. Peter gave the impression of languidly accepting the inevitable. What did I think of him at this time? I liked him, but I was sad that he wasn't going to be the love of my life because he had spots. I think we didn't dance. It was very much foxtrots and things. It wasn't even jive although jive had arrived by then, because I had taught the girls at Cheltenham Ladies' College how to do it. I had brought it back from Beirut, where the American sailors did it.' Jenifer suspects they must have looked a snooty couple.

'We must have been obnoxious really. We both leaned back against the wall. This was the beginning of the Peter Cook humour. I remember giggling a lot about what he said about the people there and then coming home with him and it seeming slightly wistful that it wasn't going to lead to anything. I had had a first kiss somewhere else by then, but I was feeling sad that there was this beautiful family that I had fallen in love with and that I wasn't going to fall in love with their beautiful son.'

At this time Jenifer remembers Peter as shy and unlikely to take the initiative. For one person these visits home from Peter were even more exciting, spots or no spots. His sister Elizabeth, fourteen years his junior, regarded her brother as the epitome of style.

'He was always semi-adult when I knew him and he was a terribly glamorous figure to me,' she says. 'It was always terribly exciting when he came home. I used to go into his room and try to get to know him in his absence during the term by just being very nosy and going through his chest to look at these wonderful items which I often took out: these shells and this beautiful sandalwood soap box, which smelled of the soap which used to be in the box. The shells were tenderly packed with wads of cotton wool. I think he found those shells in Gibraltar. Lovely, lovely shells, which to me seemed quite miraculous. They were translucent. And there was this pale blue, satin kipper tie with jazzy musical notes on it, and this cartoon which he had sent to *Punch* of a fakir sitting on a pin. And a rejection note from *Punch*. I thought it was a very good cartoon. I thought it was brilliant. I just thought he was brilliant. So I would ritually go into the room and look at these things when he was away.'

Back at school Peter was taking equally illicit pleasure in sneaking to the radio to hear *The Goon Show*. He would regularly fake an illness in order to be admitted to the matron's room at the right time of the evening.

For Christopher Booker, discovery of Peter's schoolboy love of the Goons fits in with the sense of humour he came to know.

'*The Goon Show* was interesting,' he told me. 'I never really liked it, but if you look at what they were doing, a lot of it was making fun of the army and the Empire, Victorian values. In that sense it was very much of its time. Peter would have liked the freewheeling zany stuff. The silly names and so on.'

Inspired in part by the surreal world created by Peter Sellers, Spike Milligan and Harry Secombe, the Radley schoolboy fired off a series of original cartoons and comic essays to the *Punch* editorial team. Eventually something was accepted for the Charivari section, earning Peter four guineas. He also confidently sent scripts off to the BBC and, although they were never used, his Goon hero Spike Milligan asked him to lunch on the strength of one of them.

By the time Peter left Radley, at any rate, it seems he was the embodiment of its Latin motto *Sicut columbae sicut serpentes*. He was as 'innocent as the dove, and yet as wise as the serpent'.

He was able to put some of his theories about the world into practice in the next twelve months. Not due up at Pembroke, the Cambridge college his father had attended, until October of the following year, 1957, he took a trip to Germany to improve his grasp of the language before starting his degree studies as a linguist and to see how Britain's former enemy lived. After a dull stay in Koblenz, he transferred to Berlin and managed to get arrested in the Eastern Zone after taking an alcohol-fuelled excursion on the S-Bahn train. It seems Peter was developing a taste for misadventure that I don't think ever left him. He once told me that while staying in Berlin he had noticed an attractive girl at the railway station one day. He had just deposited his suitcase in a locker together with some precious newspapers and made the unorthodox move of thrusting a ticket and a note with his address on it into this girl's hand, before going on to tell her that he was being pursued. He said he had left some secret documents in his locker and that she should wait ten minutes, then open the locker and bring the contents to the address on the piece of paper. He delivered all this in breathless German; whether or not it was a successful ploy history does not relate.

The real significance of Peter's stay in Berlin was a visit to The Porcupine Club. This was a famous political cabaret, with origins dating back to 1949, and it inspired him later to set up his own satirical nightclub in London. The Porcupine, or Die Stachelschwein, traded in spiky political parody, the kind of subversive humour, as Peter was to drily remark, that had done so much to prevent the rise of Adolf Hitler.

The German sojourn was followed by a stay in France which was also designed to improve Peter's fluency in the language. During this time in Tours he struck up with his first girlfriend, the daughter of a shoe manufacturer from Milan. She was called Floriana and he described her in a letter to his parents as 'very attractive'. The two of them obviously had some good, if fairly innocent, evenings out together, although he talked later of the relationship being rather one-sided. He used to quote reams of Blaise Pascal in an attempt to woo Floriana.

Once back in Britain Peter took a summer job as a beachfront photographer down in West Bay in Lyme Regis. This was a period he often referred to as one of the happiest in his life, suggesting he could go back to it if he ever fell on hard times. His plausible manner and sense of humour meant this highly seasonal line of work brought him a princely £20 a week, which was quite a lot of money then. He said later that he capitalised on the situation once again at the end of the summer when he sold off his supply of unsold photographs in brown envelopes as if they were saucy pictures. Most of them, of course, were of holidaying families on the prom. Peter was to go up to Cambridge a worldlier, if not a more sensible, teenager.

He had escaped National Service – still in existence then – because his asthma was enough to convince the interviewing officers that, were he to enter a dormitory where there was so much as a single feather pillow, he would immediately collapse with an attack. His mother and doctor had backed him up on this, establishing one of the leitmotifs of his life – the bypassing of unpleasant things he was not minded to do. Friends of Peter's from Radley who did not get out of their National Service stint were astonished to go up to Cambridge two years later and discover their former classmate had become the toast of the town.

Aside from provincial fame, the early years at university brought Peter a few close friendships and a growing interest in evolving a new kind of student cabaret, or revue. One of the closest of these friends, and the one who was to be at his side at the opening moments of our courtship, was Jack Altman. They had a nicely balanced friendship. Jack suspects now that Peter, having missed out on National Service, was dealing with the British class divide for the first time in his life.

'Like so much in Britain at the end of the 1950s – now, too, for all I know – the beginning of my friendship with Peter was a story of class,' says Jack. 'With the meticulously graduated social thermometer that Cambridge used in those days, I was a working-to-lower-middle-class scholarship boy from Watford Grammar, and Peter middle-to-upper-middle-class from a public school – but as he liked to say, as if to lighten any possible smear, only a *minor* public school.'

Jack remembers that he and Peter started out with the accents appropriate to their backgrounds. 'At least at first. Strangely, for a while, we proceeded to change places, Peter adopting some of the vowels and disappearing r's and t's of my Metropolitan Line "Bayka-Stree'-ool-chaynge", while I painstakingly sought to move "up" to what I imagined to be pukka – before we both seemed to settle in between for something nondescript, classless.' Jack points out that this sort of class mix later became a substantial part of the chemistry of Peter and Dudley.

'Yet it was I rather than he who was the snob. Peter had more sensitive antennae for cant and hypocrisy, with respect only for the authentic.' Jack remembers that on a visit to his home in Croxley Green, Peter managed to charm his parents without 'losing his edge'. 'When my mother apologized that our bathtub might have been too short for him, he said: "Not at all, Mrs Altman. Never mind, I'll wash my knees some other time." He appreciated her then telling him to muck in with the rest of us: "As I always say, 'When in Rome,' she declared, 'do as the Romanians.'"'

Both studying at Pembroke, Jack and Peter swam against the tide of what was 'a relentlessly jock's college – rowers and rugby men, who could manage only a few bemused smiles for clowns like Peter and self-styled "journalists" like *Varsity* editor, Martin Page and myself, the three of us huddled together in one corner of the dining hall'. According to Jack, fellow students never got Peter's early Common Room imitations of a man they had never heard of, 'some Yank called Elvis Preston, Prescott or whatever his name was'.

One of Peter's other great friends from this period, Colin Bell, was encountered outside the confines of Pembroke, at a place he was increasingly making a second home – the Footlights club. 'I must have first met Peter – who was a year below me, missing lectures in another discipline – through the Footlights,' recalls Colin, reminding me that at this time Footlights was not just an Annual Revue, but a small clubhouse which held regular 'Smokers', or evenings of 'cabaret, booze, and tacitly, auditions for greater things'.

Colin had joined the Footlights in his first year and found no shortage of talent among those offering 'turns and sketches' for the membership. 'This membership would be clad by custom in black tie and still largely adhering to comedy conventions which would have not surprised Noël Coward, Hermione Gingold or Joyce Grenfell, despite most of us having been brought up on the Marx Brothers and the Goons.' Although Colin had watched more sophisticated pieces by Bamber Gascoigne, Joe Melia and John Bird, he had seen dozens which still clung to tired routines relying on 'camp, pastiche, and poking fun at lesser breeds'.

Peter, he says, was quite obviously something else. '*Sui generis*. Almost the fully formed E. L. Wisty from the first moment he told us that if all the Chinese held hands, they would girdle the earth three times.' His style of comedy, even then, was clearly defined. Talking about it recently with Christopher Booker, and explaining that Peter had always told me he was afraid of analysing his sense of humour, or his personality, in case his muse disappeared in a puff of smoke, Christopher said that Peter almost seemed to be in a trance when he was being funny. 'It was as if he switched on to the unconscious. I mean, obviously he was very personable and had a lovely style to him, but it was as if he was speaking in "orphic utterances", which is the Greek phrase for the way the priests would speak at Delphi. On automatic pilot: as it came.'

If the political cabaret of Berlin had whetted Peter's appetite, there was not much radical zeal in his comedy. He attacked political targets, but not from a particular position. 'Peter was, in his Cambridge years, an unabashed Conservative,' Jack Altman remembers. 'This never precluded his abiding contempt for the Tory party – saying in the 1959 elections: "Of course, I'm going to vote for that dreadful old shit Macmillan, I've got some stock to protect" – and for all the other parties, too.'

Very quickly Peter began to dominate the Footlights. There was little resistance, at least as far Colin Bell was concerned. 'There was really no question about any further rites of passage or audition. From the start, Peter was obviously going to be not just in the Annual Revue, but at the heart of it. We both served on the Society's Script Committee, which had until then been a kind of MCC, passing judgement in a senatorial way on the year's crop of little numbers and deciding whose county performances might merit a Test appearance. In the Age of Peter, the committee simply became a sounding board for his boundless invention.'

The committee still held regular meetings, but gave up the formality of debating the merits of anything else which had been tried out at a Smoker. 'It boiled down to which of Peter's numbers we thought best – for the Revue of 1960, which was directed by John Fortune (or Wood, as he was before Equity told him the name was already taken), every single number was written by Peter alone, save one: the shared credit was with me, of which I am still proud, just as I recognized when we had to cut the running time, that that would be the one to go.'

Colin reminded me too that even back then several of these committee meetings took place in the rooms of another committee member, David Paradine Frost. 'At the time, we thought it would be an amusing opportunity to visit Gonville & Caius, if the cab driver could find it, and let David show off his enormous tin of biscuits. We later realized that Frostie had probably pioneered Richard Nixon's bugging techniques, and was simply accumulating the material for his own career.'

In rehearsal it sounds as if there was never much done to Peter's pieces. Friends and fellow performers were rapidly gauging that if you worked with Peter, it was his comic world view that won through. 'John Fortune made the occasional suggestion, but if Peter didn't fancy it, he'd simply send it up,' says Colin, plaintively. 'I tried to make him a better dancer, but that too was rather pointless – the way he did it wasn't what I wanted, but then, it worked perfectly well on Planet Cook.'

Learning to Stand Out

Wonderful Mrs Howe, the Domestic Science teacher at my new school, first taught me the joys of adventurous cookery. We pupils shared a well-equipped kitchen cubicle in pairs and made the kinds of exciting dishes, like koulibiaka (a Russian fish pie with capers), that my mother would never have dreamed of. We invited staff members for lunch so that we could learn how to lay the table, make nice flower arrangements that didn't obscure the diners opposite, serve our guests and develop conversation. This was to be the most useful of all courses for me, as it turned out. We also learned to starch and iron our father's shirts (the boys too, accompanied by great giggling from the girls) and how to clean a room properly.

One day I was called to the study of the headmaster, a Cambridge man called Mr Blayney. It had been drawn to his attention that because of my bronchitis I didn't enjoy the tougher sports like hockey. He said to me, 'Wendy, I can see that you are artistic. I am going to offer you the chance to do extra art lessons instead of some of the games. I could be accused of special treatment, but I'm prepared to do this for you. So when your name is up in lights somewhere, please remember me.' Of course I never forgot. It was such a gift to do more art, as well as sewing with Miss Friend, who must have put a word in for me. I really started to thrive.

My best friend, Diana Moles, was the naughty, funny girl in the class. She made all the others laugh and was constantly sent out. I was her sidekick. I always seemed to play second fiddle, never daring to be as outrageous as I would have liked. There was, though, an exceptional incident when I was caught drawing nudes in the break to amuse the boys. The deputy headmistress came in and gave me a proper dressing down in her study. 'You, Wendy Snowden, of all people!' she shouted. (I was something of a goody-goody, having won the prize for Speech.) I was gutted. I did not want to fall from grace. Round about this time I had my first period, an event that was only ever whispered about. When I embarrassedly told my mother about it, she simply handed me a sanitary towel and said that if I kissed a boy I could get pregnant. Perhaps you can picture the various images that arose in my mind. I had even thought that women bled from the armpits or breasts, as these seemed to be the places where changes most visibly took place. Such was my ignorance. Diana Moles, who was going to be a nurse, professed to know more about these things, but even she turned out to be ill informed. It was all very frightening and I was not to learn much more until I was seventeen and living away from home. This may sound unbelievable today, but that was how it was. Peter's sketch, 'Facts of Life', in which he was to take the role of a father informing his son about human reproduction, was actually not so far off the mark. The son is dutifully told he is the result of a 'very mysterious, rather wonderful and beautiful' event that followed on naturally four years after his mother sat on a chair that had only recently been occupied by his father.

I hardly need say that I was constantly in love at this age, usually with older boys upon whom I could have a secret crush.

All this burgeoning emotion found another outlet too – in religion. I was now teaching in Sunday school at the Methodist church. I also sang in the choir, often performing solos.

The fifties saw some of the old Victorian values return for a brief last hurrah; they were something to grasp onto in response to the disruption of the war years and to all the change that was clearly coming. Churchgoing was part of this search for reassurance and a new crusading phenomenon from America appeared in the form of Billy Graham who, with his good looks and punchy evangelical style, was recruiting millions. He called to people to 'come up and be counted for Christ'. In 1954 he came to the UK and, using the huge efficacy of the American advertising machine, he filled football stadiums and concert halls, as well as churches and cathedrals. People were singing hymns – good old-fashioned hymns – in the churches, in the schools, in the workplace. Diana Moles got me to go to a Graham meeting in London and we stood up and were among those who were counted. It was, of course, an emotional setup, but we were both very sincere. For a while goodness and light and helpfulness seemed to flow from every pore. Nothing was too much trouble and life became gold-tinged. Even the customary quarrelling at home seemed to abate. It was a period that set up a pattern for my life: I swung between the reverent and the irreverent, somehow drawn to both extremes.

As a Sunday school teacher I felt inspired by the Gospels and parables and the Methodist church appealed to me, I think, because of the fellowship. They loved a good hymn and a good sermon, but the normal trappings of the High Church were missing. This shiny period lasted for some time and led to me being asked to contribute some lay addresses. My parents were proud, but I was nervous and always felt as though I was receiving an invisible helping hand. At school Diana Moles and I discussed having some sort of career, yet deep down we suspected it was just a matter of time before we found good husbands, leading, of course, to lovely homes and babies. This dream was fed by our favourite pastime in the fifth form which consisted of poring over every woman's magazine we could find for pictures of fabrics, furniture, wallpaper, light fittings and bathrooms; the aim of having a sumptuous bathroom after a childhood of tin baths was paramount. The folders that contained our future ideal homes became bigger and more extravagant and soon it became a bit of a craze throughout our class; nesting desires triggered by hormones, I suppose. By now my family had, in fact, moved to a larger, old house with our own spacious bathroom at last, in a village called Potton ('Potton Much-Manured' in the Doomsday Book, to my continued delight). How I enjoyed my bubble baths in the new bathroom.

I read *How Green Was My Valley* at this time of romantic stirrings and something in it must have been erotic. I hid the book under my pillow, feeling that if my parents caught me reading it I would be scolded. I had breasts now and had been cautioned by my mother not to appear before my father in my nightdress, I imagine for fear that I might excite him. Puberty was full of contradictory messages. Here I was, full of love, which naturally wants to give and share, but also full of secret fears of the unknown. I had a crush on a boy in the village called Mick Coote. Slightly built, with fair wavy hair and grey eyes, he had already left school and seemed rather grown up. He sent me a note to ask if I would like to go to the cinema with him. Our local cinema was in the Village Hall and showed Saturday matinees of Doris Day and Gordon MacRae-type American musicals. So that my parents wouldn't know, I suggested we meet inside the hall.

We sat together in silence. I was electrified by his nearness; then, after an honourable amount of time, he very gently and cautiously took my hand in his. The whole world seemed to throb and explode. Nothing else existed but those two tingling hands, the rest of physicality dissolved into the ether. How romanticism invests the simplest of acts with overwhelming emotion. Do we all come with this same propensity? In my case it was like a great underground well opening up.

Something always spoils paradise and in this instance it was my sister Patsy. When the lights came up I realized she had been sitting behind and spying. She took to her heels, rushing home to tell tales. When I arrived at the house I was given a severe grilling by mother, clearly anxious that anything of this nature might lead to an unwanted pregnancy. She needn't have worried. Fear and circumspection would win over desire for some time to come.

At sixteen I took a Saturday job in a lingerie shop in Bedford. I loved the lacy silk petticoats, bras and nighties, folding them with care. I usually ended up spending my meagre wages on these scraps of femininity. I learned a lot about dressing from Mrs Sheldrake, the manageress, an elegant woman who had been a corsetière at Harrods. It was now 1956 and we were putting the war behind us with a great sense of relief, but also with a real, naked horror – a horror engendered by the spectre of the mushroom clouds that had risen above Hiroshima and Nagasaki. Those clouds used to feature in my dreams and now, with Anthony Eden as Prime Minister, we faced the prospect of war again, this time with Egypt, initiated by Britain in a bid to regain control of the Suez Canal.

I returned to Stratton Grammar School that September not looking forward to the prospect of classes without Diana Moles. Although we had both made plans to return for A levels, over the summer Diana had decided to start her nursing training. I had signed up to do Art, English and French, but that first term was a lonely and restless time. How dependent

I had become on this outrageous, yet idealistic girl. The friendship revealed my tendency to want to be in the company of someone with the courage, or gall, to be more outspoken than I was. It is a two-way process though, and every Don Quixote needs his Sancho Panza. Despite teachers counselling that I was university material, I chose to leave before taking A levels. My father advised me to join the civil service, the old hypocrite. He had been made manager of the Biggleswade benefits office and had changed his tune somewhat. He'd forgotten how much he had hated it. I would earn a reasonable salary and get a pension at the end of twenty-five years' faithful service. What more could I want? I don't think my mother was at all convinced. She had other ideas for me. Still, at seventeen I applied to the GPO in Cambridge and was given a job as a junior accountant. Each day I travelled by train to a large square building overlooking the grassy stretch known as Parker's Piece. The office was brown, the manageress wore brown, the tea lady and the tea, all brown. I wore a heather tweed suit and attached a bunch of artificial violets to the lapel. With my auburn hair, I was the only bit of colour in that place. I learned to add up long columns of figures in my head and also learned all the names of the telephone exchanges, making up poems with the quaint names to alleviate the boredom: Sawbridgeworth, Saffron Walden, Snettisham and Sawston – they all came alive in my imagination. Meanwhile, I looked enviously at the undergraduates in their medieval black gowns as they strolled by, chatting nonchalantly, across Parker's Piece. I was in the right place, but just in the wrong environment, so I whistled to cheer myself up (I had developed a powerful whistle, thanks to the tutelage of a boy from my youth). Before long I was hauled up to Miss Snipe's office and told severely it was inappropriate to whistle at work. Soon after that I went home in tears and told my mother I was really unhappy.

Always a woman of action, she got me to gather the artwork
I had done for my A level studies and to do some fresh drawings
and paintings. An application was made for a place at Cambridge School of Art. I was granted an interview and went with
mother and portfolio to the John Ruskin School. I longed to
be able to be part of that colourful ambience. There was a
nail-biting period after this while my application went through
the various channels, but I eventually got a scholarship for
four years. Our delight was palpable. There were celebrations
and a party at home for friends.

There comes a moment when every young person should fly
the nest. Now it was my turn. By September 1957 we had
found a bedsit near the station in Cambridge so that I could
get home easily for weekends. My mother and I sat sewing
together so I could start my new life with some suitable art
school dresses and skirts. (I don't remember girls wearing
trousers much then; it really hadn't become the fashion yet,
unless you were a land girl.) So I headed off to my new life of
freedom, driven by my father with suitcases and belongings.
Without a record player of my own, I reluctantly left my
Tommy Steele, Bill Hayley and Elvis Presley records behind.

Art schools were still teaching real art in those days and I
was in seventh heaven. There were large, light-filled studios
reeking of oil paints and printer's inks, with couches for the
models to recline on, swathed in velvets. There were rooms
for sculpture, with armatures, blocks of Portland stone and
large bags of plaster of Paris and, best of all, people – fellow
students – who had a spark of real enthusiasm about them. It
was daunting but exciting.

Roddy Maude-Roxby, the actor and comedian who was
later to become a good friend, was also at art school at this
time and has pointed out to me how the revolution in visual
arts was a driving force, or perhaps an emblem, of all the other

54

changes going on at this time. We know about the impact of feminism, of the dawning of the age of Aquarius, and the hope, in the shadow of the nuclear threat, that there would be peace and no more war. But art was also nudging in a quite different way of thinking.

'Abstract expressionism had an impact too; Debuffet, Jackson Pollock and De Koonig too,' says Roddy. 'It was a relief from all the very dark, turgid paintings after the war. A feeling of achieving enormous work achievable without any money. There was a feeling that this also would have a political effect.'

One of the first people I noticed at art school was Roger Law. Handsome, six foot four inches tall, the dimpled 'Fen Tiger' was gnawing on what looked like a leg of lamb that his mother had put up for his lunch. Peter Fluck, later to become Roger's partner in creating television's *Spitting Image*, used to sit so close to the nude model, regarding her every contour, that I thought his intensity would be bound to have consequences. I honestly think I had never seen a nude adult in the flesh before and this one looked like a Toulouse-Lautrec brothel maiden, with scarlet lips and dyed hair. She chewed garlic too, and the fumes increased as the room became hotter. We were an oddly assorted bunch. There was John Williams, who both looked like and painted in the style of El Greco; Andy Cooper, who also played the clarinet with a band and later went off to join Kenny Ball; John Holder – a Norfolk man with Elvis sideburns who was a gentle, strong presence and played bluegrass on his guitar; Rosemary Onyett, all-English maid with a peaches-and-cream complexion; Annie Watt who looked Middle Eastern, and her friend Tina, who was also rather exotic in that she already had a Greek boyfriend whose family owned a restaurant in Cambridge. Rosemary Myers, who is still a good friend, joined us from Harrogate. She had a well-developed illustrative sense, using intricate fabric and drawn collages. Then there was Deidre Amsden, a dark, curly-haired enigma who wore trousers even then. She was later to marry Roger Law and become a renowned quilter, stitching the clothes for the satirical puppets that Roger and Peter created. I found another Diana Moles in Penny MacClean. Outrageous, with a wicked sense of humour, Penny had the plummiest upper-class voice I'd ever heard. She was the first person to wear 'the sack', a style of dress which became a fashion hit in the late fifties. An only child, she was doted on by her genteel widowed mother, whose hair had turned white prematurely, probably as a result of her daughter's escapades. Penny had been allowed an account at Joshua Taylor's, the smart department store in Cambridge. This was probably a mistake as she frequently convinced herself of the need for the latest French perfume and the odd little Susan Small frock. Penny taught me quite a bit about fashion and about upper middle-class mores. Roger Law remembers me as 'vivacious':

'You were the centre of that group of girls. All sorting out which party, and what party, and when you would be there – and lots of giggling and whispering. It was fun. You were very colourfully dressed all the time – reds and stuff. You were far too girly for me. I couldn't deal with it. I liked girls who were boyish and not so threatening. I had to be much older to deal with it. You were a Good Time Girl. You probably couldn't fit the art in.'

Roger was right that my social interests proved rather strong competition for my interest in art. Attentive young men were quite a distraction.

'I didn't think you were particularly interested in anyone, but you were quite interested in all the activity that involved. You were very social. Well, you certainly got about more than I did.'

The foundation year meted out a traditional old-school art

Roger Law, Peter Fluck and Deidre Amsden, Aldermaston Protest

training, headed up by John Bowlam and Bill Darrell, both excellent painters in the traditional English school. We had lectures from Jasper Rose and Christopher Cornford and were often taken for sketching to the marvellous Fitzwilliam Museum, where I always made a beeline for the Egyptian Department and would sit, transfixed, drawing the figures and life depictions of the ancient Egyptians, the plant and bird life, the shadoof, those mysterious almond eyes. It all seemed so familiar; I knew it all intimately from somewhere. I returned time and time again. I loved having my own bedsit where I could cook and invite my friends (discreetly, of course). On Saturday mornings I polished the furniture and then went to collect my weekly food parcel from home. This was a godsend.

It contained things like tins of paté and pearl barley and dried lentils to make soups.

I found an old sewing machine too, and started to collect interesting remnants from the wonderful Cambridge market. Brigitte Bardot was becoming an icon at this time. She popularised gingham and full-skirted dresses with matching headscarves, so I bought some lavender-check gingham and made a dirndl skirt and headscarf. The fashion was to have 'waspie' elasticated waistbands and miles of tulle hooped petticoats – not very practical for riding a bicycle while balancing a drawing board and other accoutrements. The petticoats were usually swirling in the wind and caused something of a stir, particularly among the undergrads who were, in turn, rather more alluring to me than our home-grown Cambridgeshire and Norfolk lads at art school.

The expression 'town and gown' highlighted a real divide between the university and anybody 'other'. However, when it came to women, the physical attractiveness of the average university female was generally summed up by the word 'bluestocking', meaning brainy but unattractive. So if you were a pretty art school or foreign language student your chances of having multiple suitors were very good. How breathtaking it all was to be in such a contrasting milieu, only thirty miles away from Potton-Much-Manured. This could have been another continent.

I started out as one of the promising students and I really did enjoy the classes, but soon the parties and social scene took centre stage – perhaps not surprising after seventeen years of rural Bedfordshire and the stern protocol of my Victorian-minded parents. Wellington boots were ditched in favour of pointy shoes. Penny MacClean and I were by now quite firm friends and so, when one of her two flatmates left, I was invited to take her place.

Three pretty eighteen-year-old girls together proved to be a magnet for the far-from-home undergrads and all sorts of admirers started calling. We didn't have a telephone, so lots was done with handwritten notes and personal calls – tricky if one was encouraging several suitors at the same time. It was all fairly innocent – there was kissing and fumbling – but we really didn't know what fire we were playing with. Penny got hold of a book, I think by Marie Stopes, which provided some fairly graphic descriptions of sexual intercourse; sentences such as: 'The woman must lie with her knees bent and thighs open and close to her breasts.' I was horrified. I had no preparation for this kind of information. You would think it would have been impossible to arrive at the age of eighteen and be so utterly ignorant. It is hard now to believe my state of unpreparedness. I had a strong determination to remain a virgin until I married, but the other two girls just giggled and seemed much more knowledgeable than me.

Of course, one couldn't carry on like that without some kind of 'incident', and one night a young man, Peter from King's, took me to a party and then, on the way home, kissed me passionately and made me touch him outside his trousers. I couldn't believe this was genuinely part of his anatomy. I was shocked and thought he must have had a piece of piping down his trousers. For a while this put a brake on my flirtatious ways; then, by way of contrast, I came to like the polite John Pleskett. The son of a Trinidadian tea planter, he had a car and drove me to a nice pub in Trumpington. He opened doors and pulled out my chair for me, and went on to suggest that I might like some smoked salmon as a starter. I had never eaten smoked salmon before. Translucent quills of beautiful pink, it was delectable. I certainly preferred this impeccable treatment to the smash and grab tactics of some chaps. At the end of the evening he kissed me on the cheek at my doorstep and drove off having asked for another date. In fact, I had found his conversation dull, so that was that, but he had given me an indication of how properly brought-up young men behaved.

Not wishing to lose touch with my spiritual life, I took to attending evensong at King's College Chapel. The atmosphere engendered by soft lighting and sacred music floating up to the magnificent fan-vaulted ceiling of Henry VIII's extraordinary chapel worked deeply on my impressionable young soul. But, of course, there were young men to tempt me there too. The older choristers looked adorable in their cassocks; quite angelic in fact, but they were certainly not so pious when you got to know them. Lindsay, Cliff and Robin became frequent visitors to our flat in Warkworth Street. I would rustle up special dishes, like the huge salad I created with tiger prawns and passion fruit (not bad on £4 a week). Now my cooking started to take wings: my flatmates were only too happy to let me take a lead in the kitchen and there were plenty of young undergrads, refugees from college fare, to be my guinea pigs.

At the end of my second year at art school I narrowly failed to get through my intermediate exam. This would mean resitting it and taking another year. It was a real wake-up call and I had to go home to face the music. My father was furious and I realized that I would have to take my studies much more seriously. Helpfully, there was an influx of new teachers at the college. The new head, Alex Heath, led a team who were all successful in their own fields of design: among them, Paul Hogarth was an internationally famous illustrator and entertained us with his adventures, including his stories of the Spanish Civil War. Many students came to be influenced by his unique style. Looking back, I think Roger Law is right when he says that we had 'the best of both worlds' at art school. 'We had a traditional background to our work and then the new tutors came in. It gave us a head start,' he says.

I opted to study theatre design and developed a flair for costume. I got involved with a Chekhov play, *Uncle Vanya*, which I found absorbing, designing model sets and costumes.

So many influences swept through Cambridge at this time. Miller's Jazz Club was a favourite haunt and the jive was becoming popular too. I fell under the spell of Louis, a handsome singer with a silver stripe in his hair who sang Nat 'King' Cole numbers with his band. I also attended art school gigs where I drank scrumpy with Roger Law. Many of us also joined the Aldermaston marches and CND protests. A country weekend away with Penny in her mother's beautiful thatched cottage near Newmarket made a lasting impression too. We went to a point-to-point and I was aware I didn't have quite the right gear, but we did eat asparagus and then fresh lychees, something else I'd never had before. These were simple but defining moments. I was learning a lot about good taste and proving a willing pupil.

Love in Never Never Land:
Peter and Wendy

An old black-and-white photograph is lying on my desk. John Bulmer, the photographer and cinematographer, an old friend from Cambridge days, has sent it to me as an *aide-mémoire*. It shows a disreputable young man whose sharp features are almost entirely masked by a hat. Draped over his side is a young girl, a teenager, with dark hair, wearing a dramatic ball gown. The girl is me and the young man is Peter. But the picture is something of a fake. We posed for it together but at the time we didn't know each other from Adam or Eve. Let me explain.

The summer term of 1958 was drawing to a close and for undergraduates the end of the year is always punctuated by a succession of May Balls, Bacchanalian affairs featuring, in those days, roasted swans and boar, jazz bands and ballroom dancing. Black tie and beautiful ball dresses were *de rigueur* and well-groomed fiancées were summoned from home – much to the chagrin of the 'fill-in' girlfriends. The balls were advertised that year, as usual, in *Varsity* alongside a piece about a young writer and Footlights star, Peter Cook, who had already distinguished himself by contributing material for the West End revue *Pieces of Eight*, starring Kenneth Williams. John Bulmer was taking the photographs for the story and was looking for a suitable girl to be photographed with Peter in evening dress. He asked me if I'd like to be that girl. 'But I don't have a ball gown,' I pointed out. 'Surely you can borrow one,' he said. I went home and told Penny about the offer and she generously offered to lend me her special Susan Small ball gown. She had stuck it on her account at Joshua Taylor's and hadn't even worn it yet. It was strapless, with a hooped skirt and covered in blue and white tulips. It fitted perfectly. I can't remember whether I cycled over to the *Varsity* office wearing said garment, or carried it in a carrier bag and changed there, but once I got it on I felt like a million dollars. I had learned how to use eyeliner and my hair was shoulder-length at the time.

So, dressed up to the nines, I was introduced to a skinny young man with an acne problem. He was so full of himself that I was instantly quite put off, though I rather stiffly allowed myself to be wrapped around him on a sofa for the photo shoot. I was glad when it was over. I had picked up on the intensity and ambition of this young man, along with a glimpse of the media buzz that even a university magazine can engender. I have to admit I was quite chuffed to see myself in the paper, especially since it led to an invitation to the King's May Ball for Penny and me.

This time I had my own ball dress made by a local dressmaker from a *Vogue* pattern, in black crepe silk with white chiffon across the shoulders. It was very elegant, and my mother paid for it! The ball was incredibly romantic – dancing in great marquees, tables groaning with luxurious food, an attentive partner in Tommy Lung Lee, the son of the Malaysian Finance Minister who taught me how to nose kiss. We ended the evening in the traditional manner, with a moonlit punt down to Grantchester. How grim it was to come back down to earth after that, particularly as Penny and I had vacation jobs in a factory to go to in only a few weeks.

As summer approached, I would spot Peter Cook at student parties. He was usually in animated conversation with impressive university women like Eleanor Bron or Margaret Drabble. We would wave to each other, but that was all. I didn't find him that attractive. Another of our early Cambridge encounters is recorded for posterity on film. I had the opportunity to be an extra in a movie called *Bachelor of Hearts*, written by Leslie Bricusse and Freddie Raphael and starring Hardy Krüger and Sheila Sim. Most of the filming was at night, after art school, so I had to stay awake constantly over four days. To help, somebody gave me some purple hearts, pills used by the US armed forces to keep them awake. Quite a few girls I knew were on purple hearts for slimming purposes, but because the effects were rather scary I decided not to take them again. I became very spaced out. I felt a kind of bodily disassociation, and yet was very hyper. I took time off to recover and slept for three days. Peter Cook was also an extra and appears in shot repeatedly. He pops up all over the place in the film, his first screen appearance. He was so obviously pushy, it put me off even more. Afterwards It had been an exciting experience with the cameras, spotlights, the director shouting through a megaphone and everyone milling about. I believe we got the princely sum of 10s a night.

Came the end of term that summer of 1958, and Penny and I donned pink overalls to work in Pye's television factory in Cambridge. Not quite the type of TV work we'd hoped for; rather, making printed circuits, learning how to use a soldering iron, working on a production line and being chatted up by the workers. They loved Penny's posh accent.

Thankfully, the King's choristers had stayed on to keep the services going through the summer, so we had company; without them Cambridge would have been a little bleak. Some of them took us punting on the Cam on long summer evenings.

Cliff was Welsh, slight, blond and a countertenor. Sometimes he'd let forth an Elizabethan love song in castrati tones, surprising unsuspecting passers-by. Lindsay was a bass – and dark, with great black eyebrows, while the third of our choristers, Robin, a tenor, was very English and wore well-cut tweed jackets.

When we weren't being punted, the *modus movendi* was bicycle, and what good things they are. I painted mine purple and wrote my name on it in gold. It was my number one piece of equipment. It was also a wonderfully egalitarian aspect of Cambridge life, The Bicycle.

Penny now seemed to be getting serious about a cool and seemingly hip Cambridge figure called Peter Brimacombe, while I quite liked his friend George Chilcot. But George was to plump for our flatmate, Marian. This meant the equilibrium in our flat was somewhat changed, so I decided to move out and found myself living in what had once been a pub called the Prince of Wales. It was owned by two philosophy graduates, Stuart Anstis and Arden Lyon. Stuart had a glamorous girlfriend, Glenys Roberts, who proved that university women could not only be bright but also attractive. Glenys, now a successful Fleet Street journalist, says the two young men were hoping to make some money out of the place.

'The pub was owned by Stuart, who was a graduate student in experimental psychology,' she reminds me. 'He and his friend Arden, a philosophy student, had the idea they would become rich as property developers. So they bought this down-at-heel, disused pub on the wrong side of the tracks and rented out rooms. They never did become property tycoons, but they set a benchmark for bohemian living in the days when the sexes were strictly segregated in the Oxbridge colleges and you got thrown out for the slightest bit of canoodling.'

The pub was one of the few places where you could get

away from the prying eyes of the guardians of morality. She suggests it became 'a bit of a knocking shop', although we didn't see it that way. 'We thought we were frightfully intellectual,' she says, 'with our beatnik outfits and our high-minded conversation about free love and feminism.' The other residents were graduates and mostly had partners with whom they slept. Glenys remembers me as one of the founder tenants. 'We tied ourselves up into knots talking about all these things so there was not actually much spontaneity in our lives. We were all weighed down by expectations. You'd never have thought we were on the brink of the permissive society.'

According to Glenys, as an art student I seemed free of these hang-ups. She remembers me as 'earthy and colourful' and a favourite with the boys, in part for my cooking skills, 'We couldn't do any of that, but you even knew how to wash up while we sat round drinking gallons of filthy white wine and filling up the ashtrays discussing the meaning of life.'

I wore my long red hair with a deep fringe at that point, right down over my eyes. My clothes were 'arty' and I came across as sure of myself and opinionated. Glenys recalls 'Arden and Stuart used to flirt with everyone and make fun of them with their cold logic and philosophical in-jokes, but you would not take any nonsense,' Glenys adds.

At nineteen, I was the youngest and still protecting my virginity. This soon became known to the residents of the Prince of Wales and in due course there was a 'Meeting of the Elders' on the subject. Out of this conference came an agreement that it was about time Wendy had a proper lover. As Stuart and Arden spoke in philosophical riddles, it took a while for me to catch on. Eventually I got the message and started to review my situation. If these sophisticated, well-educated people thought it not only right but beneficial to be in a full-blown relationship without necessarily being married, then perhaps I had better reconsider. It was a crossroads. I had to face down years of indoctrination from my parents, my church and all the people that I had grown up with, voices that told me you simply did not have sex before marriage. Their reasons had been many, but chiefly fear of unwanted pregnancies. Now easily acquired forms of contraception were changing all that.

This energetic explosion of sexuality was certainly evident in Cambridge. Young people, away from their own small communities, felt liberated after the deprivations of the war, while at the same time the widespread amorous activities of American GIs had also had their effect. So here was I being counselled by people, all over twenty, who listened to Georges Brassens and Edith Piaf and went to see foreign movies. They must know a thing or two, I thought. The trick was to find someone I could entrust with my first sexual experience.

Once a decision has been taken, circumstances often contrive to produce appropriate situations. Penny and I used to go to watch the boat races and there one young man caught my eye. He rowed for St Catharine's College and had soft brown hair, deep brown eyes and the most amazing broad shoulders. His muscles rippled as he rowed. His name was Barry and I learned that he was going out with a pretty blonde nurse. Nurses were supposed to be rather sexually advanced, so I assumed they were in 'that kind' of relationship. Whenever I saw Barry I would smile provocatively and it worked. He took me to Miller's Jazz Club and we danced. He was sweet and gentle, as well as being very masculine, and he was going to be my first lover. One evening at his digs he played a record with the beguiling title *Red Bird Dancing on Ivory*. It consisted of the poet Christopher Logue (who, coincidentally, was later to become a good friend) reading his poems in his sexy, gravelly voice over a musical background played by Tony Kinsey. This record became a real cult item in Cambridge. I melted and

I don't think that I could have had a more caring partner. I've come to the conclusion that Englishmen are not very good lovers, but Barry was an exception. We were together for the best part of that year. It had a stabilizing effect and even my artwork benefited, but I realized deep down that, since we had few interests in common, he was not husband material.

That Christmas, after spending time with my family, I came back to Cambridge to take a holiday job in the Kenya Coffee Bar, the first coffee bar to open in the town. It was the trendy place to be seen in, despite the black nylon overalls the waitresses had to wear. I customized mine with a 'waspie' belt to show off my nineteen-inch waist and piled my hair up like Brigitte Bardot's.

One Saturday there were two customers I recognized: Peter Cook and his friend Jack Altman. Peter was proudly sporting a new charcoal mohair overcoat and carried the customary roll of newspapers under his arm. Jack, with his black curly hair, had keen, jet-black eyes. There was an air of excitement and intensity about them and they were in fits of laughter when I went over to serve them. I was embarrassed about my subservient role and the black nylon uniform, but rather wrong-footed when Peter said: 'Are you going to buy me a coffee, Wendy?' 'Well!' I thought. 'This is a bit of a novel tack.' Having had my fill of doting men, I was ready for something different. When the pair got up to leave Peter said, 'How would you like to take me to the pictures tomorrow?' I was beginning to be pulled in by the Cook charm. (Thankfully, the acne had abated too.) So I said, 'Yes'. What makes one say yes rather than no? That response was to change my whole destiny and somehow I knew it. ('So she didn't know how she knew, she just knew,' says Wendy in *Peter Pan*.) All the same, I felt uncomfortable. I was cheating on Barry. I was also aware that Peter was the sort of twitchy person in whose company one would hardly ever relax. Despite these misgivings I was ready when he called to pick me up. He had the loan of his parents' car while they were abroad.

I don't remember the film, but I can, however, remember that he didn't waste much time trying to put his hand down the front of my dress. I was embarrassed and tried to wriggle away. Not much finesse, I thought. I grabbed his hand and held it so it couldn't get up to more mischief. I didn't like him being so forward and I showed it. Did he think that I was some kind of tart, just because I was an art student and had allowed myself to be photographed lying across him? Well, he had got me wrong. Emerging from the cinema Peter looked sheepish and I felt awkward. There had been no preamble, no 'getting to know you', but pretty soon he made some outrageous joke to take ease the atmosphere. This was a key strategy of his, as I was to learn. He suggested we go to Stavros's Greek restaurant, Varsity. Throughout the meal he made me laugh nonstop; not too good for the digestion, but that's how it began.

I somehow let him know I was in a relationship and suspect this only served to make the chase more exciting. It was flattering, of course, as he was already quite a personality in the university, but I wanted to put the brakes on his ardour. He wrote me notes and once even sent flowers. I found his attentions unnerving, but when Barry returned our conversations seemed mundane in comparison with the gaiety of Peter's talk. I told him I was being pursued by Peter Cook, perhaps wanting to make him jealous. How heartless! He responded with amazing equanimity: 'You must do what you think is right, Wendy.' It made things worse in a way; I felt awful, but not awful enough to cut myself off from Peter's advances. How blind we are in youth. Only later did I realize how hurtful my behaviour must have been for Barry. I sometimes wonder what my life would have been if we had stayed together.

For my nineteenth birthday Peter planned to take me out to dinner, but was mysteriously taken ill. I was quite volatile in those days and we must have had a row the night before. The next day I received a note on Cambridge Footlights Dramatic Club headed paper from a bedridden Peter. It explained in a plaintive tone that he had rushed out into the cold night to look for me after I had 'huffed out (rightly)'. Still clutching my birthday present to his chest, Peter said he had then collapsed in a heap on the pavement and stayed there until eventually some kind passing gentleman asked if he was all right and took him home. Full of apologies for 'lousing up' my birthday, he then begs to be forgiven and asks me to pop in to see him before I go out to celebrate with someone else that night.

Appeased, I went round to his digs early the next morning and found him in his dressing gown, looking rather sorry for himself. I grilled bacon on his gas fire and made toast with a toasting fork, Girl Guide-style. Peter was impressed and, for once, dropped the funny voices long enough to tell me in the most passionate way of a desire to create a satirical nightclub, of the kind that had inspired him in Berlin. This is when I began to drop my own defences. I was caught up in his idealism: the wish to tear down the hypocrisies of our culture. Here was a young man who was going to make a difference and, at that moment, something inside told me I was going to be by his side, helping him to do it. When he had recovered from his strange attack of fainting, I invited him to supper at the Prince of Wales. All the residents were there, for we had a kind of cooking rota that brought out the competitive spirit among some of us. (Maggie Angeloglou, who was later to become a food writer, was one of the protagonists.) That night it was my turn and I had made a great cassoulet, cheap and filling, with a huge Caesar salad. We had a carafe of wine too.

It turned out to be a hilarious evening. Such a benevolent

and creative atmosphere had been engendered by the food, the wine, and the stream of surreal flights of fancy provided by Peter (some featuring the Holy Bee of Ephesus) that it seemed appropriate he should be allowed into my bed that night. I was full of trepidation about seeing him without his trousers since he was extremely skinny in those days, but candlelight softens all. And, as Peter was to go on to say in a sketch, spindly legs need not hold a person back: Mahatma Gandhi, he points out, was not deterred if people shouted at him: 'Goodness me, you've got spindly legs!'

I was still very shy about my own body too. I can't say that Peter was an experienced lover. In truth, women were still strangers to him, despite some previous, fumbling affairs. We were both untutored, but he was keen.

As you might expect, it was Peter's ability to make me laugh that won me over; for such a serious young woman it was the best therapy. Laughter makes you drop your defences and challenging ideas can sneak in surreptitiously. There was great joy in making fun of things together, especially in that post-war atmosphere when so much that was traditional now seemed so ridiculous. Peter was provocative too, and there was an unpredictability about him. Right now I'm trying to imagine him buying one of his first presents to me, a black, frilly, nylon nightie. He must have discovered underwear shops on one of his trips to London (he discovered the strip clubs too, I was to learn much later). Next I was given one of those black, lacy Folies Bergères-type corset bras that gave you a cleavage. I laughed at these presents, I suppose because I was embarrassed and didn't quite know what to make of them or their donor. Here I was, a romantic young girl, steeped in images of courtly love. How could I deflect the more lurid tendencies of this apparently polished and sophisticated twenty-one-year-old? He carried an enormous amount of perceived assurance and glamour, but clearly also had some slightly odd ideas about courtship.

Yet we got on well and were good together. The one supplied what the other did not have. I appeared to be fairly stable and had a strong wish to nurture others. I was also a dreamer, and felt that Peter would lead me into adventures. In return, I wanted to smooth his path if I could.

Aside from complementing each other, we shared a fear of abandonment and quite a lot of hidden anger, something which would erupt from time to time. I knew that Peter was danger-ous, but that was exciting. After all, I had always been drawn to the naughtiest people and I felt a lot of pride in his talent. I would often spend a couple of hours getting ready to see him in the evening. And, anyway, who could resist those head-lamp-blue eyes with their thick fringe of lashes? It wasn't long before Peter moved into the Prince of Wales with me. He liked my cooking as well as my company and made the most of the ready-made audience of graduates who supped together nightly. He kept on his own rooms for appearances' sake, though I think he stopped paying the rent as I remember he had to deal with an irate landlord at one point.

Glenys Roberts was introduced to Peter properly at the Prince of Wales, although she had previously spotted him on one of his rare academic sorties. 'Peter and I both read Modern Languages and I first set eyes on him in one of the few lectures we went to, so contrary to popular opinion he must have gone to some. He was good-looking, rather romantic and sensitive, and there weren't too many men like that around. The lecture was probably about Sartre or Gide. I am sure they had a good deal of influence on his comedy of alienation. He must have felt an outsider just reading French at Cambridge, because everyone else seemed to be reading English or sciences and to have their lives mapped out for them.'

To some, Glenys included, Peter and me seemed a strange match. She saw me as straight-talking, while Peter was all wryness and guilt and inhibitions. 'You didn't seem like a natural couple on the face of things,' she says now, 'but you certainly had a vigorous sex life. I couldn't ignore it because I was sleeping in the next room. You had the room off the kitchen where everyone ate, so it was pretty hard to disguise what was going on.'

Glenys remembers Peter being angst-ridden about his sex life, but, as she points out, this was the way it was for everyone in those days. 'Sex was still a big thing – and anyway Peter was angst-ridden about everything: relationships, exams, parental expectations. Nagging angst was the definition of those years: there was a lot of worry about getting it right. Peter worried about his background and what people expected of him and what he felt best doing.'

The great thing about the Prince of Wales – or the PoW, as we called it – was that you could say and think what you wanted. 'That's why we all liked it so much. Nothing was expected of you there but an open mind,' recalls Glenys.

Freedom of speech was often rather restricted, however, if Peter was talking. Melanie Rouse, the girlfriend of another pub resident with whom I am still in touch, says nobody else got to speak when Peter was in the room, he so utterly dominated everyone's attention. On the whole, though, people were quite happy to be entertained freely by such a genius with words.

The E. L. Wisty character, based as it was on that Radley waiter, was already there in embryo. Kenneth Williams was performing Peter's 'It's not an Asp' sketch in the West End revue *Pieces of Eight* using a similar persona, and the idea behind 'If Only I'd Had the Latin, I Could Have Been a Judge' was being formulated before the eyes of dinner guests at the Prince of Wales. There was a sense that there were many unruly characters inhabiting the one skin of Peter Cook. Best of all for me, though, were the surreal, impromptu digressions about the sort of little animals with which he had been preoccupied since childhood: some bee, lizard or snake would materialize in front of us, drawn out by the power of an audience, making our own everyday conversations seem banal in comparison.

As mentioned, Peter had regularly developed a mysterious high fever at Radley at the time *The Goon Show* was being broadcast so that he could repair to Matron's sick room with its wireless. This show certainly helped Peter form his own stream-of-consciousness material. I watched how, by emphasizing a particular syllable, a word could take on a new, bizarre, not to say unsettling, meaning. For instance, Neasden – the area of north-west London to which Jack Altman's family had relocated – was arbitrarily seized upon by Peter as the funniest place-name in the universe. Researching this book I have discovered that there are at least two counterclaims for the roots of this comic association with the place. According to the late Sidney Gottlieb, who was to become Peter's close friend and his faithful football-going companion, the significance of Neasden was based on their frequent north London trips to watch Tottenham Hotspur. Alternatively, the *Private Eye* team claims that Neasden earned its place on the map of British comedy because this is where the magazine was printed. All I can say is that Jack Altman's claim pre-dates the others.

One morning at the Prince of Wales, as Peter studied the racing form at the breakfast table – something he did every day – the Cook comedic tour reached another milestone. Melanie remembers witnessing it. She was cleaning up around Peter, and the radio was tuned to a documentary programme about a group of people who had climbed a hill to await the end of the world; they belonged to the Doomsday Movement or something similar. Mel says she was reduced to hysterics as

Peter took up the theme, embellishing it, twirling it around. It turned up in *Beyond the Fringe* in the form of a sketch in which Peter tells a gloomy band of crouching followers about the 'mighty rending in the sky' that is to come. It is an influential bit of work which was notably revived later for performance at one of the Amnesty International gala nights.

It was only at a recent reunion with Mel that this story came out. Thank God for friends who can come up with cherished pieces of the jigsaw so long after it all happened.

Through Peter's friendship with Nick Luard, the treasurer of the Footlights who was later to become his partner in The Establishment Club, he had been invited to join The True Blue Club. As far as I could make out this was a dining club for the sons of the rich and privileged. The young men admitted to its inner sanctum dressed up in seventeenth-century costume, with breeches and powdered wigs, and then consumed a fifteen-course meal, along with numerous bottles of the best claret. They, of course, then got up to the sort of thing that drunken young men always get up to. On one particular night, after Peter had gone off to one of these debauches, I was woken in the middle of the night by loud voices. The noise was coming from an inebriated Peter and two policemen who had followed him in his car down Norfolk Street, as he seemed to be all over the road. They had come inside the Prince of Wales to apprehend him. Peter, still in costume, with periwig askew, was saying, 'But officer, I swerved to miss a cat which ran across the road.' I don't know how he did it, but somehow the officers left without charging him; they didn't have breathalysers in those days and the police gave a lot of slack to the young undergrads. It was the only time I ever saw Peter really drunk.

Peter, who had grown up with a largely absentee family, now entered a ready-made family of sorts and those evenings at the Prince of Wales became legendary among our friends. Helen Nicholl, the author of the *Meg and Mog* children's books, says she still remembers a good meal eaten outside the pub on 'one of those winter days you sometimes get that are suddenly like summer', with Peter as something of 'a glamorous peripheral'.

On other nights we would all repair to Stuart and Glenys's room. Stuart had kept the bar part of the pub and it looked a little like a high-class brothel, with pink Regency striped chaises longues and a chandelier. Once ensconced at the pub, Peter continued to make a big impact on everyone around him. Glenys remembers listening to him honing what were to become his famous comic personas.

'The rest of us got to know Peter at breakfast or dinner, one of those endless PoW meals round the kitchen table – well, not really know him. I don't think he let anyone know him very well, apart from Wendy, but we got to know his act, though we did not think of it as an act then. It was far too soon to realize he was going to do this for a living.

'He would practise on us, though not for effect, just because it came naturally. He couldn't control himself – and yet it was completely controlled. He could do a verbal riff completely off the cuff, always with that slightly sardonic look on his face that would have everyone under the table. It could be about something as simple as "pass the salt". Nowadays only Paul Merton comes anywhere close to what Peter could do with words and surreal ideas. But Peter was even better. Perhaps because we had never heard it done before, never heard words used like this. And he was at his happiest doing this. It was not showing off, it was just doing what he did best.'

I was twenty now and Peter took me to see *Pieces of Eight* in the middle of its run at the Apollo Theatre. The popularity of the show had brought Peter to the attention of the theatrical agent Donald Langdon, who took him on as a client. Other contributors to the *Pieces of Eight* script included Harold Pinter and Sandy Wilson. Kenneth Williams starred on stage, alongside Fenella Fielding, around whom there were constant dramas. The show was hilarious, glitzed up with lots of singing and dancing as revues tended to be in those days. We went backstage to meet Kenneth and Fenella: two more over-the-top performers you could not hope to meet. I came to like Kenneth Williams. He had some sweet and endearing ways, when he wasn't being waspish. He often came to dinner when we moved to London: he was one of the very few people who really could upstage Peter.

Back at Cambridge, Leon Brittan was President of the Cambridge Union Society and we often went to listen to the debates. At student parties we would meet the people who were to go on to be so prominent in the arts world, among them Trevor Nunn, Derek Jacobi, Ian McKellen and Corin Redgrave. The atmosphere was usually animated: ideas were exchanged at high velocity. I was rather shy of these over-powering characters, yet at the same time I was attracted to the liveliness and fun of it all. Until now Cambridge revues had been of the blazer and straw boater genre. We had been treated to Bamber Gascoigne's *Share my Lettuce* and *Salad Days* by Julian Slade, but I could see the new generation of Footlights was revolutionary. Eleanor Bron, who was then, as now, a dark 'Edwardian beauty', to use a descriptive phrase of Alan Bennett's, says she remembers first hearing about Peter from John Bird, one of the brightest theatrical undergraduate talents around. Bird, who always wore black and smoked Gauloise, had approached her to ask if she would take a role in a show. 'He said to me, as the story goes, "I have just met the funniest man in the world",' Eleanor reminds me. 'And that, of course, was Peter.'

Peter and Eleanor appeared together at the Arts Theatre in a play by N. F. Simpson. Called *A Resounding Tinkle* it was directed by Bird. The piece was one in a stream of challenging, surreal plays coming from the pen of authors such as Harold Pinter and Samuel Beckett. 'It was hilariously funny,' says Eleanor. 'We played for one night at the Royal Court [Sloane Square] and they couldn't believe it could be done so fast. It went at a tremendous lick in John Bird's production. We had such fun.'

Eleanor also remembers Peter's determination to entertain, wherever they were. 'On the Tube Peter would do that Mr Grole thing of going "ooweeeeweuu", and he would lean back slowly, making this funny noise. It was scarcely perceptible to anyone but me and John, but we would just fall about laughing. It is a daft memory.'

The Footlights put on a show entitled *Pop Goes Mrs Jessop* in which Peter featured, as did David Frost, who had been trying to get into the Footlights for some time. I was aware of him as an ingratiating but determined character who had Peter firmly in his sights. David was to organize several cabarets at private parties and he'd invite Peter to participate. Often this was just an excuse to stay in hotels at the host's expense. Girlfriends could come along and David derived enormous pleasure from manipulating the bedroom arrangements so that there could be a good deal of creeping about in the night. All this seemed rather childish to me, now that I regarded myself as a 'woman' and since Peter and I were an established couple who had no need for this subterfuge.

You may be tempted to ask if any college work got done by either of us in this flurry of extra-curricular activities. Good question. I did enough to keep my place, whereas I can't think that Peter attended many lectures at all. He did read Proust and Voltaire, though, and made jokes about them. From the outset of our relationship he was also preoccupied with Goethe's great Faustian theme.

That Easter Peter was to go to Tripoli to visit his family where his father was now working as an economic adviser. The visit was ill-starred. Unfortunately, Grandfather Mayo (Margaret's father) was dying and his mother was called back to England. Their journeys crossed in opposite directions. Once there, Peter almost immediately contracted a bad case of jaundice and his father and younger sister Elizabeth were left to nurse him. Never a good patient, he wrote me several sorrowful letters. I felt rather helpless with no possibility of telephoning. I relied on the lengthy process of airmail delivery to stay in touch. I still have his first letter and it let me know, tempered with some wit, just what a grim time he was having . . . He starts off by warning me the contents will be of a low calibre, barely legible and interspersed with gratuitous 'darlings'. The Ghibli, he continues, is blowing desert sand across their little garden, the extent of which is as far as he has been so far. He tells me a little, characteristically, of the pets and animals he has come across and closes the letter with protestations that he misses me and loves me very much. Having planned to fill the remaining page with kisses, he gives up explaining that his strength is flagging.

A second letter to me charted the progress of his illness with customary good humour, but it was clear to me now that he was seriously sick. His fever, he says, had wavered 'monotonously' between 100 and 105°. The doctor in charge of his case was charming but seemed to rely on a method of 'lulling the disease into a sense of false security', he complains.

These letters are so hard to make out now, because of Peter's idiosyncratic hand, that anyone who wasn't used to his screed would find them impenetrable. Even at this early age, unless Peter was in a high fever as he wrote each one, it seems he believed the harder it is to read a letter the better. Looking at the pages now reminds me of something Paul McCartney, who was later to become a friend of ours, recalls Peter advising him: 'I had to write something out for Peter once, an address or something, and he looked down at my handwriting. Now my handwriting is not sort of doctor's, grown-up handwriting, it is very schoolboyish. I used to pride myself on my handwriting as a kid, but I never realized it would be a lot cooler to scrawl a bit. It was rather, sort of, legible. And I remember Peter saying, "Oh God, Paul, you have got to scrawl a bit. You have got to do something about that. It is really grammar school."'

A bout of jaundice was eventually diagnosed out in Tripoli. At his bedside, Elizabeth and Alec fed Peter endlessly on Marmite sandwiches in an effort to pull him round.

'I am not sure whether Peter wanted Marmite sandwiches or whether Dad and I thought that was what you had to give an invalid. Anyway, we went around Tripoli desperately trying to get hold of Marmite, I remember that. We just got fixated on the idea that Marmite would make him better,' Elizabeth says. 'Peter was very ill. He lay in a darkened room a lot of the time and my father was quite worried. He felt quite a sense of responsibility and probably he was quite worried about Mum as well, with her father dying over in England. It was a difficult time.'

I was never sure what Alec Cook had been doing in Libya at this period and it turns out, according to Elizabeth, that neither was he. 'Dad was working for the United Nations and this posting was when he was semi-retired. He had a number of commissions after retirement; one was going around the West Indies, the Caribbean, helping to decide which island should become the capital. I remember that one because he was away for around three months and I was terrified of forgetting who he was. I kept going into Mum's bedroom to look at

Above A city girl who took to country life: Claire Snowden, my mother, aged 20.

Above Always a dapper man: William (Bill) Snowden, my father, aged 35.

Right Making the best of ourselves: my mother and I wearing her latest fashions, 1948.

Above Peter's family, from left
to right: Sarah, Peter, Elizabeth,
Margaret and Alec with the
pet dog.

Right The charming schoolgirl
Elizabeth Cook with her big
brother, Peter.

Above Behind the mike: entertaining a crowd at the legendary Cambridge 'smoker', 1959.

Left An art student at last: me at Cambridge, 1959.

Below Already making his mark: Peter at Cambridge, 1959

Above Peter in the Pembroke Player's production of *The Merchant of Venice*, playing Lancelot Gobbo, 1958.

Three Success Stories

David Frost and Peter Cook

THE first impression one gains on entering Mr. Pules' vast office is one of spaciousness. Head of Digital Pressure Ltd., makers of the new pull-out Automatic Bread Computer, he left school at the age of 18.

"Never fluffed myself up—just take care of myself", are often his very words.

He started life on the shop floor, earning what he now laughingly terms "the princely sum of three and fivepence" an hour.

Gradually he worked his way up through the Egg Department to the Bread Division, where his experience with eggs proved to be of little value.

Undismayed, Pules carried on, and soon word came from the Ruhr. War had been declared. Essentially a man of peace, Pules steadfastly refused to be caught up in the ensuing turmoil and pressed forward his own campaign for increased production, efficiency and wealth.

Soon he was put in charge of the new Digital factory at Ashford. Then in 1942 came news of the death of his father, and Henry succeeded to his present position.

Pules likes boxing, enjoys a good crossword puzzle, and writes cheques in his spare time.

It is to the wide experience he gathered during his apprenticeship that he modestly attributes much of his success.

"Workmen, foremen, threats, complaints, strikes—they're all the same to me," he will tell you. And who will argue ?

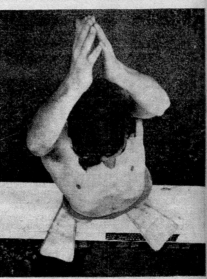

BRIAN POCK, 7-year-old teenage swimming sensation, has an old head on his shoulders; I found this likeable British lad drinking in the garden of his house, 9 Great Band Walk, Snain. In three short years this unspoiled coil of dynamism has toiled his way to Snain's premier diving team. I asked him to what he attributed his present state of success.

"I owe most of it to my mother, Mrs. Pock," vouchsafed this modest bundle of bounce. "When I was only two she threw me into the sea at Yaberleigh; I'm truly grateful to all that what mum's done for me and I visit her once a week."

Brian has not yet been selected for the Olympics and it is still too early to say that he has broken any records, apart from the Snain and district closed backstroke over 40 yards, and it was Brian himself who remarked, "I shall need training if I'm going to smash the Hungarians; what we want is a Minister of Sport."

His aged, spry but bearded father, a placid man living on his nerves, wryly divulged, "As far as Brian goes, why, he's a game little beggar, always up to his neck in cold water."

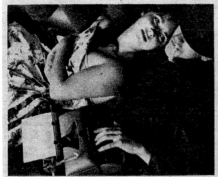

"THE man they poked in the eye in Bermuda" they call him. And rightly. Jack Rune is the sort of man who must by the very nature of his calling be somewhat unpopular.

"Jack Rune's Diary" concerns itself not with dreary platitudes, but with outspoken social criticism. Rune eschews the conscious pleasantries of seventy years ago.

"We present unpalatable facts in palatable form," he rejoins.

Few indeed are the famous who can run far amok without the Rune typewriter being in pretty close pursuit.

Actor, parson, deb—Rune metes out to them all the same characteristic treatment. Yet his attacks are not indiscriminate. "In all good journalism, truth must be selectively represented," he avers.

The untrained eye may see no news at all, but still Rune brings home the uncensored bacon. He even claims to know about oncoming babies before the fathers do. Which is no mean feat.

He works a punishing three-hour day, and spends much of that dictating to his secretary. His leisure-hours he divides between darts and billiards—for he is at root a man of simple tastes. He is not, however, entirely averse to politics, and was responsible for the new slogan, "Life is better under the Conservatives—so don't let your daughter marry a Socialist." "And that's no idle boast," he told me calmly.

Above A page from *Varsity* newspaper, June 1959. Clockwise from the top: David Frost; Peter Cook; myself and Peter.

Above From left to right: Stuart Anstis (landlord), Glenys Roberts and Peter Rowse, outside the Prince of Wales, the pub in which we first made our home. Cambridge, 1959.

Above Peter (right) and Tony Howarth at the Pembroke Garden Party, 1959.

Above Two from Oxford, two from Cambridge: the brilliant *Beyond the Fringe* team, put together by luck and good judgement.

Left Contemplating the past and the future: me in the Temple of Knossos, Crete, 1961.

Below Peter, typically with an English newspaper, Crete, 1961.

his photograph because I was so frightened I would forget what he looked like.'

Libya came along after this trip, at a time when Sarah, the elder sister, was at boarding school at Sherborne. Peter had gone up to university, but managed to make the one visit out.

'Mum and I were there for nine months and Dad was there for a year. That was enough. He could have stayed there indefinitely, drawing a large salary and doing very little. But he didn't like that. He was too honest. There was an awful lot of graft, if you wanted to get into that system. He just felt terribly frustrated and didn't want to be corrupt and so he left. All that bribery. He hated that. It was terribly lonely.'

The Cook's Libyan home was a rented bungalow three miles outside Tripoli on the main road. 'It had stone floors and tile floors. It wasn't a very beautiful looking place, actually. Mum loathed it. There was an outbuilding where we kept this poor little kitten, which I think had been taken away from its mother far too young and died. It was awful. Peter describes this kitten in a letter as the smallest kitten he had ever seen.'

This strange little home, with a flat, dry garden all around full of orange trees and cacti, is still clear in Elizabeth's mind's eye. For her, one of the country's most enticing landmarks was a market stall on the road nearby. 'It sold sticky sweets and Mum wouldn't let me buy them. She thought they had too many flies landing on them, but they always seemed really inviting, and much nicer than the kind of sweets that were wrapped up.'

Elizabeth, at school only in the mornings, also used to cycle off to visit a Bedouin family with her father, stopping to look at the camels on the way or to mend punctures caused by the cactus thorns. She thinks Peter visited the more conventional landmarks on his stay, like the Roman ruins and a stylish hotel on the seafront in Tripoli, although she and Alec would also have taken him see to their favourite beach once he was well enough.

'He must have been able to get up and write,' she says. 'We hadn't met you at that stage, but it wasn't going to be long before we did.'

Although I had never been abroad, I too managed to enjoy little tastes of foreign climes and cultures while Peter was away, however indirectly. For a start, I helped develop some amazing photographs of African wild animals in the bush when I worked for a while with photographer Tony Howarth, who had recently led an African safari. Tony shared nice premises in Park Street, Cambridge, with an Indian architectural student called Kamal Mangaldas and I got to know some of his relatives. His mother came to visit and made a wonderful curry. There were cousins, too, studying at Cambridge and I was treated as one of the family. We would sit on the floor and help ourselves from saucepans. I was astonished to see my Indian friends eat daintily with their fingers, using chapattis to scoop up the dhal. I was later to learn that the family, so cosy and egalitarian in their hospitality, actually lived in a Le Corbusier-designed house, had started their own Montessori school, had an enormous modern art collection and were one of the most prestigious Jain families in Ahmadabad. I was so interested to learn about the Jains, a vegetarian sect of Hinduism. They go to great lengths to avoid killing anything, including insects, to which end the strict ones sweep the ground before they tread upon it and wear special face masks to avoid breathing in microbial life. (Kamal's grandfather had made news because he was the first Jain to kill an animal – a rabid dog.)

Peter at last returned and I was glad to see him back. He was an interesting yellow colour though, and still needed to recuperate. The feverish quality of this illness and its impact on his liver seemed to have somehow stimulated the creation of more and more absurd characters. This was his way of getting back to health, this, and, of course, studying the racing form and placing his daily bets, something which I don't think he had been able to do in Tripoli. Such were the key elements of his life, it seemed: Cambridge was about humour, making people laugh, acting, having an audience; racing, sex and newspapers were passions too, and part of being *au courant* with what was happening in the world in order to lampoon it.

I was now to be introduced to Peter's mother, who was coming up for one of her termly visits. We were to dine near the river at the Garden House Hotel, one of the best in Cambridge and a place where I had worked as a waitress one summer holiday. Margaret was plump with iron-grey curly hair. She had a sweet, shy smile, with a dimple. But she was also very formal and conversation was pretty stilted. Peter was on his best public schoolboy behaviour, somewhat unrecognizable, but witty and deferential. Alan Bennett really struck a chord with me when he told me of the occasion, a few years later, when he gave a tea party for Peter's mother at Peter's request. 'He was so grateful and yet it was nothing,' remembers Alan. 'It was the only time I think I had seen Peter behave like a normal person in a normal situation – being gracious and interested and easy to be with.'

My introduction to Margaret was obviously a kind of solemnization or recognition of my by now fairly important role in his life, but it also gave me an insight into a way of life that seemed to be permeated by taboo subjects. Eleanor Bron's memories of a trip she made with John Bird down to Lyme Regis to meet Peter's family also chimes with my own impression. 'It was very sort of "correct",' she says. 'They seemed upper class and there was that polish, that English thing, which I found very intimidating, of always being very polite whatever you were thinking.'

With Peter in convalescent mode, the Prince of Wales suddenly seemed like Piccadilly Circus, with a succession of callers popping in. It was especially disturbing as our room was on the ground floor, so Peter and I decided to try to find a place of our own. I learned that Tony Howarth was going down from Cambridge and would be leaving his smart premises at Park Street. Peter decided to take on the lease. I went to auction rooms and found some interesting pieces to furnish the upstairs flat. I also found some gorgeous fabrics on the market to make curtains and lots of squidgy cushions. Peter had been only too happy to let me get on with this and I was in my element. Soon we had a nice little nest. Because it was so central to all the colleges we always had people dropping by for food, company and laughter.

As Peter's time as an undergraduate drew to a close our relationship took another step forward. He took me down to meet his parents on their own ground. I can still feel the nerves now and the whole daunting experience, from my point of view, was later transformed into a surreal sketch in which a young man presents his fiancée, Deirdre, to his parents for the first time. She spends the entire encounter inside a cardboard box and converses through a slit in the top. A slight exaggeration, but I can't say I was at ease.

They were so different from my own rumbustious family. The only part of the trip I really enjoyed was the journey down by train. While we progressed through Dorset towards Devon Peter would mimic the station masters' accents at each stop. As the miles passed, they got broader and broader, ending up in a rich Devonian burr: Crewkerne, Axminster, Lyme Regis. This happened every time we were on that train subsequently.

He had an incredible ear, in spite of the fact that he was musically tone deaf.

At the end of the summer term the moment of reckoning arrived. It was time for Finals. Had Peter done the necessary work to get him a reasonable degree? Not really, and although I was an accomplice in all these jolly extra-curricular activities, I did nag him to go to lectures. Perhaps he went to a few when I wasn't looking. What he definitely did do, however, was to borrow Eleanor Bron's notes and spread them out on the bedroom floor. Then he simply walked around, staring at them in a kind of trance. He appeared to have a totally photographic memory. (How generous of Eleanor this loan was! She says now she did not resent it at all.) There were essays on Proust, Voltaire and Goethe; the entire contents had clearly clicked into the camera-like mind of this extraordinary young man because he came out with a lower second, a miraculous result given the circumstances. (It should be recorded here that the exams themselves were also marked by a dramatic incident in which Peter blacked out and fell on the steps of the examination hall. Some said then that he had induced the collapse to get more time for a difficult paper. We will never know, but I wouldn't put it past him.)

Edinburgh or Bust

Peter's career path in the Foreign Office had been encouraged by his father, it seemed to me, although his sister claims there was no definite plan. Certainly I was never aware of Peter making any job application in this direction. I do, however, remember him being rather disdainful about his friend Adrian Slade, Julian's brother, who had an excellent degree and yet had gone off to write advertisements. (Adrian later went into Liberal Party politics.) Another friend joined Beaverbrook's newspaper empire as a way of earning enough money to write his own books; Peter made cynical remarks about that, too, and went on to parody his decision in a sketch in which an apologetic hack protests that just because his name's at the top of the column, 'you mustn't think I have any connection with it.'

Peter's own future career was about to be decided by a quirk of fate. Out of nowhere an invitation to take part in a new revue at the Edinburgh Festival dropped on to the doormat at Park Street one morning in the early part of that spring term. The fateful letter came from the office of John Bassett, assistant to the director of the Festival. He was an Oxford politics graduate who also ran his own jazz band, in which another Oxford man, Dudley Moore, sometimes played piano. Both of them had heard of Peter as an up-and-coming cabaret talent and had seized upon the name because John's boss, festival director Robert Ponsonby, was keen to come up with a fresh piece of challenging comedy for his Festival programme. So, rather like putting together a kind of intellectual boy band, they were trying to find a small team of clever, funny young performers. John already knew about Alan Bennett's entertaining line in 'constipated vicars' because they had both been up at Exeter College, Oxford, at the same time. He had also come across Jonathan Miller's startling brand of verbal and physical humour. Jonathan, a medical student, had been known as 'the Danny Kaye of Cambridge' but was by now working as a junior doctor at University College Hospital in London and was finishing his medical training. Alan, meanwhile, had completed a first degree in Medieval History at Oxford and stayed on to do further research. They received letters of invitation at the same time as Peter.

In his critique 'Beyond the Fringe ... and Beyond' Ronald Bergan makes a valiant attempt to put John Bassett on the map for posterity. The part he played in bringing together this foursome was crucial and Bergan writes, 'If Hal Roach gets the credit for teaming Stan Laurel and Oliver Hardy, then the unsung and unknown John Bassett must accept the laurels for bringing these four very different young men together.' So who exactly was John Bassett and how did he come up with the idea?

John had been running his jazz band for three years by then, initially performing almost every night in the Union Cellars under the Oxford Union, a venue opened by Michael Heseltine, the Union President at the time. Dudley Moore, officially the pianist, had soon started 'opening up', doing impromptu cabaret, while John began to invite noted jazz musicians down from London to guest with the band, building up a contacts book of musicians and comics and also building up the size of the band so that they could play at big London hotels, as well as at the enormous number of debutante balls still being held. 'Most of the debs' parents hadn't the first clue as to how to book a band,' recalls John now, 'or what was the popular music of the time, let alone how to venture into the world of cabaret.'

Working for him in this way, John says, Dudley, Alan and Jonathan had all begun refining their acts and earning quite decent money for students. The only person none of them knew, or had even met, was Peter Cook, although Jonathan had watched him performing and had declared his 'Titanic' sketch 'electrifying'.

Once he had taken up his £11-a-week job helping to plan that year's Edinburgh International Festival, John Bassett's close association with Dudley meant that Ponsonby, the director, had what John now describes as 'a gradual and in-depth acclimatization to up-to-the-minute intellectual student humour' of the day. (Dudley, it seems, called in at the Festival Offices in London more frequently than was strictly necessary once he had started to conduct an affair with the director's secretary.)

At that time, just as now, the 'Festival proper' was threat-ened by the growth and anarchic life of the Festival Fringe. John explains: 'Despite calling itself an "International Capital City", Edinburgh's restaurants closed at about 9.00 p.m., the bars were usually homes to drunken local violence and closed all day on Sundays. There was nothing to eat, drink, do or see after leaving all the concerts and theatrical performances of the main Festival. This was where the Fringe came in, having a life of its own up to about two in the morning. Robert Ponsonby decided it was the responsibility of the main Festival to offer late-night entertainments as well – and on a bigger budget.'

Robert Ponsonby confirms to Ronald Bergan that he can claim some of the glory for the impulse to prick the cultural bubble that year: 'I always had a naughty corner in my mind and it seemed to me that we were a bit pompous and that late-night entertainment, which was of course flourishing on the Fringe, was something the Festival proper ought to be doing itself.'

John Bassett argues that the cheapness of the idea also appealed. Going for 'a not particularly expensive but brainy student show' would mean more money could be spent on the other professional performers.

When questioned about the idea Jonathan, Alan and Dudley reportedly said they felt they could not 'hold' an evening and so John penned his invitation to Peter on Festival paper. He still has the reply which he says was 'very enthusiastic'.

So the four young men agreed to meet up for the first time just off the Tottenham Court Road. Jonathan says it was at a Greek restaurant, John Bassett says it was Italian and Peter once described the place as 'an Indian'. One thing all agree upon, though, is that it is not there any more and, let's face it, the food is not what it is remembered for in any case.

Jonathan says they all took an instant dislike to one another and John Bassett admits that things were tense. 'The beginning was hesitant insofar as all of them had a reputation for intellectual humour to live up to and none of them wanted to make the first joke in case it fell flat. Dudley saved the day by lecherously following the waitresses in and out of the different doors to the kitchen, in the Groucho Marx manner – going in with a brunette and immediately coming out with a blonde. After such a non-verbal icebreaker, the lunch took off and lasted something more than three hours. As usual, absolutely no content of the revue was discussed, nor any notes taken.'

Dudley later claimed, 'We were all very competitive when

we met. We had had some success in our respective fields, but I couldn't compete on the literary, philosophical level at all. I had no knowledge there.'

Class was a contentious element from the first too, with Alan and Dudley coming from significantly humbler backgrounds than Peter and Jonathan. While Peter's father was in the Foreign Office and Jonathan the son of an eminent psychiatrist, Alan's father was a butcher and Dudley's a railway engineer. There was a genuine division there that they went on to play with so deftly in the famous sketch 'Real Class' from *Beyond the Fringe*. Peter started this sketch by pointing out to the less observant members of the audience, 'and God knows it is apparent enough', that he and Jonathan were both from a public school background, while the other two had clawed their way up from the proletariat. The experiment, he summed up, had been a success: all four were working together as equals.

That winter John Bassett was engaged to play with his band at the coming-out ball of Lord and Lady Ismay's daughter. He also persuaded Jonathan, Alan and Dudley, as well as Peter, to do the cabaret. I came along too and when we arrived we were shown to a large, grand bedroom dominated by a great four-poster bed. Upon this bed, in foetal position and clearly gripped by the medieval history book that he was reading, snuggled Alan Bennett. My first sighting. He was oblivious to the cacophony and excitement below and his hiking boots and knapsack were resting on the floor beside him. He looked up at me, owl-like in his heavy-rimmed spectacles, and said in his soft Sheffield accent, 'Oh hello, is it time to do our bit?' I thought him so lovely and unpretentious. In fact none of us, Alan included, was going to be let off without doing some hobnobbing that night before their performance. There was a grand banquet to be tackled first.

John's band struck up, with Dudley at the piano. He was a scrap of elemental, dark-haired musical energy and he seemed to become a different entity when he played. (During this period he was also playing with Johnny Dankworth and Cleo Lane, I believe.)

Peter and I went down into the banqueting hall first, spotted a table with two empty chairs and assumed we could sit there. Some moments later we realized we had placed ourselves at the main family table. It was a mistake that brought me my first taste of really immaculate upper-class manners. Instead of saying, 'I'm sorry, you're the cabaret. This is family!' more chairs were simply called for and everybody shifted round to make room. I personally wished the floor would open up, I was so embarrassed, but of course Peter, unperturbed, came up with some side-splitting quip and suddenly everyone appeared grateful that this couple of cuckoos had landed in their nest. Jonathan arrived for the show with only minutes to spare, looking like a demented scarecrow and going in six directions at once. His reddish tousled hair surrounded a face that might have been made of rubber. He was always a little breathless and a little apologetic, but comic dynamite, despite his slight predisposition to stutter. The audience applauded crazily as they finished and the evening had wings.

Alan tells me he went to several of these 'warm-up' gigs before the Edinburgh run and that if he had had any idea at the time that Hastings Ismay was Churchill's former right-hand man he would have been much more interested in this particular ball.

'Back then I would have just thought it was another upper-class affair with a cabaret-type thing. We did another one at some architect's in north London before Edinburgh as well, and the others all came over to do one at Exeter in Oxford where I was living. It was a Commemoration Ball, I think. I always remember it because there was some Mahler on the gramophone in my rooms and Peter was very sniffy, implying this had been set up to show how cultured I was. He was probably quite right. He would always regard any appearance of culture as being a total sham.'

Jonathan, although paired with Peter as one of the two well-to-do members of the team, tells me now he also felt looked down upon, or at least rather different from Peter. 'He was always immaculately dressed, in the way that none of us were. His suits were always good and he looked fantastically handsome. We always thought that I was a Jew and the other two were proles. We all just felt different from him in many ways. He had already had a show on in the West End. He was already in show business.'

While all this was going on I was attempting to sort out my own career prospects. Now in my fourth year, I needed another year to graduate, but had really had enough of being at Cambridge School of Art. Most of my friends would be leaving, so I applied to a London art school just for the hell of it. I approached the Central School of Art, despite the fact that part of me was still very attached to Cambridge life. The place had given me the most incredible education, on every level; I loved the history and atmosphere. I had friends who roomed in St John's College in the very rooms where William Wordsworth had penned some of his poems; we often took tea in Rupert Brooke's Grantchester Meadows tea rooms; and, of course, I had recently been enjoying the company of people who were to become modern giants in their fields. I loved it all, from evensong at King's to the social whirl. I'd really enjoyed my time at art school, but I knew I lacked the focus that would make me a successful freelance artist or theatre designer. I rather preferred to use my talents to help another; I certainly had lots of drive, but it was channelled into ambition for Peter.

I began to have some influence on his style of dress. The mohair coat that had impressed me originally was, unfortunately, where his fashion sense began and ended. So we made a trip to London and the trendy shop run by John Michael in Carnaby Street, where jackets, crisp shirts with button-down collars and the must-have skimpy ties were all procured.

The four young Oxbridge men came together in London in the early summer of 1960 to rehearse and develop a new show. Alan says everything was decided by committee. 'We didn't actually vote, but there was a consensus as to whether something went in or went out. Jonathan would change his mind from one meeting to another. He would say, "Oh, I think that was very good", if I read him something and then, "Oh, I don't like that" later. So you never knew where you were.'

In the years that followed it seems to have been agreed among the cast that Peter contributed about a third of the ideas in the script, with the remainder shared between Alan and Jonathan. Dudley's input was to create a masterly series of comic musical numbers, parodying stars of the day such as the pianist Dame Myra Hess.

Today Jonathan is magnanimous about Peter's role: 'In a way I have to admit, looking back on it, that the edge in all the humour really was Peter. We all contributed. I wrote the Shakespeare sketch and I conceived the end of the Second World War thing, and I thought of the civil defence sketch. But Peter wrote most of the really funny things. I almost think he was a sort of ventriloquist's dummy. Things spoke through him. He became them. I never had a conversation with Peter outside one of his accents.' His judgement on Peter as nothing more than a vessel struck me as harsh at first, but perhaps it merely harks back to what Christopher Booker had noticed at Cambridge when he spoke of 'orphic utterances'.

In August Peter and I drove up to Edinburgh, where a large, fourth-floor furnished apartment overlooking the castle had been taken for the cast. It had a piano and space to rehearse. Jonathan and his wife, Rachel, stayed elsewhere, but he came round every morning to 'rehearse'. I slipped easily into my role of den mother and cook. There was a fantastic bakery on the corner of the street and I would go out early each morning to get fresh baps and muffins. Edinburgh seemed like a fairy-story city, precipitated out of granite, with rolling hills surrounding it and a castle with battlements and flags flying. A buzz of excitement pervaded the city during the Festival, a mysterious combination of both antiquity and modern culture. I could always hear the sound of laughter in the flat as the four worked on the show, but John Bassett says there was, in fact, virtually no rehearsal at all, ever. He says that when the journalist Alan Brien came round to do interviews and for an article on the Thursday, he couldn't believe there could possibly be a show on stage by the following Monday. 'But what with their own couple of solos each, plus their ability to busk just about anything – there was.'

I bought a new dress for the opening night, a dark magenta watermarked taffeta with a full skirt which I thought looked good with my auburn hair. Friends from Cambridge had come up to support us, some even forking out for the tickets, which were 10s upwards. And so, on Monday 22 August 1960 at 10.45 p.m., *Beyond the Fringe* first pushed its way on to the stage, sandwiched as it was in the Festival schedule beside upmarket fare such as Alexander Dumas' *Les Trois Mousquetaires* and *An Evening with Beatrice Lillie*. Dudley, who was always late and paid little heed to the half-hour call before the show began, went off for a pee in the dressing rooms, which were stuck at the top of the building. His own trio was supposed to play for a quarter of an hour before the curtain went up, but Dudley only arrived, whistling as he came down the stairs, once Peter, Alan and Jonathan were on stage and already doing the mannered 'harrumphing' that opened the show. Despite this sticky start, the audience roared throughout the hour and next day the critics raved. Under the headline 'Midnight Gaiety in Edinburgh', *The Times* review ran: 'The pleasingness of this revue is difficult to pin down in words. It keeps the midnight audiences in a continual ripple of easy laughter. The reason may be that each performer is coolly confident of his own power to amuse and also that the comedy is ruled by a nice sense of proportion.'

We had the sensation of overnight success but John says the audience for the first night was only 38 per cent capacity. Word of mouth was so good, however, that the show played to 120 per cent over the week, 'which probably means it was illegally full on occasions'. The *Edinburgh Evening News* trumpeted that the show was 'convulsing Festival audiences' and slaying 'everything it touches'. It pronounced Peter, Dudley, Alan and Jonathan the 'hit of the Festival'.

Peter's agent Donald Langdon, plump, tanned and camel-hair-coated, magically appeared on the second night. He had been reluctant to treat this revue with any degree of seriousness; his client after all was already a professional writer with contributions to a successful West End show under his belt and the rest of the cast were young, inexperienced graduates. They were all to have been paid £100 for the week, including writing fees. Langdon negotiated Peter's fee up by £10 so that he would be paid £110, but by the time the agent's fee had been paid Peter ended up with £95. This proved to be a source of great mirth for the other *Beyond the Fringe*-ers and has made me suspicious of agents ever since. After reading the reviews Langdon at last took notice of the production. He made a promise to Willie Donaldson – a would-be West End producer

Edinburgh Festival programme

of little experience but the man who went on to write the bestselling *Henry Root Letters* in 1980 – that he would hie himself to Edinburgh and secure the show for him. But was it a foregone conclusion that the four would want to take up a life on the stage?

Both Peter and Dudley were very well disposed towards taking up an offer to appear in the West End. Their friendship, founded on shared ambitions and their delight in each other's silly flights of fancy, was deepening and I was pleased. In fact I felt included, as they used to perform for me. Their lives were already pointing towards the entertainment business, but Jonathan and Alan had different considerations and showed initial reticence in the face of several potential offers.

Peter commented once to the press on the predicament he and Dudley found themselves in: 'Jonathan had this doctor–comedian conflict and Alan had this academic–comedian conflict. I had no conflict whatsoever, nor had Dudley. It was rather boring. We kept trying to think of something such as "By day he is a Trappist monk, by night he is on the boards."'

In fact, of course, this was not quite fair to the musically gifted Dudley: he had won an organ scholarship to Oxford and had at one time considered a career as a classical organist – or, failing that, as a full-time jazz musician and composer. Certainly, though, it was true that Jonathan was well on his way to becoming a medical doctor and this vocational call was strengthened by the fact that his wife, Rachel, was also a doctor. Her influence, we all felt, might sway the balance against the show. Alan seemed a little more malleable, but it would have been unthinkable to do the show without Jonathan – indeed, without any of the four. The mix of diverse and uniquely complementary ingredients in these four young men could not have been reproduced. It was a kind of alchemy of incompatibility. So when Rachel and Jonathan closeted themselves in a bedroom together to thrash this one out in destiny-changing deliberation, a torturous and pregnant silence fell over the room where the rest of us waited with bated breath.

Jonathan says he remembers walking all night around Edinburgh with Rachel trying to decide what to do, but I am sure the denouement took place inside the apartment. Occasionally Dudley or Alan would creep up to try to listen at the keyhole to determine which way it was going. Peter pretended to disdain such activity, but was just as keen to know the outcome as the others. So was I, but I just observed with great interest, not knowing what it might mean for the future.

Eventually Jonathan and Rachel emerged, flushed. It had clearly not been a straightforward decision by any means. 'Medicine was becoming boring, which was part of it,' says Jonathan. 'And we had no money. So we thought, let's just do it for a bit.' I believe Rachel really wanted Jonathan to continue with medicine, but since humour is one of the best medicines known to man, somehow I feel the right path was taken, although Jonathan, reflecting now, wonders whether it was indeed the right choice. 'It changed the course of my life in ways that I regret. I wanted to be a clever doctor and I became a clever director. I was brought up to admire nothing but science. It changed my life completely. It didn't change Peter's life because that is what he was going to do anyway. Yet it was a sort of catastrophe for me, although I enjoyed it in many ways.'

Think what the world would have missed if he had gone down the other route. He has become one of our greatest intellectuals, the man behind some mind-stretching documentaries, a writer of books and a director of opera. His contributions have frequently caused controversy, but he has made us think and laugh and appreciate beauty. I have often thought about his decision-making process. The huge impact on my own life aside, it threw together four extraordinary people for a period of four years. They were not even friends until John Bassett introduced them and Alan Bennett still questions whether they ever really got close to each other. 'When we were in *Beyond the Fringe* none of us really ever knew one another,' he says. 'We were together for three and a half years but we never had any discussion about our inner lives really at all. We never talked about Dudley's disability. We never talked about me being gay. We each of us had a slightly jokey personality and so it wasn't real life. If Peter and Dudley went on like that, I don't know.'

Alan harboured doubts too, back then, about whether he had chosen the right path. 'I took my degree in 1957 and I was at Oxford all that time until we left for America in 1962. A car would come for me after the show while we were in London and take me back to Oxford. I still thought I would go back to Medieval History.'

There was rejoicing that day nevertheless, and, borne on this tide of excitement, Peter and I decided to get engaged. This, too, was a bit of a group decision. His mother and sisters were arriving at the end of the week and, since we were quite obviously cohabiting, it seemed a good idea to give a degree of respectability to our situation and for me to be presented as his fiancée. We did all thrive together as a group, but, looking back, it was also a bit tribal. I seemed to be working out my unconscious destiny of becoming Peter Pan's Wendy, looking after any amount of lost boys. I found myself growing into the role and I think they all really appreciated being cooked for and collectively mothered somewhat. Peter and I went out to look for a ring and chose a pretty, fairly inexpensive moss agate and silver ring. We had been together for about a year already, but this was to be a long engagement. That same day Peter rented some fishing tackle and drove me out to a nearby loch to give me a lesson in fly-casting for trout. I found this wonderful, being in that soft, watery greenness of Scotland, the future stretching out unimaginably rosy before us, and then to go home with freshly caught trout for tea.

Peter's mother and sister Elizabeth duly arrived, all excited. I rather fell in love with seven-year-old Elizabeth with her big eyes and open face. She had thick pigtails and was wearing her school hat. She told me that she wanted to be a ballerina and I bought her a book about Margot Fonteyn. It seems the immediate affection I felt for this unusual schoolgirl was returned. Elizabeth says now that I seemed interested and unpatronizing: 'Because whatever age you are you think you are as old as you will ever be in terms of awareness, don't you? There is nothing worse than grown-ups who talk down to you and call you "little girl".'

Apparently the trip up to Edinburgh in the car had been long and seemed even longer. Elizabeth says her mother proved hard to please when it came to accommodation too. 'She would say, "Oh no! We can't possibly stay there. It smells of cabbage."' They eventually stayed in a B&B. 'It wasn't very near you. I went back recently and I was trying to picture it. I thought I could see where your lovely flat was.'

Elizabeth was taken to the Tattoo for her eighth birthday and met Alan, Jonathan and Dudley for the first time. 'It was terribly exciting, although I had this great sense of mournfulness that I was never going to be seven again. I just felt life rushing away from me.'

Peter's other sister, Sarah, had come up for the show too, and as a teenager she was allowed to see it more than once. 'It was thought she would understand it and I wouldn't, which was probably true, but I thought I understood it all,' complains Elizabeth now. 'I thought it was very funny. Even the bits I didn't understand. It was funny that Dudley Moore was announced as "playing with himself", even though I hadn't a clue what it meant. I had no idea of the innuendo of it. All sorts of things went over my head; Dudley singing Little Miss Muffet was funny, yet I didn't know it was a parody of Peter Pears. I liked him sitting with a wig on the wrong way round and I liked it too in the wartime sketch when Dudley said he wanted to be one of "the few" and Peter said he was afraid there were too many.'

She also particularly enjoyed the sketch about the way the road signs had been altered to fox the enemy during the war. 'One sign had Lyme Regis on it, which I liked. I was so proud. I wanted to tell everyone in Edinburgh that my brother was on the stage.'

There were national celebrities circling the cast by this point, she remembers: Fyfe Robertson of the television show *Tonight*, for instance. (Elizabeth got his autograph. 'I got all your autographs. You drew a nice picture for me. Alan Bennett drew a picture of himself.) Cliff Michelmore also approached Peter about becoming a reporter for *Tonight*. 'That seemed fame indeed. Peter was being headhunted.'

Margaret Cook showed herself to be happy about our engagement, but then she was a supremely polite woman. It was rather a public occasion, but luckily there were no private reproaches either. Peter had been obliged to cope as an independent force from childhood, so they probably thought it ill advised not to give their approval. Besides I hoped they quite liked me, even if I appeared a bit of a loose cannon. There was plenty of champagne that night, and I decided I liked champagne.

Negotiations for the London run were now in progress. Donald Langdon, so late to appreciate the project, swiftly cut John Bassett out of the deal. 'Over the six years of its run I calculate I should have received over half a million, so I'm not that enthusiastic about him,' he says now ruefully, remembering that Peter explained to him he felt it 'vital to have an agent for whom he could have no respect at all' so that he wouldn't mind 'bollocking' him. Jonathan and Alan are also still annoyed about how little they were paid at this point. For them, Langdon was also a big mistake, although John Bassett claims he has a contract that shows they earned £180 a week plus a quarter share of the author's royalties of 2 per cent and not the paltry £75 a week that has sometimes been recorded.

All this was academic for the moment, however, as no London theatre was available until the spring of 1961. So Peter and I, the engaged couple, made our triumphal progress back to Cambridge.

Stepping Beyond the Fringe

Peter's restless personality required a constant fix from an audience, so he appeared in many Footlights' 'Smokers' at this time. Now honed for the stage, 'The Holy Bee of Ephesus' had everyone falling about. The salon atmosphere we had developed at the Prince of Wales was carried over to our Park Street flat. I had decided not to return to art school and my application to the Central School in London was to be deferred until the spring term. I put together some designs for a few undergraduate theatre productions and continued to work on my cooking skills. I rode my bicycle, visited friends and stayed up talking until the small hours.

I had also encouraged Peter to allow the use of the downstairs offices to Roger Law and Peter Fluck as a base for their anarchic, creative company. This soon became another repository of rapier wit, out of which later sprung *Spitting Image*. David Frost would often visit too, preceded by an overwhelming whiff of Old Spice. (David was someone who continually and energetically pursued all avenues of enquiry in his determination to make his mark on Cambridge, and indeed the world, and since he cycled just about everywhere, he was inclined to sweat.) He would happily use anybody's telephone and I often heard him in the office below, sounding as if he had six secretaries bustling about him. Christopher Booker, who went on to work at *Private Eye*, also remembers David at this stage:

'He was a strange, pushy little character. It was very rare for undergraduates to have a phone then, but we had one in our hostel, and Frostie, being Frostie, as you can imagine, also got a phone pretty quickly. I was the only person he could ring up though, so he would ring up for about an hour and we would have meaningless conversations. I did know him quite well and I had a half-affection for him, because he was such an absurd character. He was so utterly in Peter's shadow. I put it in print somewhere at Cambridge: "Recipe for a bad joke, De-Frost and leave to Cook for ten minutes."'

We celebrated my twenty-first birthday that January at Park Street and Jonathan Miller came up for the party. I had made a dress in green satinized floral cotton, I remember, and had spent some days preparing the food. I had a wonderful evening and people stayed until the small hours. It was a foretaste, I felt, of the sophisticated London lifestyle awaiting me.

My place at the Central School of Art was duly awarded. I hoped to continue with stage, film and television design, but Peter dissuaded me from taking up the place. He thought we would have such different daily rhythms that we would never see each other. He said he could keep me busy enough and offered to finance both of us. Agreeing to this was probably a mistake, because I became financially dependent upon him. Although he was earning well by now and could afford it, I had surrendered my own independence to a degree and given up my own chance of a career. The trouble was that the opportunities being offered to us were so exciting and so glamorous that I was just carried along. Besides, I knew that Peter had by no means forgotten his heart's dream: the creation of a political–satirical nightclub. There would be plenty to do then.

We were ready to leave Cambridge. The satire boom was in

its infancy and the West End was calling. Peter was twenty-three and I was just twenty-one: mere saplings. John Bassett had invited us to share his flat in Hampstead until we found somewhere of our own. His place was just opposite the Everyman cinema, which showed excellent foreign films. It was a good area in which to begin our life in the metropolis because Hampstead still had the air of a village and the lovely heath was nearby. It was full of atmospheric pubs and nice little bistros, restaurants and delicatessens. The residents seemed quite bohemian too, so, as 'theatre people' we felt at home. (Little did we think that within three years we would have our own home in that Georgian gem of a street, Church Row, just around the corner.)

This is as good a moment as any to pay due respect to another man without whom the success of *Beyond the Fringe*, and perhaps the entire London 'satire boom', would not have been possible: Harold Macmillan. Aside from having become a key element of Peter's repertoire of comic characters by this point, Macmillan was surely one of the most extraordinary men ever to appear on the British political scene and was the first Prime Minister of the television era. An upper-class, patrician figure, he changed the cut of his hair and his moustache, as well as his suits, in an attempt to fit in with fashion trends. His teeth too, were reorganized, but none of this helped to change the platitudes he uttered. He was dubbed 'Supermac' by the cartoonist Vicky, who ridiculed his efforts to impress his public. It seemed he was filled, as Bernard Levin said, 'with a sense of ubiquity, omniscience and supernatural powers'. He seemed to think that life should be fun and what didn't please him was a bore. In his first year of office he wrote to the Director of Conservative Central Office with a rather unusual request: 'I am always hearing about the middle classes. What is it that they really want? Will you put it down on a piece of paper and I will see if I can give it to them?' Later, of course, he announced to the British people 'You've never had it so good!', forcing them to face the fact that life actually was rather fun. But it was also true that Britain no longer ruled the waves and the 1960s were to be full of arguments about our national identity – with Harold Macmillan muddying the water still further by launching Britain's attempt to join the Common Market. There was even wild talk of building a Channel tunnel in the hope that some kind of physical link might provide a cultural umbilical cord with the rest of the Continent.

Rehearsals of *Beyond the Fringe* now began. After fairly unsuccessful tryouts in Cambridge and Brighton, it was to be staged at the Fortune, Covent Garden, an intimate theatre, perfect for such a show. I watched some of the rehearsals, as Peter was interested in getting my feedback. He was certainly the most prolific contributor of material (although in such an alchemical process I think it would be difficult to separate out whose ideas metamorphosed into which sketches). It was mesmerizing to witness such a kaleidoscope of characters and topics, all brought to life with stingingly funny dialogue. Then came the counterpoint of Dudley's unique musical contributions, his classical pastiches and naughty impersonations of performers of the day.

Roddy Maude-Roxby, later to appear in the show in America, remembers initially being considered for the role of director for the extended London production, but eventually this role went to Eleanor Fazan, who had just directed *Share My Lettuce*. Fairly quickly she discovered the revised version of the show was too long now, rather than too short.

'She said that as she edited it down, or got them to edit it, it bulged out somewhere else,' remembers Roddy. 'Peter on a good night would just extend down the line for half an hour.'

Sean Kenny, the young Irish designer, devised a stunningly

simple yet versatile set in dramatic black. Well known for her clever visual sense, Fazan got her cast garbed in charcoal-grey sweaters and trousers and moving about in a more deliberate manner. In spite of a regional warm-up tour that had been received less than warmly, lots of pre-publicity in London let the world know it was about to be woken up by these young men. Peter was photographed with Jean Shrimpton and pictures of all four seemed to be everywhere.

The show eventually opened at the Fortune Theatre to a full house and rapturous reviews. Milton Shulman in the *Evening Standard* declared it: 'A rare delight, brilliant, uproarious and wonderfully mad.' Bernard Levin, in the *Daily Express*, referred to the cast as 'The four good, great men who have done this thing to and for and in the name of us all', adding, 'The satire is real, barbed, deeply planted and aimed at things and people that need it.' But perhaps most famously of all, Ken Tynan wrote in the *Observer*: 'Future historians will thank me for providing them with a full account of the moment when English comedy took its first decisive step into the second half of the twentieth century.' All credit to Tynan that it doesn't seem as exaggerated today as it did then. This really was the kind of intelligent humour the world had been waiting for.

Jonathan Miller has always felt the show was a symptom of the changes that were going on in the 1950s, rather than a catalyst. He believes that until the 1960s England was effectively stuck back in the 1930s.

'The deference and proprieties all began to crack like tectonic plates,' he suggests. 'They had begun to move as a result of the Labour government coming in. People had expected Churchill to get in, so there were already all sorts of shifts in the public understanding of who had a right to rule. Things started to crack just before that, with Suez in 1956, which showed up an incompetent government.'

Theatre was reflecting these changes: John Osborne's *Look Back in Anger* too had come to the Royal Court and the Theatre of the Absurd came into ascendance.

'We were symptoms of the end of the war, really,' says Jonathan. 'I don't think we were responsible for the change. Although, of course, the word satire got attached to us, we didn't consciously indulge in satire. We just indulged in being funny. Because we were educated, university people, we addressed topics that had never been seen on stage before. We also had this retrospective irreverence about the heroic mythology of the war. That was why we called that sketch "The Aftermyth of War". I look back on it with some guilt. Peter and I did that scene with the line "We need a futile gesture at this time". It was funny at the time, but looking back I can understand why people who had fought in the war, or who had relatives who had laid down their lives, were upset. I realize now if they hadn't laid down their lives, my parents and I would have been gassed.'

At any rate the show was a sellout; tickets were at a premium. I think that the Fringe Four were equally astonished and delighted to be handed such laurels by the best critics in the land.

Peter and I now moved in to a large mansion flat in Prince of Wales Drive in Battersea, sharing with old Cambridge friends Colin Bell, Ian Davidson, Roger Hammond and Peter Bellwood. Colin and Ian were now journalists, and Peter Bellwood, a Footlights alumnus, was in advertising, a burgeoning industry. Roger Hammond was an aspiring actor and later married Margaret Drabble.

It was a bit of a bachelor pad, so I was given the remit to make it more homely. The antique shop owners in Portobello Road got to know me quite well as I scoured their stores for stripped-pine Victorian furniture of the kind that was becoming rather chic. I found lamps and a rocking chair and a beautiful Edwardian rocking horse which our children would come to love riding. An oak dining table was central to the plan and a large comfortable three-seater sofa, a new purchase from John Lewis and an item still in service today.

'We all mysteriously assumed that we'd have to go to London,' recalls Colin Bell. 'Peter, of course, already had scripts being performed in the West End, and *Beyond the Fringe* looming. Nevertheless, when I told him I'd found a huge mansion flat in Battersea, which Ian Davidson and I were looking to fill, he immediately agreed to join in. Until then, I now suspect, he'd never found the time or interest to consider where he and Wendy would stay. I've rarely met anyone with such a low boredom threshold, and frankly, viewing flats and negotiating leases fell way below it.'

The 'substantial Edwardian mansion flat' was on the south side of Battersea Park in what was not yet south Chelsea, even to the most unscrupulous estate agent. Apart from the core residents Colin is quite right to point out that there were quite a few fleeting tenants: 'a shifting crew of extras who were either sleeping with the residents, or stopped sleeping with their usual cohabitees, or had just forgotten how to get home after a Battersea party. I do remember bumping into Gerry Mulligan in the kitchen, who generously offered me a lucky dip into his enormous bag of grass.'

Colin's girlfriend and later his wife, Rose, was not supposed to be living with him out of wedlock so to keep up appearances for her parents she kept on a room elsewhere that was actually sublet to Alan Bennett. Colin had just started working for the *Scotsman*, while others were also making careful steps towards careers in the media. Peter, in contrast, was already working to a showbiz clock.

'God knows how the rest of us got to work in the mornings,

but it is a tribute to the solidity of those mansion blocks (or the tolerance of our neighbours) that I don't recall a single complaint about the noise. Of course, I might easily have forgotten any, even the next day.'

Helen Nicholl remembers a typical piece of silliness. Apparently one evening Peter rang up the duty officer at Rediffusion, the television network, and told them he had just missed a bit of *Coronation Street* because he had had to answer the door: could they let him know what had happened? 'While I have been talking to you I have missed the next bit,' he went on to complain.

Peter's daft displays aside, life for the residents at Prince of Wales Drive was not without its rules and regulations.

'There was a kind of logbook in which communards noted their needs or expenditures,' according to Colin. 'It was just that these were curiously imbalanced. If the booze ran low, you could guarantee that someone would either note it, or reveal that they had redressed it. Wendy and I both bought food, which she mostly cooked, but I have a feeling that if we ever stocked up on lavatory paper, Ajax or soap, I was the only compulsory neurotic who would have attended to it.'

For Colin, Peter and the other 'boys' there were gestures in the direction of healthy living – the ritual of Sunday morning football in the park for instance. This was followed by the ritual of Sunday morning boozing. This was followed in turn by the hope that Rose and I might have whipped up a traditional roast.

We all regularly visited the fun fair across the road too, a relic of the Festival of Britain. It boasted all the usual showground attractions but with the added bonus of a freak show. 'Unthinkable now,' laughs Colin, 'but irresistible then. Star of the Freak Show – The Wowl, half-woman, half-owl.' It might sound made up, yet this was not a concept Peter had invented, but something to which Colin is right to note I was 'enslaved'. Inside a dimly lit room it was possible to espy a feathery figure and a pair of human eyes. Not very convincing, but I used to visit once a week, to try to cheer her up, I think.

There was little or no jealousy from the others, but it was clear Peter was on the fast track to success. 'We knew, because on the hall table in that gigantic flat there piled up everybody's post,' says Colin. 'For most of us, strained letters from Cambridge wine merchants and booksellers whose patience was wearing thin, snubs from potential employers, or stunning offers from magazines. For Peter the picture was slightly different as we discovered one morning when trying to clear up the mess. Many of the envelopes he'd chucked aside in boredom contained substantial cheques from agents, broadcasters and publishers which he'd felt no immediate necessity to cash.'

It was a happy time and I began to give the kinds of dinner parties that were to become my main creative satisfaction in those years. Christopher Booker kindly says these evenings were among the happiest memories of his life.

'You would bring some new dish to the table and there would be twelve or fifteen people around the table. They were terrific. I don't know why, but they were absolutely magical, those evenings.'

Venetia Mooreshead, now Venetia Parkes, one of the *Private Eye* 'irregulars', has also written to me recently to help jog my memory on a few details and says how she was struck, as a young, impoverished girl about town, by the way that Peter and I entertained – grandly and yet without ceremony. 'Yours and Peter's domestic life was an eye-opener,' she writes. 'In those days I could just about boil an egg, so your glamorous and delicious dinners were heaven, and seemed so normal and fun.' She also recollects my trademark repertoire of hats.

By April 1962 word of my enthusiastic hostessing had got

around and *Queen* magazine invited me to cook a dish. I chose to do salmon in sauce genevoise; rather adventurous. John Bulmer took sultry photographs of me too, one of which appeared on the cover of *Town* magazine. My improving cooking skills allowed me to become ever more ambitious and the talented Bruce Copp (a restaurant manager then in the early stages of being head-hunted by Peter to be the manager for his future nightclub) came along one evening and ended up helping me make a casserole of pigeons.

'You were getting quite a reputation for your cooking,' he says. 'It was quite a big dinner party and you were slaving away, so we worked on it together.' Peter and I were devoted at this time, Bruce attests, and the evening was informal although 'elegant'.

But Bruce's clearest memory from that night was a simple and stunningly sad exchange he had with Timothy Birdsall, a brilliant cartoonist and artist, there that night with his wife Jotty. Tim was a good-looking and gentle man, a friend from Cambridge who had won fame as the first to draw caricatures live on television.

'I was sitting next to him and I adored him. He used to do these quick cartoons on television. He was the sort of boy everybody would like to have as a son. He was good-looking and talented. "I hear you are not terribly well," I said to him, "but it is not the time to talk about it now." But he said: "I don't know, Bruce, I would actually like you to know I am dying of something which is apparently incurable."' Seen as a 'young Hogarth' in his day, it was tragic that Timothy died at twenty-eight from leukaemia.

During the London run of *Beyond the Fringe* I would usually go to watch the performance, meeting many of the visiting guests backstage. Famous fans of the show ranged from Peter Sellers to John Gielgud and even the Queen herself, who was observed to laugh out loud. After the curtain fell I would join the cast for a supper at Chez Solange, the French restaurant tucked between theatres in a West End alley. We were regularly served in an upstairs room by a diminutive and feisty French-woman, in Alan's words 'almost a caricature of a French wait-ress' and who quickly came to know what everybody liked and kept a table for us. Sometimes Rachel Miller would join us, but I was often the only woman present: Dudley chose to keep his women friends apart at that time. (Despite his growing friendship with Peter, if he had a date we would not see him for dust.) What a privilege it was for me to be repeatedly, personally, entertained by this group of intriguing characters. Alan, I will never forget, was peculiarly devoted to artichokes. It was pure theatre just to watch him engaged in the meticulous ritual of deconstructing one, daintily dipping the leaf in French vinaigrette and then, after biting out the delicious soft base, reconstructing the flower in a mandala around the edge of his plate.

'I was always really proud I knew how to eat the globe artichokes without being in any way intimidated, because it was quite a complicated affair with a finger bowl,' he says. 'There was no sense of being out of your class there. I know we were in a hit show and all that, but actually it was a classy restaurant and yet there was no sense of being on your best behaviour.

'We sat on those long banquettes and I remember once Dudley was there and he sat next to Nureyev. The next day he came into the theatre and said how wonderful Nureyev had looked. He said, "I have actually turned." Dudley, who didn't have a gay bone in his body.'

Jonathan was not much of a foodie, as I recall, but more of an ascetic. Dudley was the complete opposite. He liked creamy dishes, comforting foods. Peter just liked all food and was a voracious eater. In that lovely period I sampled hitherto unknown delicacies such as frogs' legs, confit, escargots and sheep's brains.

Much of the fun was had at the expense of Jonathan's former patients. He used to entertain us with lewd stories from the casualty department, genuine encounters with the public, according to him, which even then I thought rather doubtful. But it didn't stop us laughing. One involved an old man complaining that he had 'pins and needles in his balls'.

> NURSE: Yes, dear, never mind, I'm sure it will pass.
> OLD MAN: But Nurse, Nurse [getting louder] I've got pins and needles in my balls, look, look!
> NURSE, upon inspection: I see what you mean, how on earth did this happen?

Jonathan claimed this old guy had visited a prostitute and, after pleasuring himself with her, had tried to leave without paying her the agreed price. Her revenge had been to use his balls as a pincushion.

Apparently on another occasion a man was admitted with severe anal burns:

> DOCTOR: My goodness me, what have you been up to here?
> PATIENT: Well, you see, Doctor, I came upon my wife having it off with the lodger. So I went out, bought a rocket, stuck it up my arse, lit the touch paper and went fizzing around the room, saying 'I'll show you! I'll show you!'

Jonathan told these unlikely stories with such conviction that we were left wondering whether indeed there might be some truth in them. Alan Bennett tells me he has since come to realize that a lot of Jonathan's tales were rather taller than even the good doctor himself: 'He told so many lies. He was a romancer and he just made things up. I used to think I was going mad.'

An even more dubious post-show entertainment was organized for us one night by Willie Donaldson as a surprise. We were driven out to an address – somewhere off Bond Street, I think – and shown into a large, pink frothy boudoir presided over by a French madame who was going to show us a special film. You can imagine what it was: a laughable pornographic film depicting a well-endowed Frenchman and two blonde companions. Alan stuffed his handkerchief in his mouth to stifle his protesting shrieks; Peter and Dudley were absorbed; Jonathan, I think, viewed it as an opportunity for anatomical study; but I was absolutely shocked and horrified and hid my face for most of the showing. I wouldn't let Peter touch me for some days afterwards; I thought it so utterly cheap and denigrating of an act I thought was a very private affair. You may call me prudish but that was my reaction; I was only twenty-one and pretty green. On Willie Donaldson's death in 2005 Alan recorded his own version of the incident for the *London Review of Books*. He writes that the madame tut-tutted at him because he looked so young, although he was actually the oldest of the four. The films 'were silent, jerky and with nothing subtle about them at all, the participants anything but glamorous, one of the men resembling a comic villain in a Chaplin film. Still, we managed to find the films exciting.' He confirms the atmosphere was nervous and strained. 'At the finish the madame was insistent that we should not all leave together so we separately filtered out into an empty Bond Street with me wondering if this at last was "living".'

Beyond the Fringe went from strength to strength, but all revolutions devour their children and this was no exception. The very people the sketches were attacking crowded in to see themselves being parodied. During the run the show was attended by HM The Queen, R. A. 'Rab' Butler, the Home Secretary, Roy Welensky, the leader of Southern Rhodesia and Iain Macleod; and, of course, Harold Macmillan, whom Peter impersonated at length on stage, eventually turned up to show what a good sport he was.

That evening the sketch began as usual with a silly bit about Macmillan meeting John F. Kennedy, contrasting the two leaders. Peter's much-admired joke about Britain as an honest broker followed; that is, a country that could not be more honest or, indeed, 'broker'.

Then, famously, Peter adapted his script for the occasion. He said, still in Macmillan's persona, that whenever he had some time on his hands he liked to stroll into a playhouse and take a seat among the audience in order to sit there, listening, 'with a stupid great grin spread over my silly old face'.

Christopher Booker still reckons this Macmillan takeoff, performed with gusto by the twenty-four-year-old in front of its powerful target, was the defining moment of the satire movement. 'It is very hard now to reconstruct for a modern readership just how extraordinary that was,' he says.

Alan Bennett, waiting in the wings, remembers the hush that accompanied this bit of ad-libbing. 'There was a difference between how it was perceived outside and how we perceived it, because I think we thought he was insane. He went on and on, well beyond what he needed to. The audience had stopped laughing and he still went on and on.'

Summer was approaching and two of my art school friends and some of our tutors were planning to meet up in a little fishing village near Malaga, called Los Boliches. They had taken a house there and everyone was invited. I had never been abroad before. *Beyond the Fringe* was set to roll on through the summer, so when Ros Myers and her boyfriend offered to drive me there in his trusty Morris Minor it seemed a good opportunity for my first adventure across the Channel. Peter demurred only a little – he was probably worried about having to fend for himself for a month. I got one of those pink temporary passports and prepared myself with bottles of Ambre Solaire, sunglasses and other necessities for fun in the sun.

Our first stop in Normandy was at a typical French *pension*, where I had the opportunity to practise my French at table. It was fascinating to find we were served every element of the meal separately: first a garbure (vegetable potage), then a plate of exquisite tender French beans, sautéed in butter, then an escalope, a salad, some cheese and a dessert, plus metres of crusty bread; all part of the menu. Whitewashed bedrooms furnished with brass beds were simple, cheap and charming, except that we'd agreed to share a room to save money, so I had to play gooseberry. The next day I took a stand on having my own room whenever possible.

Our journey to Madrid took us through wonderful scenery, travelling through the medieval towns of Biarritz and San Sebastian and across dusty plains. We saw the threshing of grain performed by donkeys walking in a circle – very biblical – and watched little ragamuffins playing at being matadors, one way of getting out of the grinding poverty. The 'bulls' tied sharp knives to two legs of an upturned chair and charged each other, while the 'matador' had a tattered cloth to serve as his cloak. They twirled gracefully and swerved past the flashing knives. Although playing, they were deadly serious. We drove on, but outside Madrid the Morris started to cough and splutter and the red oil light came on. It juddered and finally ground to a halt, happily not too far from a garage. The required part would have to be ordered and might take a week . . . or maybe longer; we learned the meaning of the word *mañana*.

After mistakenly walking into a brothel with tatty red

carpets, we booked into a cheap hotel in the city and were obliged to share a room again. During this enforced pitstop I managed to see Goya's *The Naked Maja* and the paintings by Hieronymus Bosch at the Prado, to fall in love with a pair of soft blue Cuban-heeled leather court shoes that had white satin bows and to write a quick postcard to Peter – which by some chance I still have. The picture is of a bull ring and on the back I have written: 'Darling, Now in Madrid. What a marvellous country this is! Fantastic scenery – we have just about one more day's driving to Fuengirola on the South Coast. Have stayed in some rather good hotels. If only you were here. Be good! Write you a long letter tonight. All love, Wendy.' Strange how a handful of commonplace phrases can take you back.

The car was ready the following day, so we prepared to leave Madrid in high spirits. A glittering sea on the horizon told us we had arrived in Malaga, a city we found in its week of fiestas. Spain was still ruled by Franco in those days and a signs of poverty were still visible, but even the poorest knew how to fiesta. I was stunned by the beauty of the women with their lace mantillas, sitting side-saddle next to their black-sombreroed men, proud and straight-backed, their steeds nervously prancing Arab stallions. There was guitar music and the smell of cheap olive oil was softened by a heady waft of gardenias, sold by old ladies from brimming baskets. All was movement, colour, excitement. This was Spain, still authentic, still bewitching, the blood and passion – *orgullo* – were palpable. I had waited all my young life to be introduced to this beating pulse. It was like the reawakening of a love affair, a contact with the gypsy in me. It changed my life.

We found a small house for the equivalent of £6 a week near our friends. It was primitive – certainly the plumbing was – but I had my own room and that was something. Our elderly landlady, given to foul-mouthed ranting, told us there was a market in the village that day, so off we went down the cobbled streets among the donkey carts. By ten o'clock the sun was hot and I was glad to have brought a sunhat. The market announced itself with the hum of excited: housewives clucking like the hens they held, feet tied, wings flapping, tinny flamenco music emanating from the cafés where old men sat with their coffee and cheap cognac watching the world go by in a spirit of equanimity. The stalls were heavy with juicy fruits, salad and vegetables. We filled our baskets, amazed at how cheap it all was, but avoided the butchers' stall where meat hung black with flies. This was an unbelievable sight and reminded me of the Sartre play *Les Mouches* I had recently been working on as a student designer. Instead, we bought cheeses and salted anchovies and went home with all our purchases – only to find that there was no fridge. We immersed our fruits and salad in bowls of cold water and then, fixing up a picnic, set off for the beach.

Los Boliches was a tiny fishing village with a beach of white sand and a sea of deep hyacinth-blue. Fishermen mended their nets on upturned boats and on the beach was a little group: a black-haired woman, bronzed, with the look of Nefertiti, sitting on the white sand threading a necklace with the black seeds of a watermelon and her two naked, white-haired children cooling themselves with crimson slices. This was my first meeting with my friend Janet Allan and her children, Louise and Arum. Before taking her children off for lunch and a siesta she advised us to adopt a similar rhythm, since the sun was crucifyingly hot in the middle of the day, and then she invited us to dinner.

It was a wonderful evening, eating outside under the stars with jasmine and honeysuckle scenting the night air. Huge carafes of wine had been set out that could be refilled at the village bodega for a few pesetas. We talked about everything under the sun and then went skinny-dipping in the sea. London felt very far away. Travelling overland in a car really had underlined the geographical and cultural differences that were now making such an impression on me.

We visited friends in Mijas the next day and were told there was to be a bullfight that evening in Torremolinos. The bullring was historic and the best matadors came from all over Spain to fight there. That night it was to be Antonio Ordoñez, one of the country's most respected bullfighters. I had been reading Hemingway and was drawn to the startling ethos of the bull-fight. Today I couldn't face one, but back then it seemed exciting and brave and honourable. There were two corridas that evening before the great Ordoñez came on. The age-old ritual was impressive: the special music, the fading sunlight, attendants in seventeenth-century costume and the excited crowd, sensitive to every pass, like a stringed instrument as it registered each gain and every loss. Before the last and most important corrida we piled down to the bar, dazed by the late-afternoon sun and the theatricality of it all. Standing at the bar was an extraordinarily handsome young Spaniard with straight nose, dark hair, proud bearing and the most beautiful eyes – looking straight at me. I felt myself tremble.

Michael, the American writer we were visiting, said, 'Let me introduce you to Angel Risueño, Wendy; he's a bullfighter and he speaks a little English.' I was tongue-tied for a while, but like many Spaniards Angel was at ease with the opposite sex and asked me if I had ever seen a bullfight before. 'No, never,' I responded. 'Would you like to know more about it?' he asked. What an offer. 'I shall be fighting in here on Sunday, but perhaps we could meet before. Here is my card; give me a ring.' Once we had taken our seats again for the main fight the picadors and attendants paraded round the ring with the matador. When they dispersed, he was left alone in the ring with his cape and sword. The picadors sat on their blindfolded horses and the foot fighters hid behind wooden screens. A hush descended as the bull was released into the arena; it stamped and pawed the ground, bewildered, looking for its tormentor. Then, seeing him, it thundered towards him. The matador parried him with his cloak and the dance of death commenced.

The crowd immediately sensed that this was an especially mean bull and, sure enough, within ten minutes Ordoñez had been seriously gored in the groin and rushed to hospital. I imagine Angel Risueño accompanied him. There was mayhem after that. The ring was closed down and for the next four days the entire country tuned in to monitor the fight for life of one of their greatest bullfighters. He had been so close to death, but clawed his way back to life with the help of an entire people praying steadfastly for him.

We met up with Angel Risueño again before the corrida on the following Sunday. He was in his *traje de luces*, 'the suit of lights'. The sight of him, serious and focused, was moving. That whole week with Ordoñez fighting for his life had been taxing; there was a great brotherhood among the men who had chosen this dangerous occupation. Angel explained to me the genuine respect that the matador had for the bull – it was an enormous dance of courage and dexterity, a moment of glory for the animal, whose entire purpose in life had been for this brief hour. A priest blessed both matador and bull. The modern bullfight is a tradition made more decadent, in my opinion, by the picadors and lancers on horseback. Originally it was simply a man and a bull.

I had been given a front seat, close to the president who arbitrated the fight. When it came to Angel's corrida, he entered the ring and walked over to where I was sitting and dedicated the bull to me. Then began an extraordinary dance of grace and tension and I was electrified. (My first time out of

Angel Risueño showing the two ears and tail of his bullfight.

the country and look at what was happening to me.) The crowd roared: the bull died cleanly and honourably in their eyes. The president awarded Angel two ears and a tail, which he then presented to me. I can't remember what I did with them. Writing about this long-ago event now it seems barbaric, but for a twenty-one-year-old who'd grown up in drab, post-war Britain, how could it have been anything but an exciting adventure?

I was invited to join the bullfighting crowd for dinner after the corrida and I might have been in another century. The costumes and dignity of those men, the respect they showed me, were unforgettable. Angel had to leave that night and I never saw him again, but occasionally, down the years, I would see bullfighting posters bearing his name. The entire episode became a cameo in my life, something to take out occasionally and recall, when the gypsy in me had been stirred by exposure to the passionate atmosphere of southern Spain. The food, the wine, the guitars, the musk, the careless laid-back attitude of the Spaniards, the sexual charge between men and women – all these elements were laid down for me to return to some day.

I flew back to London but when I reached home there was no sign of Peter. I had wanted my arrival to be a nice surprise. He appeared eventually, in the early hours – and wanted to make love, or, rather, to have sex. The way he did it made me realize immediately that he had had another woman. I was pretty devastated. It was so obvious, but Peter denied it, foolishly. I found that everybody seemed to know about it. He had not been home for four days. The woman in question was a rather glamorous journalist, who had worked for some top fashion publications, older and more experienced than me. There followed months of further deception and exposures. I remember finding florists' bills, showing records of flowers sent to her address, and I remember confronting him with such a receipt as he sat, like Jean-Paul Marat, in his bath.

When he was brazen enough to look me in the eye and deny it, I slapped his face hard, and left. I just couldn't bear the lies. Eventually he sought me out and apologized and said it was all over, but it wasn't and I continued to find letters from her. It was ludicrous how careless Peter was at covering his tracks. But I would have known anyway, as women do . . . and so, a bit later on, I felt justified in getting to know the journalist Jeffrey Bernard a little better.

At around this time the *Observer* offered Peter a regular satire page which he put together with Michael Frayn and Roger Law. The idea came to grief after a few outings, however, when David Astor, the paper's editor, objected to the depiction of the Home Secretary's wife in one of the cartoon strips. Peter really had taken too much work on at this time anyway, but was starting to see himself as the spider sitting at the centre of a complex, web-like empire of satire.

Establishing The Establishment

Not satisfied with going to bed at one or two in the morning, Peter wanted to create still more seductive ways of spending the small hours. Now had come the time to incarnate the long-cherished ideal of his political–satirical nightclub. Peter aimed to set up an intimate, membership-only salon where he could go on sharpening his tongue and pushing the boundaries. He despised powerful regimes of every description, together with the secrecy, pomposity and hypocrisy that propped them up. So, despite claims that Peter was not a politically driven humorist, the moral elements that suffused his humour in those early days did lead him in a political direction.

This creation was to be a theatre/dinner club with a jazz club downstairs (Peter had already persuaded Dudley to play there with his trio). Peter and Nick Luard, whose friendship had grown from Cambridge days, spent some time trying to find the right premises for what was to be a joint enterprise. Elizabeth Luard, who was to meet and marry Nick through *Private Eye*, says it was a partnership built on their conflicting skills. She wrote to me recently explaining how she viewed it: 'The relationship was close; ideologically and politically far closer than might be supposed, far more than front man and moneyman, since each provided what the other lacked. Nicholas was the consummate insider, socially adept to his fingertips – Wykehamist, Coldstream Guardsman, Magdalene, Cambridge, scholar with a Masters in Medieval English – choosing his friends from among the sons and daughters of the rich and powerful. Peter's early success at the Cambridge Footlights had already marked him as unreliable, iconoclastic, too-clever-by-half.'

Because Peter was unruly, Elizabeth argues, he would not have been able to get as much done as he wanted to without an 'insider' like Nick working on his behalf.

'Peter was clearly not a man to be trusted in the corridors of power – he might sneak in and blow up the filing cabinets – while Nicholas had access to whoever he chose.' Nicholas had inherited some money on reaching the age of twenty-one, through a trust fund set up by his grandfather, the industrialist Sydney Lamert. 'It wasn't a fortune – Lamert reckoned daughters and granddaughters were in need of dowries, but grandsons (there were no sons) were better fending for themselves. Nevertheless, £20,000 was a tidy sum.'

Eventually Nick and Peter chanced upon No. 18 Greek Street, which they rated a real possibility. I remember going there and being assailed by the seediest of beer-sodden atmospheres. The windows were swagged in oceans of red velvet curtains (some of which somehow ended up in Melanie Rouse's London flat, courtesy of an opportunistic friend of Ros Myers); there were discarded G-strings, used condoms, plastic chandeliers – all the tawdry remnants of a former strip club. But this could be changed.

Bruce Copp, who we head-hunted from the Mermaid Theatre where he worked for Bernard Miles, was to become the inspired manager and head of catering. He still has total recall of the interior of the site (and of plenty of the strange things that went on inside it).

'We took on this old strip club, along with another house

behind it. You could go up the steps behind one house and there was a sort of well between the two. If there had been a fire, people would have been hopelessly trapped up there, so I had all these roll-up fire escape ladders put up under each window so you could have lowered yourself down into the yard of St Martin's School of Art, behind us in Charing Cross Road. I remember we used to see odd bits of sculpture lying around in the yard there.'

Jean Hart, the singer who joined The Establishment team, was a comparative veteran of the nightclub scene and has reminded me that the government's Wolfenden Report had just moved prostitutes off the streets and into the architecture of Soho. Unbeknown to these Cambridge grads the area had become the centre of a gangland struggle. 'The girls were forced indoors and this put tremendous heat on Soho. It turned from being an old French London village into sex city. It was being fought over by the gangs. I think the club's membership kept them secure for a while, but all these clubs bought their liquor on tick, so you were immediately in the pocket of the criminals.' The threat of violence of sabotage from the gangs was a problem for the club throughout its history. Christopher Logue, the poet who, back in Cambridge days, had inadvertently provided the soundtrack to the loss of my virginity, was to write the words for some of the songs Jean would to sing at the club. These days he is lauded for his painstaking version of *The Iliad*, but then he was a satirical lyricist. Jean and Annie Ross sang his sour lines beautifully. One song tackled the dangerous idea of marrying a crusading 'Liberal Man', who would 'tell you how to change the state by fighting for the cause and you feel confident he'll do nothing less', that is before, of course, he eventually buys a car and takes a steady job, deciding that:

And little Mark must go to Winchester ...
   But when he finds his tongue is nailed to the floor
By the steady job he cannot do without,
You'll hear that non-conformist-who's-conforming roar
'and it was you and your damn child made me sell out!'
Then he whispers: 'Do you love me?'
And you have to answer 'sure'
Your husband hides his face in the *Observer*,
   And you, my dear,
   You cry into the *Queen*.

Christopher remembers the occasions when gangland thugs turned up at the door and asked whether we had 'fire insurance'. 'Once Peter brought them all in and he threatened to put them all on stage. I thought that was absolutely brilliant. Of course, they became terribly embarrassed and left.'

The club itself, billed as 'London's First Satirical Nightclub', was soon taking shape. Bruce Copp paints the picture:

'There was a long approach as you went into the club; it was a long building, in fact, as most are on Greek Street. A good half of it was given over to the theatre and restaurant and the stage was at the far end of that. The first half was a long bar. As you came in the door, the bar used to be very crowded and yet you would recognize every face.'

Bruce had to build a new kitchen in 'a terrible cupboard downstairs' while Sean Kenny (who had just designed the sets for Lionel Bart's *Oliver!*) was involved in choosing our decor – black again, of course. Roger Law was to have a nightly cartoon space on one of the walls near the entrance. Membership application for the new club, which with some ironic panache was to be called The Establishment, was piling in as soon as word got out, quickly rising to 7000. In gratitude every life member received a portrait of Harold Macmillan.

Bruce says that Peter was underconfident at the outset about the number of members he would attract. At our first meeting with him in a French restaurant in Wardour Street Bruce had to reassure us both.

'It was a nice lunch and Peter told me what he had in mind. He said that if anyone joined The Establishment on trust at that point they would get it a guinea cheaper and I remember I said, "You will have twenty-five thousand members when you open", to which Peter replied: "I think you have had too much wine." But I wasn't far out in the end.'

Bruce's decision to jump ship and join us at a nonexistent club in a grubby part of town was a lucky fluke. 'Peter told me how much he wanted the club to be in Soho, because of the dodginess, although this turned out to be its undoing. Still, something appealed to me about the job on a political level. Six and a half years in the army had made me absolutely pacifist and Peter was too, in his charming way. When I met Peter for that first time, that is what drew me to him: a feeling that things could change.'

Before opening night Venetia Mooreshead, Elizabeth Luard and myself were dispatched as lures up to Cambridge to gather membership among the undergrads. We stayed at the Blue Boar Hotel and spangled ourselves up for the fray. I'll never forget watching Venetia back-brushing her jet-black hair into a bee-hive, now becoming fashionable; it stood out in a veritable halo around her dainty, finely chiselled face. I'd never seen that before. We were outrageous – and very successful; the memberships flowed in.

Publicity, organized by Colin Bell, could not have gone better. As Elizabeth Luard points out, there was as much media fuss about the potential audience at the club as there was about the performers involved.

'The membership included Edward Adeane, son of the Queen's

Private Secretary; Adam Butler, son of "Rab" Butler, who was now tipped as the next Tory leader, Timothy Willoughby, heir to the fortune and title of the Earl of Ancaster – old money, the stuff which still owned much of the country,' she says, adding that this impressive roll call had its unforeseen consequences: 'And that was of interest to the Special Branch at Scotland Yard. By the time the club opened its doors, Nicholas – and presumably Peter – was already on file as a danger to national security.'

The evening the doors of The Establishment swung open was quite extraordinary and I am pleased to say that Bruce, who was effectively managing it all, confirms my recollections: there have been times when I wondered if I dreamed it all.

'The opening night of the club was something else. I have had to organize quite a few in my time, but never one like this. Applications from people who wanted to be there came from all over the world. From the beginning I said to Peter, "My proposal is first-come-first-served", and he had said, "Quite right".'

One or two gatecrashers, however, did make it past Bruce: 'One of the people who didn't book was Margaret Argyll, the Duchess of Argyll, who was notorious at the time, and another notorious man-friend of hers, Dominic Elwes. He was the black sheep of his family. She arrived with him quite early, when I was just seating people. Suddenly she was there and she brushed passed me and sat at a table without even asking.

'When there was a lull I went over and said: "This table is already reserved for other people. You will have to leave", to which she said, "I will stay". Eventually they moved on to another empty table. They went on doing this, as guests arrived, until there was only one free table left. When the people for that table arrived I thought, "I have had enough of this". I was totally exhausted. I was losing my grip on the whole thing. I said to the lord who had booked it (possibly it was Viscount Ancaster, Tim Willoughby's father), "Now, I have got a very nice table for you, but a lady called the Duchess of Argyll refuses to move from your table. I don't even want them here at all." And he said, "How wonderful!" Then he walked up to her and said something in her ear and she blanched and got up with Dominic and left.'

Christopher Logue says I used to sit at the door of The Establishment at the beginning: 'I remember you being on the door with a very low décolletage and I used to come in looking down your front.' Cleavage aside, it is certainly true that once the club was up and running I operated as something of an unofficial hostess. There were usually two people manning the box office, because of the threat from the protection racketeers and from people trying to get in, and I would divide my time between the door and the bar areas. We hired a tough doorman too and Bruce occasionally wielded an antique Russian truncheon, tapping belligerent patrons on the shoulders. He too stayed in the building nearly all the time the club was open, presiding over the food service.

'People were served at table twice-nightly and so there was the problem of not having clattering cutlery while people were performing. Everything had to be cleared away and I had to handle this team of Italian waiters.

'There were lots of things we couldn't cook because it all had to come up from the subterranean kitchen in a lift into a little servery right outside the restaurant itself with no room for more than two people in it.'

We were limited, of course, by the lack of space and time restraints, but actually the food was quite good. We served soup in special casseroles with lids and handles, and rabbit too. There was one shady patch on the bill of fare, however; because licensing laws meant alcohol could only be served with food after midnight we had to provide what Bruce describes

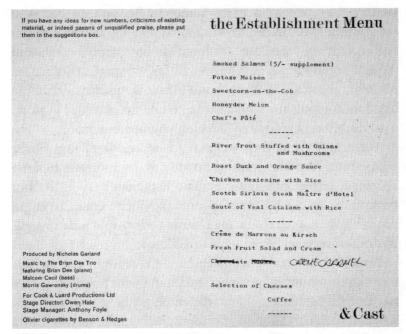

The Establishment menu

as 'awful curling sandwiches' in the upstairs bar. Nobody ate them anyway.

The first sitting in the restaurant was at 7.30 p.m., before the early show began at 8.15, and Bruce was strict about keeping time: 'If people hadn't quite finished their dinner, they just had to wait to have their coffee. I wouldn't allow any clatter and carry-on during the show. I said to the waiters: "The show comes first and if they can't wait, they are philistine and they will have to go. If they have come here just for the food, they must be mad."'

The show lasted around an hour and a half and then a second sitting was served before the late show, which started at about 10.45, or even later. Audiences and cast members of the big West End shows used to fill the club for this sitting.

Dudley, fresh from his performance in *Beyond the Fringe* at the Fortune, would go downstairs to join his trio in the jazz bar around this time too. (In later life he complained that he did not see anything that happened on the stage upstairs, but his own musical dominion down below quickly became a London hotspot in its own right. While he played, his piano was always surrounded by adoring young women.)

'After 11.00 p.m. the place really went to town,' says Bruce. 'Only Peter had the stamina to do ten or fourteen minutes on stage in the late show at The Establishment as well as performing at the Fortune Theatre. Who else could have got up in front of that distinguished audience – and it was distinguished quite often – and ad-libbed?'

Peter did have a magnificent arrogance that carried him through the daunting prospect of dealing with Soho gangs and the British Establishment at the same time. Jean Hart, who went on to marry another comedian, Bill Oddie, watched with an approving, wry smile as Nick and Peter took on the world.

'These young people came down from a provincial place like Cambridge, where they were gods, and they came to Soho, which is quite dangerous. I knew a bit more about it than them because I was a little older and I had been singing in jazz clubs around the place, but they just swanned in. Their confidence bowled people over. Even the villains in Soho were bowled over by the confidence of these men.'

Jean regarded the new club as an expression of the impatience felt by our generation. 'I don't think they really were trying to change people. I think they had a point of view. They saw the world in a particular way. And I think they were right – I went along with their view of it – but I don't think they did it to change the world. They did it to demonstrate what they could see. It was a quite narcissistic thing they were doing.'

The club opening and *Private Eye* starting up happened within three weeks of each other, Elizabeth Luard recalls, and their histories were to remain entwined until the club eventually went under. While The Establishment was packed out from the first, Elizabeth says the *Eye* was soon finding itself seriously underfunded. 'Print bills were an issue, let alone wages (for me, a fiver a week). Andrew Osmond, the original Lord Gnome, was heading for the Foreign Office and hoped for a return of his investment. The *Eye* looked to The Establishment. On the face of it, the theatre club was successful, apparently fearless, well funded – there was a chance Cook and Luard might bite. A meeting was held, the project discussed, account books examined – not good, as well I knew. In the *Eye*'s rent-free offices, above a warehouse in Neal Street at the time, we awaited an answer. Cook didn't bite; Luard did. Peter didn't rate the *Eye* – too soft: a bunch of schoolboys. And anyway, *Beyond the Fringe* was heading for New York. But Nicholas, who was toying with the idea of launching an arts magazine, thought the *Eye* worth saving and repaid Osmond his original investment, clearing the magazine's overdraft. The *Eye* moved – albeit briefly – into the Green Room of The Establishment till a lease came up at 22 Greek Street, just down the way.'

Venetia Mooreshead heard about a job on the *Eye* at this time and climbed up to the temporary first-floor office above The Establishment where she had a typically bizarre induction. She was told to wear horn-rimmed glasses and to say, 'It is Miss Rigby speaking' when she answered the phone. Apparently there was not much work done, but a lot of free refreshment from the club below.

'One never stopped laughing. We would sort of finish work, as it were, at 5.30 and then we would go down and prop up the bar,' she says. 'I started doing evening work a couple of hours a night and the waiters would always give you free food and free booze.' Elsewhere in the building Sean Kenny kept a studio, as did Lewis Morley, the photographer who became famous for his image of a naked Christine Keeler on that chair. The venue was a kind of subversive mecca and offered a compact social life for us all. 'I was a hobo around London,' recalls Venetia. 'I occasionally got into a flat, but it never worked out for long, so I used to carry around my personal doss-down pillow and I remember I dossed down in Sean Kenny's studio when I thought it was too late to get the Tube. I didn't mind discomfort.'

I, too, seldom went to bed before 4.00 a.m. What energy! And Peter and I would often take in whatever the late debate at the House of Commons might be on our way home to Battersea. (It was usually on gravel or some such fascinating thing, providing good material for Peter.) This daily pattern meant sleeping until midday, when Peter would get up and read all the newspapers, do the horses and then prepare for the show and sort out whatever might be needed for the club. It was a pretty unhealthy rhythm, but I guess you can do it when you're young.

Jean Hart, observing from the stage itself, sums up how exciting it all was at its height: 'There was an energy there. A really powerful energy. That it is why Jonathan Ross and all the other devotees today still love the idea of this club. It is almost like a holy grail of entertainment: an ideal. That connection with people, with a real live audience, as there is in theatre, but it was better than theatre because it was intimate, because it was around food. Now that is very special. It was like having a giant dinner party with the best minds and the funniest people.'

The small scale of the enterprise helped build an incredible atmosphere, she thinks. 'It was a tiny little room, so you are having a person-to-person chat, and you are eating food, and you are being entertained in an extraordinary new way by young and beautiful people who are master and mistresses of what they are doing because they invented it. No wonder people keep talking about it! I am so pleased and grateful that I sang there. It was in the most exciting part of London and it had the best music downstairs afterwards or you could sit at the bar.'

Soon people flying into London from abroad were directed to The Establishment as the hottest place in town. Bruce Copp was constantly being offered bribes to let people in. Since it was a membership-only club, anybody wanting to see the show or buy liquor had to go through the process of joining. Visiting celebrities tried to press money on the box office person, but the policy was fairly egalitarian. Even Jack Lemmon and Robert Mitchum were quite happy to be seated on the stairs one night when it was standing-room only. We had plenty of regulars, but there was always an unexpected element to the clientele on any night. Alan Bennett says he was once delighted to spot John Sparrow, the warden of All Souls, Oxford, and he has held on to a memento of a visit from the maverick travel writer Patrick Leigh Fermor. 'I still have a note that he sent in asking, could we get him in?' says Alan. 'It was an immensely smart place to be and one forgets that. People today just think of it as being very satirical, but there was also this social thing.'

One of Bruce's most thrilling memories of the club is an unexpected evening spent with his literary hero, E. M. Forster, an honorary fellow at King's College, Cambridge.

'He was one of my idols. I loved him. And one night Peter came to me and said E. M. Forster wants to see the show. I received him and we had dinner together, but I can't remember a single thing he said. I was in such a dazzled state. It was one of the greatest moments of my life.'

The black American writer James Baldwin also crossed the threshold, as our friend the actress Gaye Brown, who sometimes worked on the door, recalls all too well: 'James Baldwin was sitting with the singer Annie Ross in the club one night and various other people were standing there. We were talking about something to do with performing and I said to him, "Don't you find that too?" He said, "Yes, I do. What do you think I do?" and I said, "You are her drummer, aren't you?" And Annie said, "No! This is James Baldwin. He is a writer."'

Paul McCartney, on the brink of fame, tells me he was a frequent customer at the club too. 'I went to The Establishment quite regularly actually. You would drink at the long bar upstairs, with all the drawings on the wall. Then we would go downstairs to listen to Dudley and his drummer.'

Among the more regular regulars were Terence Stamp and his brother Chris, Jeffrey Bernard, Michael Caine, Peter O'Toole, Tom Driberg, Mary Quant and her husband, Alexander Plunkett Green, Francis Bacon, Kiki Byrne, Rudolf Nureyev, the cast of *Oliver!*, Georgia Brown, Barry Humphries (whose Australian housewife, Edna Everage, later appeared at the club) and Ron Moody.

George Melly and his wife, Diana, had their own table kept aside for them. 'George was there almost nightly,' says Bruce. 'He was very kind about the food, which encouraged me enormously because he knew about these things. He had been around. There was a certain table he liked which was raised up on the side of the stage.'

But the joy of the place for Bruce, and for me, was that you never knew exactly who you would see. 'All the big stars were there alongside all the roughnecks. Young actors used to come in every night though, because they could rub shoulders with famous actors and advance their careers.'

Politicians came along too and on one triumphant night

Randolph Churchill actually got up on the stage. He told Bruce he would like to try and so Bruce mentioned it to Peter. 'He did ten minutes ad-libbing and he was only slightly drunk. He was usually totally drunk . . .' Romance seemed to blossom under that nightclub lighting too. Bruce remembers that the actor Sean Lynch used to come in every night because he was in love with Annie Ross. 'When she was doing her stuff, he used to be there every night.' He eventually married her.

My friend the poet Adrian Mitchell and his wife Celia were also frequent customers. 'We loved The Establishment. The acts were great and I adored Annie Ross. She used to sit on a stool and say, "And now it is medley time" in her lovely voice.'

Adrian even toyed with the idea of performing a comic monologue at the club: 'I once said to Peter that I would love to go on. I had been writing this monologue and listening to all these American comedians. It was all about a man living in the suburbs with the hobby of washing his car and it built up somehow to nuclear war. Peter asked me to do it for him and Nick, so I went along, very nervous, up to this attic above the club. I sat there with the script and read it and Peter said, "That's fine. How about 12 January at 1.00 a.m.?" But then, on the day, I thought, "I can't do that. That is not my thing." So I rang up Peter and said: "I have got this terrible 'flu." I was terrified about going on. I would have had to learn it all. He forgave me.'

Anneke Wills, a young, blonde actress with no need of false eyelashes, was one of the attractions of 'the scene' at the club, spending a lot of time, like many glamorous ladies, dancing in the basement to the music provided by Dudley and his trio. She was the first person to learn the Twist and was happy to teach anyone who wanted to learn. She was also to become the first in a long line of Dr Who's beguiling assistants on television, working initially with William Hartnell and then with Patrick Troughton. Anneke, who later married Peter's good friend the actor Michael Gough, now lives near me on the wilds of Dartmoor. She remembers The Establishment Club days, or rather nights, as some of the best of the sixties.

'We were all getting it on with each other and it was great,' she says. 'It wasn't that you and I were unique – we were all doing it, I think. I didn't have the moral thing that you did, though. I wasn't brought up morally. There was nobody in charge of me saying "You can't do that". We were breaking out of those restrictions that our parents had and we were all getting to know each other, in and out of bed. And it all felt so innocent and fun.'

Anneke, a girlfriend of Anthony Newley's at one point, was described recently by my friend Venetia as 'a beautiful Dutch doll'. She was certainly a head-turner and the experience, she suggests, may also have turned her own young head. 'It was so heady. The fact that we could attract the fella with our long eyelashes and our bodies, this was an amazingly heady experience. It was exciting and very dangerous also because you thought, "I could have anybody if I put my mind to it". But I was completely inexperienced and didn't know how to get rid of a married guy or to attract the right ones.'

It was a period when everyone seemed to be living at a tremendous pace and, for me, Peter's sudden national fame gave it a surreal quality. As Anneke points out: 'You happened to be living with the most successful man in England at the time. Before I met you I was sitting in Vidal's one day and I opened up *Queen* magazine and there was this picture of Peter in this suit, this incredibly tall, brilliant man, and I thought, "I want to meet him". Then within weeks I had met both of you at The Establishment – and this was incredible to me.'

Perhaps the most notorious and glorious guest artist who

appeared at The Establishment was Lenny Bruce. This was the New York comic's first and only London run and for some of the time he stayed at our flat – when he wasn't out on the town that is. A registered drug addict back in the United States, Lenny took excess to new heights in most areas of his life. Several of my friends remember being dragooned into picking up drugs from one shady doctor or another during his visit.

Harriet Garland, one of my best friends in those days, was one such stooge: 'I just was so innocent. I was sent off to Harley Street: "Go on, little woman, go off to pick up the drugs. Go to this doctor and he will give you a packet and then you can take it to Hyde Park Square." And when I got to the flat Lenny Bruce would be there and he would be so desperate for his drugs that he would have left the door open and locked himself in the loo. And he would just say, "Leave it there and go".'

One night in our flat Lenny's normal heroin supply was not available and he had got hold of some prescribed narcotic, which I remember him heating in a silver tablespoon over a candle as I watched, hypnotized. At that point he was like a marionette whose strings had been cut. He applied a tourniquet and injected himself and within moments became like Superman. Somehow we thought it all rather glamorous, but looking back it was tragic to see him slumped like an invalid and then transformed in a matter of minutes. That night I remember I had made a rabbit pie and the leftovers were in the kitchen. He piled on marmalade, added some marzipan candies and a quart of chocolate ice cream and then downed the lot like a boa constrictor. He then wanted to go out and party!

Jean Hart was on stage too for some of Lenny's London dates at the club. 'I sang a couple of nights when Lenny Bruce was there and it was awful,' she says. 'This creature was almost being eaten up. He was huddled in the corner like a little rag doll. What had happened was that in Britain at that time if you were an addict you could get your prescription from a doctor. So they took him to someone, but what he was getting in the States was much stronger than anything you could get given in London, where addicts were a new phenomenon. So nobody knew how to deal with this man whose habit was a hundred times bigger than anything our doctors had seen. He was going crazy, poor man.'

For Bruce Copp, however, Lenny was a star through and through. And he was not the only one to be star struck. He claims the singer Alma Cogan had a huge crush and came along every night of the run. 'Alma used to say to me, "Bruce, make sure I have that table tomorrow night", and she used to bring a different friend along. At that time the Café de Paris had just put a plaque up on the wall to mark the spot where Marlene Dietrich stood before going on stage, so one day when I was passing one of those amusement parlours where they had those machines where you could stamp out a metal nameplate, I stamped out one that read "Alma Cogan sits here" and then I put it on her table at the club. And, of course, when she came in that night she put her handbag down right on top of it. I was watching from the back to see her reaction. She didn't even see it until she took her handbag off it as the meal was coming out, quite a while later, but her laugh then could have been heard in Shaftesbury Avenue. She threw her head back and screamed and had everybody come and look, because we all knew what it was alluding to and knew about this plate that had just been put up in the Café de Paris.'

We don't know if Alma's devotion was reciprocated by Lenny, but Bruce thinks not.

'He was so used to that kind of thing. He was very lovable and I'd take him out around the town. At the end of the show he would say, "Come on, Bruce. Let's go out". He used to love the greasy spoon places all round Leicester Square – really nasty little caffs that were open all night. He would say, "This reminds me of my early days in New York", and he loved it. I never knew him to take anything when he was with me and I spent several hours in his company. He never even smoked a joint. I think once he had his fix, he was all right for a day. He was wonderful company and on stage there was nobody to compare. He was brilliant. Brilliant, because he had this wonderful, radical attitude.'

A couple of the shock tactics that Lenny used to wake up an audience that wasn't listening properly come back to me now; one was a remark about the difficulty of cleaning snot from a suede jacket and the second was to talk about cancer. Other Establishment patrons heard him ask the front row: 'Hands up who has masturbated today?'

One of the innocent bystanders called upon to guard Lenny during his explosive time at The Establishment was Venetia Mooreshead. 'Lenny Bruce was a complete nightmare, although he was a deeply charming man,' she says. 'I was camping on Nick Luard's sofa and Lenny was in the back room. I was delegated by Nick to be his minder and to get him to the club on time in case he went off anywhere, getting dope or something.'

Christopher Booker has a memory of the strange mood in the club during this period. 'I loved it, but I was slightly worried by the atmosphere some of the time; the menace of it. I went almost every night when Lenny Bruce was there.'

After completing his short run of dates Lenny went back to the States. He had been such a success, though, that Peter soon negotiated for him to come back again. He accepted immediately because he had loved London and Bruce Copp went to meet him at the airport.

'Lenny felt very free here, you see,' he said. 'He didn't have to put up with the prejudices in the States, but then the Home Secretary issued a statement saying that Lenny Bruce was unacceptable in this country and he was not to be allowed in. He was detained at Heathrow Airport and, as I was there to meet him, I said to an official, "Can I see him? He is friend of mine. Can it be arranged for me at least to see him?" And then, about six doors down a corridor from where we were standing, a door opened and Lenny leaned out and said "Hi, Bruce", and that was the last I ever saw of him. He wasn't even allowed to come up and talk to me. It was awful – it was the very thing we were trying to fight.'

Aside from the unforgettable impact of a one-off performer like Lenny, the stamp of Peter's sense of humour and personality were all over the club's acts and this was no accident. Roddy Maude-Roxby, who went on to perform in Peter's New York venue as well as in London, clearly remembers his 'boss's' technique for handling and developing stage material.

'Peter could take anything that was happening in the world and transfer it very quickly into comedy – often by going into something in minute detail.' Peter always 'chunked down' with his comedy, Roddy says. 'Chunking up is going up, towards "god", and Peter chunks down, where you go down to minutiae and to ingrowing toenails and things like that. He will keep narrowing the field. Jonathan Miller and I, for example, moved sideways with a comic idea very quickly instead. I remember when there were clashes about work, I would go round to ask Peter what we were going to do and he would be very accurate about keeping in what he wanted so that you never got your own way really. He always established what it was that he wanted, then, as you were leaving, he just entertained you – just as you were getting to the door. So everyone left crying with laughter. Everyone felt affection as they went out, and yet the moment before . . .'

On one afternoon Peter's tireless efforts to entertain those around him caused a few disconcerting moments for Christopher Logue. 'I remember once coming into The Establishment in the middle of the afternoon and Peter was giving an imitation of me. I just stood transfixed in the doorway because it was so good and I had never seen myself portrayed in this way. Peter, of course, was incredibly embarrassed, but I wasn't embarrassed in the least. I felt jolly lucky that someone had done this to me. It is better than a mirror, it is a caricature. It was quite cruel in a way; on the other hand it wasn't inaccurate.'

Other tricky encounters at the club did not end so peaceably. An infamous tussle with Siobhan McKenna, the great stage actress, has gone down in Peter Cook folklore. Bruce Copp recalls the incident in more detail than most.

'Siobhan McKenna was having a West End triumph in *The Playboy of the Western World* at the time. It was the important performance of the year and she came to the club to see Lenny Bruce but was offended by the language he used. I think it must have been because she was a drunk and also, basically, Roman Catholic. She disapproved of all the "f-words" and she started to shout back. It created an amazing situation. Peter usually loved all this sort of thing because it would get into all the newspapers, but she shouted so much, it really interrupted the show. So when Peter arrived from the Fortune during the interval between our two shows he came to me first, as he often did for any information that he could use later in his act. He used to do a ten-minute ad-lib on the spot in the second show and it was always based on things that were happening around us that night, mentioning anyone who had misbehaved or drawn attention to themselves. I told him about Siobhan, who was sitting up on the raised bit on the left of the stage. She had stayed for the second house, even drunker and more

Catholic than ever. She started to shout, so Peter went up to her and said "Would you please leave?" and she caught hold of his tie. So now there was a terrible fight going on in the audience. I managed to get them out into the bar area, through the curtains, and Peter was going blue in the face. I thought I'd go up and see if Sean Kenny was in his office. He was, and he ran down the stairs and said "Come on now, Siobhan" and she immediately calmed down.'

But it seems this was not entirely the end of the matter. Bruce Copp's professional diplomacy then came into play.

'We had regular meetings with the cast and in the meeting next day Alan Bennett, John Bird, John Fortune and Eleanor Bron were all there. I said. "Look, I am twenty years older than any of you here and I have seen Siobhan work a lot and I consider she is possibly the greatest actress in the world at the moment. I would appreciate if you would write a little note of regret and I will take it to the stage door of the Comedy Theatre." And I did. She was a very important lady, artistically speaking, and also socially. We didn't want her saying what an awful place The Establishment was.'

According to Gaye Brown, Lenny Bruce himself retrieved something positive from this debacle. The next night he played a tape of the entire incident with McKenna in his show. 'It was terribly funny,' says Gaye. 'He had recorded the whole thing. He just turned on the tape and he sat down. Now that is theatre!'

During this period Peter and I were invited as a couple to many launch parties. One of them was for Vidal Sassoon, probably the first modern hairdresser to achieve celebrity status. The party was given by some minor member of the aristocracy at her home in South Kensington, I think. The only wine that was served was Mateus Rosé, for which I've had a soft spot ever since. Shortly after this Peter went to town on camp hairdressers (not, of course, that Vidal was camp!), writing a sketch for Kenneth Williams, who was himself the son of a barber. Williams plays a hairdresser who proudly trumpets the supposed English ancestry of the blow dry and other fancy hairstyles for men. He claims to have done his first blow dry at the turn of the last century: 'Henry VIII wore a hairnet in bed, you know,' he adds.

Some evenings some of us would go on to Muriel's (or The Colony Club), a tiny drinking club presided over by the autocratic black-haired Muriel Belcher, perched on a high stool. There you could see – if they weren't at The Establishment that night – Frank Norman, the playwright, Sandy and Wally Fawkes ('Trog'), the painters Francis Bacon and Robert McBride, Henrietta Moraes, Lucien Freud and Jeffrey Bernard. It was an extraordinary place where the brittle atmosphere was aggravated by Muriel's bitchy repartee with the camp barman. It turned out this barman, Ian Board, was doing his best to sabotage bookings at The Establishment. According to Bruce Copp, Board used to ring up and make phony reservations. Bruce worked hard on the seating plan each night, taking care not to put together people who had an antipathy towards each other, so when people did not turn up it all went wrong. 'This happened quite a lot, every night at one point, and I realized someone was making false bookings. We lost all that business, with hundreds of people wanting to come. It was bad for everybody, bad for the show. I discovered it was Ian Board doing it, so I went to Muriel, who I loved. She was a tough old bird, but she had integrity. There were no false bookings after that.'

Jeffrey Bernard had not yet become notorious through his drinking, betting and his column in the *Spectator*. At that time he was a rather amusing bar bum whom Bruce Copp was forever throwing out of The Establishment. He was also part of the gang of people who lived in Chelsworth in Suffolk, where my friend from Spain, Janet Allan, kept a wonderful house and garden and cured people of hangovers with a good breakfast and hard labour in her burgeoning organic garden.

Later, Jeffrey seduced me. Or was it the other way round? That kind of thing happened in quite an innocent and friendly way, or so it seemed in those days. He was married and I don't know what he'd done with his wife. We all drank too much and I used to get a little bored waiting around for Peter to be ready to come home, so I succumbed to Jeffrey's charms. His wit was dry and cruel, but he had a crooked smile and a sparkle in his eye which was pretty irresistible. I just wished he had had a better acquaintance with his toothbrush. The combination of alcohol and heavy smoking took its toll. At any rate, he was rough on his women and always broke. I 'lent' him several amounts of money which, of course, I never saw again. I don't think Peter even noticed this little interlude, so consumed was he with his show and his club, both now truly the talk of the town.

Such sexual permissiveness was pandemic, certainly in those circles. It is hard to convince cynics of today just how very puppyish and innocent it usually was then, part of a great outburst, a throwing off of inhibition and taboos, a desire to get to know people, intimately perhaps, then to part, but still remain friends. My episode with Jeffrey didn't last too long; he really was unreliable in all manner of ways – untruthful, exploitative, but still charming and funny. Better at a distance.

When I discuss these days with Anneke Gough we are not too hard on ourselves, or on those we got close to, but I think we are realistic about the dangers that were lurking.

'There we were, in this club night after night, with all the most glamorous people in London. Peter O'Toole. I mean! I

146

would have done anything. These were very exciting people to be with,' admits Anneke, acknowledging that, for her at least, there was often a price to pay.

'You put up with what you were offered because you were desperate for love. Love was what we really wanted. Women were looking for intimacy and yet once we had had the bonk, the blokes were never available. They had a taxi waiting outside, or they had to get back to the wife, or job, or whatever it was. So we were ripped off once again. Because it was in the moment afterwards, when one had opened one's body to someone, that one wanted to have the lovely, deep connection . . . and that most invariably didn't happen.'

Since the Pill had become readily available in 1960 it was gradually more and more possible for us to separate the idea of sex from the idea of reproduction. This changed everything for young women in particular, but not always for our own good. For me, though, the idea of seeking a soul mate was still paramount.

I had a little romance during this period with Tom Courtenay, who was swiftly gaining recognition as an actor from his performance in *The Loneliness of the Long Distance Runner*. Here was another man with an interesting mind and someone who reconnected me with my love of classical music. We had first met at the Edinburgh Festival and later in our time together he bought me a record of Tchaikovsky's 'Pathétique'. Whenever I hear it I still think of him. He was living with John Thaw and Rodney Bewes at the time, all really nice working-class lads making their mark on British theatre and films.

Looking back, it seems like one big party. London felt like a village; wherever I went there was someone I knew. One of the nicest of the well-known people I met was Sir John Mills. We had dinner together with his wife, Mary Hayley Bell. He was one of the few genuinely humble and charming men I have ever met and made a lasting impression on me. Talking of which brings me back to the irrepressible rise of David Frost.

All Peter's friends from Cambridge regarded 'Frostie' as something of a joke. He became allied to The Establishment without anyone quite knowing how and then made himself useful. 'They didn't despise him. They tolerated him,' says Bruce Copp. 'They thought he was a bit of an idiot and a bore – the worst thing you could be in that milieu – but whenever Peter was away for a couple of days he would say to me: "Bruce, if anything goes wrong in the show, if anyone is taken ill and needs replacing, get on to David because he is very good at stepping in at short notice. He should be able to cover." So occasionally I did this. I used to pay him five pounds out of the till.

He was always very agreeable, but later two incidents revealed more about his character to me. Once I came across him in the building at the back of the club, behind the stage, in the administrative bit which had the office for membership, and my office, and various other things, along with a meeting room. Over in one corner of this meeting room were a couple of filing cabinets in which I kept all the manuscripts that would-be writers – students and young men from all over the country, and all over the world in fact – used to send in. Peter would occasionally look through it and perhaps use some of it in the show, but they had to be carefully filed away and returned with a rejection slip once they got around to rejecting them or whatever. It was my job to organize that. I went up to the room one day and David Frost was there alone and he was lounging back on his chair with his feet on the table reading these scripts. I said, "David, what are you doing here?" He was always very temperate. You couldn't really have a row with him, but I made it clear he wasn't welcome there and I told Peter about it. Peter thought it was terribly funny.

'The second incident was not long after. Peter said, "We have booked a table at the Blue Angel", which was a nightclub right opposite the Mayfair Theatre, and he said "Would you like to join us?" So off we went, very late after midnight, with Jonathan, Alan, Dudley and, I think, John Bird. When the show began Noël Harrison, Rex's son, walked on as the compere. He said: "Ladies and Gentlemen, I have got something very interesting here for you tonight – the man who is responsible for The Establishment Club and various other concerns of that kind that have become so popular – Mr David Frost." There was loud applause along with screams of laughter from our table. I rounded on Peter and said, "I am not laughing, Peter. How can you possibly let that pass without some comment?" "I think that is extremely funny," said Peter. And I started to laugh too then, because it is funny really. But Peter was riding the crest of a wave of fame and popularity then and he could afford to laugh, but if he had known what was to come later. Nobody wanted to know Peter when he came back from America and David Frost had taken over his field totally.'

No wonder Frost came to be known among the *Beyond the Fringe*-ers as 'the Bubonic Plagiarist', a nickname which has stuck.

At this point our half-acknowledged 'open relationship', this interlude in which Peter and I had other encounters, suddenly came to a head. Peter, having tried to extricate himself from the journalist he was seeing was told by her that she was pregnant. She wanted an abortion and I presume Peter made the funds available. But, rather extraordinarily, he then had her followed by a private detective on the day she was to have the operation. No such operation took place, as I found out later when I stumbled across the detective's report. It did for their relationship and almost did for ours too. I cried and shouted and threw plates. I think Peter was inwardly stunned by the sequence of events – though he was well trained at disguising any emotions he didn't want to show. Eventually we decided we did want to stay together. We felt strongly that we had things to do that we could not do alone. For a time there was a little more attentiveness on Peter's part towards me. But he was still a driven man and his career, and the amazing acclaim he was receiving, absorbed him. I suppose it had always been this way to a certain extent; it was just that while we were students it had all been a good deal more relaxed. Night-time living in the metropolis gave a very different perspective to it all. Not waking till midday produced biorhythms which were certainly not conducive to healthy attitudes or trust. But Soho – so completely different from anything that either of us had experienced before – had become our village.

Broadway Babes

By the late summer of 1962 *Beyond the Fringe* had won awards in London. There was both a book and a record, and America was beckoning. The show had run in the West End for a year with the original cast and was to continue to pull them in, with other stars, for another four years. Two top Broadway producers, David Merrick and Alexander Cohen, were both vying for the show. In the end Alex Cohen was chosen, but Peter was, I think, rightly convinced that their agent Donald Langdon could have held out for a better deal. Shortly afterwards Peter and Donald parted company.

Before work began on a mildly Americanized version of the show Peter suggested we go away for a holiday. We both felt drawn to Crete. It was only my second trip out of England, family holidays having usually involved camping in Hunstanton or Devon, so this was a great adventure. And to be going with Peter! I was so excited. We flew to Athens and then took a boat on to Crete.

Every smell, every vital colour, enfolded me: the vibrancy of the people, with their craggy faces and animated gestures. The blue of the sea was beyond belief, incandescent. It seemed such a personal blessing that these riches had been stored up for a time when I was old enough to fully appreciate them. We stayed in a *pension*, typically Cretan in style, and the food was all new to me: spiced kebabs or freshly caught fish grilled over a wood fire, with Greek salad, fresh feta cheese and sweet tomatoes. For breakfast we ate oranges the like of which I had never tasted before with thick Greek yogurt, ladled out of a great terracotta bowl. The hospitality was overwhelming. I had brought out some of Mary Renault's novels set in Crete and her descriptions of the flowering of the Minoan culture gave me goose bumps of the kind I had felt in the Egyptian Department in the Fitzwilliam in Cambridge. There was a deep resonance of familiarity. A labyrinth, a sacred-bull cult, beautiful and acrobatic maidens, delicate pottery with depictions of octopus and dolphins, the bare-breasted snake goddess, the double-headed axe and the honey bee – and here were the great amphorae which had held the prized olive oil, exported all over the Mediterranean, and there the crimson pillars of the Temple of Knossos – all this suddenly before our gaze. Even Peter was silenced and rendered thoughtful for quite a time. He stood wordless, rooted to the spot in the King's Chamber, with a glazed expression, until, eventually, a succession of Holy Bee nonsense stories came tumbling out of him, later to be used in a sketch. While I spent hours inside the palace, still drinking in the atmosphere, he procured the English newspapers and immersed himself in those instead.

We sat beneath the throbbing stars at night trying to drink ouzo, but our time in Crete had run away from me before I could develop a taste for it. Tanned (Peter had the kind of skin which went a deep mahogany) and with heads full of potent images, we set off for Athens and home. I can't say I spotted any Cretan maidens turning up in his sketches, though bees certainly did. I also suspect he made fun of my odd experiences of *déjà vu* in a couple of pieces. We were to spend two days in Athens, staying in a small backstreet hotel and on the first day we did the tourist round. I was enchanted with these ruins too. The temples gave one such a feeling of balance in their proportions; it must have been the apogee of human endeavour. But we came down with a bump. Upon our return to the hotel we found that all our money had been stolen.

Pretty silly to leave cash in a hotel room, I suppose, but we had only recently left Cambridge where you could go out without locking your door. What were we to do? Without losing any time, Peter drew up a plan: 'I'm going to sit in the Central Plaza and see if anyone recognizes me, and then I'll ask them to lend me some money.' I thought this scheme rather flawed. He wasn't yet that well known, after all, and who would recognize him looking so tanned? I waited in the hotel room, full of trepidation. Perhaps foreign travel wasn't such a good idea. But within the hour he had returned with an air of triumph about him. 'You didn't manage it, did you?' I asked.

'I did,' he said. 'An Englishman approached me and asked, "Aren't you Peter Cook, from *Beyond the Fringe*?", and I said, "Yes, I am and I've just had my money stolen; would you be prepared to lend me £100?"' The man had generously agreed, so we ate that night and managed to get home too. What a nerve Peter had. It just shows that if you have confidence, people will always lock into it and all manner of things are made possible. Needless to say, the kind gentleman got his money back on our return, along with a little extra.

Once *Beyond the Fringe* had dipped a toe into the perilous waters of Broadway, the plan was that whole cast of The Establishment would follow on to set up a club in Manhattan once premises had been found.

So Peter, Alan, Jonathan and Dudley set off in the vanguard, rather eccentrically opting to sail together on the liner the *France*, due to arrive in New York on 28 September. Alan says the decision to go by sea was taken partly because of his phobia about air travel. 'I was frightened of flying,' he says. 'And of course there was the glamour of being on the *France*. Peter was rather taken with that. He had caviar for breakfast each morning from this big pot they brought around.'

But on board ship for the four- or five-day voyage the living was not quite as high on the hog as the foursome might have hoped.

'The ludicrous thing was we thought we would be very celebrated on the *France*, but that wasn't the case,' Alan explains. 'They had never heard of us at all and the crew, being French, were not interested. We thought we would be sitting at the captain's table and we had had a lot of discussions about whether we would sit there and how we would behave. But we weren't anywhere near the captain's table. We were put in the children's part of the dining hall. We still got the caviar and all that, but it wasn't as glamorous in that way as we thought it would be.'

I flew out to Boston for the first run of the show with Harriet Garland, wife of the theatre director Nick Garland, later to be better known as a cartoonist. I had been full of trepidation at the prospect of going to the States, so big, noisy and brash. When friends heard that we would be starting our visit in Boston, though, they were reassuring. 'You'll love it; people speak with English accents there!' All I'd heard about the place was the Boston Tea Party and I imagined it was just that – the kind the Queen has at Buckingham Palace. When we arrived the city's mood was far from genteel. The Boston Strangler was on the rampage and most people were talking about it. The city was on edge. Nonetheless, I remember enjoying my first hot beef, pastrami and dill pickle sandwich and later sharing the lift in our hotel with Anthony Quinn, who I'd idolized in *La Strada* and *Zorba the Greek*. Alone in a confined space with the great man, who exuded magnetism and masculinity from every pore, I just tried to drink in his presence.

The show moved on to Chicago next where Peter made a beeline for The Second City, a nightclub where he had already organized with the owner, Bernie Sahlins, for The Establishment group to appear. The whole warm-up tour was a huge success and in Washington in particular the show was a big smash, with even JFK expressing an interest in coming along.

Finally, in October 1962, Judy Scott-Fox, Peter's personal assistant, and I were sent on ahead to New York to seek accommodation there for the duration of the Broadway run. With all the crisscrossing streets and avenues, it seemed vast to me. My first sight of steam forcing up through the sidewalks was unforgettable. It was a relief to come across Greenwich Village with its genuine village atmosphere. If we had to live in New York, this had to be the most interesting and cosy part, so Judy and I confined our search to this area. We answered an intriguing sounding ad in a newspaper headed 'Arabian Nights . . .' and turned up on the steps of a brownstone on St Mark's Place where two gay interior designers had fashioned their basement with an exotic Arabian tent-like décor. They had bought swags of pillowcase ticking and hung them from the walls and ceilings. Too late Peter and I were to discover this had been done to mask the cracks in the walls and keep out the rats that scuttled around at night in the upper levels.

This was the first time I encountered the Fox police lock. It consisted of an iron bar that went into the floor and was wedged against the door – an ominous indication of the kind of visitors we might expect. After a few weeks I worked out that we were no more than one block away from the Bowery – 'Skid Row' – and another from the women's prison on Fifth Avenue, from where we occasionally heard screams at night. Once we returned to find a guy hacking away at our front door with an axe. He shot up the fire escape, leaving the iron bar and just a piece of the door remaining. We had to go to bed with a gaping hole where our front door had been and I shivered and trembled all night. I think Peter was scared too.

Initially, though, Peter was chuffed at the idea of living like a caliph; even the furniture was specially made – low divans and tables. So we agreed to take the place for six months; at that point we didn't know how long the run would be. As it was dark we always had artificial lighting, and took off our shoes to walk on the tatami matting, but since we mostly lived a nocturnal life, a 'tent' was a fairly suitable abode.

We had in the meantime been put up in the famous Algonquin Hotel. It was overwhelmingly hot that autumn, so when room service brought us freshly squeezed orange juice with crushed ice for breakfast, it was extremely welcome. Vanessa Redgrave and her husband Tony Richardson were also staying in the hotel and we had a happy evening together before the opening night. In the background all the time, however, was a looming dread, a crisis that had been gathering momentum down in the Caribbean – in Cuba. In April, we were told, the Soviet Premier Nikita Khrushchev had decided to site intermediate-range missiles on Cuba with Fidel Castro's agreement and so secret production had gone on all that summer. Twelve days before our 'curtain up' US reconnaissance planes had picked up the telltale images of the missiles and on 22 October Kennedy announced that any launch from the site would be regarded as an attack on the United States. On the 25th, two days before the show was due to open, Kennedy raised the status of military alert to DEFCON 2. Many New Yorkers were stuffing their car boots full and leaving in panic. The producers called a meeting to decide whether to postpone the opening, but the four plucky young British men took the attitude 'The show must go on', and so on it went. Alan Bennett, who had taken an apartment on his own on East 72nd Street, was so concerned that he didn't want to be alone.

'I stayed with Dudley, I was so certain something was going to happen. Then it seemed to have calmed down and by the time it came to the first night the feeling was actually one of relief,' he says. 'People weren't to know, but that was the actual crunch time on that night.' An American U-2 spy plane had been shot down.

'I remember a police car passed in the street in the middle of it. The audience went absolutely dead. You couldn't do anything with them. They all thought something was going to happen.'

International tension notwithstanding, the opening was certainly a star-studded affair. I went with Terence Stamp and Jean Shrimpton and I wore a long, low-cut, long-sleeved dress of navy blue wild silk, with sleeveless long coat of emerald green wild silk, which I had designed myself and had made in London. My friend Harriet was escorted by the Burmese diplomat U Thant, the new Secretary General of the UN. Bizarre, but Nick Garland was away and the publicists thought he should come along and so set up the date. The critics once more gave rave reviews, some asking 'Why can't the Americans produce this kind of hard-hitting humour?' Great celebrations and unbelievable acclaim followed, yet again. *The Fringe* was the toast of Broadway, but we had to share 'the great white way' with several other British imports who were also hauling in the crowds: Lionel Bart's *Oliver!*, Joan Littlewood's *Oh, What a Lovely War!* and Antony Newley's *Stop the World, I Want to Get Off*. In fact the invasion of British talent was so extensive that a photograph was taken by the press to record the coincidence.

Alan, who has kept the same photograph all these years too, pointed out to me there are some amusing bedfellows to be spotted in the ranks, among them John Noakes and Hermione Gingold, David Jones and Geraldine McEwan, not to mention Albert Finney, Christopher Timothy and Derek Fowlds.

All this heralded a huge wave of Anglomania in New York. We were all lionized and invited to parties by people we didn't know. The Americans seemed to like getting close to those considered to be the latest success story. Arnold Weisberger, a highly successful lawyer to the stars, gave both 'A' stream and 'B' stream parties. If it was an 'A' stream party, we had heard, Noël Coward would be there, poised on the piano stool. Clearly we had made the grade because when we arrived at a Weisberger affair, there he was, The Master himself, tinkling away and occasionally even singing. At one of these parties I remember spending quite a long time talking to Vivien Leigh. She was shy and refined, like a highly-bred racehorse with reined-in nervous energy.

Nick Garland was back in New York now directing Peter Ustinov in his play *Photo Finish*, and on their arrival in town he and Harriet stayed with us in St Mark's Place. On several occasions Nick would bring Ustinov over for a late supper. This is when I started to explore Persian and Middle Eastern cookery; it fitted in with our exotic environment after all, and I shall never forget the magic of Ustinov, a wonderful model for a sultan, reclining after supper on the divan, replete and regaling us with his wonderful stories. (In Ustinov, Peter had at last some competition as a monologuist.) One story I recall was about an elderly friend of his, the aristocratic Russian refugee Baroness Budberg, who had the somewhat bohemian habit of collecting her milk from the doorstep in the early morning stark naked. One morning she stepped out and the door slammed firmly shut behind her. So there was this naked elderly lady with pendulous breasts, locked out of her flat. What could she do? She grabbed a fire bucket and put it on her head and went off to seek help. If she couldn't see any-one, then they couldn't see her. The laughter this silly story prompted that night has stayed with me down the years.

The fashions in New York were not really comparable with those in London: there was no Mary Quant or Kiki Byrne. I remember I had bought a pair of leather high-heeled boots from Anello and Davide, the ballet costumiers in London, and was wearing them one day in New York when a woman crossed the street to ask me where I had bought them. I was rather flattered. Later, of course, long, high-heeled boots became the rage, with Paco Rabanne making them in PVC: such ideas spread like wildfire. I liked Bloomingdale's and bought some of my clothes there, but my very good dressmaker in London could make wonderful things from my sketches, so I had come prepared.

We became very good friends with Joseph Heller, the author of *Catch 22*, and his wife Shirley. For me they epitomized Jewish humour, with repartee that was so quick you'd lose the plot. Jack and Carol Gelber were also delightfully warm people. Jack had written *The Apple*, a wonderful off-Broadway play with a cult following at the time. The cartoonist Jules Ffeiffer and his wife Judy also became close. (These were the only three couples, out of all the invitations we accepted at that time, who actually cooked food in their own homes. In those days New Yorkers generally either took you out or phoned for a takeaway. Maybe they still do.)

Peter, never relaxing for a moment, now put himself to organizing the refurbishment of the El Morocco Club on East 54th Street, which was to become a plusher version of the London Establishment and called The Strollers Theater-Club. Peter's first club back home had been left in the hands of Nicholas Luard and we kept in touch with the very occasional phone call. Like the London *Beyond the Fringe* show, a substitute second team of entertainers was now in place, freeing up some of the original cabaret stars to come out to New York.

STROLLERS THEATRE-CLUB
154 East 54th Street, New York   PL 2-4711

PETER COOK and JOHN KRIMSKY

present

THE
ESTABLISHMENT

1963-64 EDITION

Written by
PETER COOK

with

PETER BELLWOOD	**FRANCIS BETHENCOURT**
ALEXANDRA BERLIN	**RODDY MAUDE-ROXBY**

and

CAROLE SIMPSON

and the music of
THE TEDDY WILSON TRIO

Directed by
WILLIAM FRANCISCO

PETER LEWIS   *Special Material by*
PETER SHAFFER   JOHN BRAINE

Songs by   *Music by*
STEPHAN VINAVER   **CARL DAVIS**

IN THE HEART
OF OFF-B'WAY

THE LIMELIGHT
91-7th Ave. So. OR 5-2212

SHOWCARD

DINNER
COCKTAILS
ESPRESSO, PASTRY
AFTER-THEATRE SUPPER
SUNDAY BUFFET

Your Ticket
Stubs From
THIS PERFORMANCE
Entitle You To A
10 Per Cent DISCOUNT
Alcoholic Beverages Excepted

December 10 & December 17

*The bill/programme for Peter's cabaret team at their New York
club home, established in 1963 in the Old Morocco Club on
East 54th St.*

The prospect of a new English-style club was anticipated with great excitement. Only one man was annoyed: the producer David Merrick, who had lost out on the show, started to bad-mouth the enterprise. Because there was a newspaper strike at the time Merrick said no one would hear about the opening night anyway. In retaliation Peter used a trick that Merrick himself had invented to drum up publicity for one of his own shows. He had found people with the same names as famous critics to endorse the production. In a naughty twist Peter turned up an unknown postman called David Merrick and instructed him to give wildly enthusiastic reviews for the show at our new club. Judy and I even paraded around Broadway wearing sandwich boards displaying these bogus quotes. The real David Merrick was furious, but it was such fun because it was dramatic and it got New York excited about the subterfuge.

In our free time Peter and I went to listen to jazz: Miles Davis, Gerry Mulligan, Nina Simone. Our apartment was opposite the Five Spot Café where Roland Kirk played nightly and Peter met up with a wonderful elderly jazz pianist, Teddy Wilson, whom he persuaded to come and play at The Strollers. He would be perfect. The new club was not to be like The Establishment with its racy jazz venue in the basement. This would be a little more discreet and comfortable, with no mafia trying to extract protection money – or so we hoped. So Judy Scott-Fox and I had a great deal to do getting ready for the opening. Again there would be a membership entrance policy, and we had to decide on the menus and generally put ourselves about.

The idea of turning New York, with its speed, violence and brashness, into our own 'village', as had rapidly happened in London, seemed highly ambitious, but in fact, with the large presence of British thespians on Broadway every party we went to was full of people we knew from home. When we were in the presence of New Yorkers, who could be so effortlessly loud and over the top, it only served to intensify our own Englishness. I found myself making a special effort to enunciate properly and I became somewhat reserved for a while, as an antidote to the let-it-all-hang-out attitude of those around us. It was therefore nice to be invited to dinner with Anthony Newley and Joan Collins, a married couple at the time. Joan was utterly sweet, wore fluffy carpet slippers and had made supper herself. The whole evening was relaxed and unpretentious. I would continue to see Joan from time to time after we had both broken up from our husbands and I found her really earthy and in reality more beautiful than Elizabeth Taylor, with whom she had been compared in looks.

I made another good British friend one night as Harriet and I were sitting at a table in The Strollers. We simultaneously spotted a handsome, debonair figure at the bar and Harriet decided he had to be English, so she strode over and introduced herself. He turned out to be Gavin Young, the intrepid foreign correspondent for the *Observer*.

We were trying to acclimatize ourselves gradually to American food, but one Thanksgiving meal at the house of Jack and Nancy Gelber was full of surprises. First there was sugar-baked ham, covered in pineapple and studded with cloves, served with sweet potato pie with melted marshmallows on top, followed by a pumpkin pie that tasted like candy floss. Some might appreciate a sugary meal like this now that the American sweet tooth has come over to England, although I don't think we have yet caught on to melted marshmallows as a garnish – thank goodness. The theatrically-themed Sardis was one of our favourite restaurants along with the plush Russian Tea Rooms, which served blinis with sour cream, caviar and iced vodka.

I find it hard now to get into the skin of that twenty-two-year-old who, only four years earlier, had been faced with a lifetime in Civil Service bureaucracy. What was it that had catapulted me, through my student relationship with Peter, into this life of lavish splendour? It had happened so quickly, so smoothly, like an arrow released from a bow. I just went along with that momentum, with no real time for reflection. At that age the future always beckons so strongly. Discussing it all with Harriet now, it was the jokes that carried us along.

'It was the laughter I remember – particularly at night in New York when we would go on to another club after The Strollers; me, you, Gavin, Peter and Dudley. I remember just begging them to stop because it hurt so much.'

Here we were – *Beyond the Fringe* was a sellout, New York was splitting its sides – despite the hysteria engendered by the Cuban Crisis. It was a fascinating time in anyone's estimation. Our literary friends were very excited by the JFK presidency; here was a man who looked as though he could extricate himself, to a greater extent than his predecessors, from the manipulation of the jostling power groups which were constantly seeking to control US policy.

Kennedy's inauguration as President had been celebrated by fifty-seven writers, composers and painters, including W. H. Auden and John Steinbeck, and this was seen as a sign by the artistic community that the arts and intellectual life would be taken seriously. A White House cultural coordinator was even appointed early in 1962 and the White House became a kind of showcase for leading performing arts organizations – from opera to jazz. After one such event Kennedy is supposed to have commented wryly: 'This is becoming a sort of eating place for artists, but they never ask us out!'

The First Lady, born Jacqueline Lee Bouvier, was a big part of this cultural campaign. She had the nerve to wear French designer clothing while presidential election rival Richard

Nixon's wife, Pat, made a point of only wearing American clothes. Friends and aides of Jackie often noted that she was also keen on poking fun at particular targets and flouting convention.

Kennedy, we had heard, had planned to see *Beyond the Fringe* on one of its Washington dates but had postponed, probably because of the business down in Cuba. Then the team was invited to perform at the White House. Peter was not keen: the idea of travelling 'like some fucking cabaret' did not appeal. 'They can come here,' he said. And so they did. Macmillan in London and Kennedy in Washington: two of the most powerful men in the world had come to see four young graduates satirising the modern age.

Soon after this, Nick Garland and Peter mysteriously suggested that Harriet and I go off to Puerto Rico for a fortnight's winter sunshine break. We were grateful, but a little suspicious. As Harriet says: 'We were flying without them so they could have extra rehearsals . . . or extra girls!'

The main thing that struck me on this trip was the appalling poverty in Puerto Rico. I felt ashamed about staying in our luxury hotel, being served fresh pineapple for breakfast. We both got rather bored too with all the pampering and so curtailed our stay, catching an earlier flight back to New York. Returning to St Mark's Place, we were welcomed by Judy Scott-Fox. Learning that I was planning to go to The Strollers that evening, she quickly warned me I might bump into Jacqueline Kennedy. What could I say? I dressed carefully, wearing a Liberty lotus-flower silk dress. It was backless with tiny shoulder straps and showed off my newly acquired suntan. Arriving at the club I noticed a buzz in the air. Peter caught sight of me and momentarily looked a little ruffled, but then greeted me with a hug and a kiss and broke the news that Jackie Kennedy had come that evening to revisit the show. 'She thought it so naughty! Come, and I'll introduce you.'

Jackie was tall and slender, with thick, black hair and a vermilion mouth; immaculately groomed. She wore an expensive looking little black dress with a diamond pin. I noticed her hands were soft, impractical, and she had a little-girlish laugh, the laugh of someone who had been cocooned from life's more arduous demands. Just as I took the First Lady's hand in greeting my fragile shoulder strap broke and I was left holding up my front with one hand and feebly trying to disengage my other hand from hers. I excused myself and rushed off to the powder room. Judy accompanied me and we both had hysterics. I did suspect there had been something going on between Jackie and Peter. Several of our friends, Bruce Copp included, remain convinced that her taste for dalliances with English public school-educated young men had certainly extended to my talented fiancé. It may have been only a flirtation, but even that was going to be a hard act for me to follow – tan or no tan.

Because we appeared to be getting along so well with at least one half of the 'Jack and Jackie' partnership, another coveted invitation came from Arnold Weisberger, to go out to some country club for dinner with Bobby Kennedy and a select group of friends. We were driven out in a flotilla of black limousines to a secret destination. I remember there were about a dozen people there. Bobby Kennedy was indeed handsome; he was in the company of his current mistress, it was quite clear. He impressed me – if that is the word – with his hypocrisy as he made a big fuss about it being a Friday when, as a good Catholic, he couldn't possibly eat meat. A special menu was duly recommended. It seemed his religious convictions did allow him, however, to fornicate unlawfully, as I supposed, without his conscience playing upon him. There was a band and a dance floor and he invited me to dance. I surprised myself by conducting a conversation about American politics as we jigged around. He was a good dancer and it was a memorable evening. There was a certain pathos about him, however, which left me feeling a little sad about all the Kennedys, with their wealth and smooth manners. They were not people around whom one could relax – they were always so busy at the charm.

This whirlwind success was getting rather out of hand. I would often go to parties alone, intending to meet Peter there. Sometimes I would even have to queue up to speak to him. Many times I left alone. In New York the *Beyond the Fringe* group took up their own varied interests: Peter was absorbed with The Strollers; Dudley was entangled with several women, as usual, but also devotedly in love with the beautiful model Celia Hammond. Alan continued his study of medieval history, using library microfilm he had brought with him. He intended to return to academia at the end of the run. Jonathan plunged himself into the heady New York world of intellectuals, writers and medical researchers. As he says, there was not much shared ground for these four stars by this point. 'The four of us never saw each other during the day before the show. We had no interests in common. I was then what I am now, which is an old-fashioned London intellectual. We all had our own activities. Peter had his. I remember him coming into the dressing room – as he had done at the Fortune Theatre in London – laden with newspapers. He was always an addict of magazines and newspapers and of horseracing.'

I became tired of the razzmatazz and the lavish but brittle hospitality. I wanted some scene of my own, not to be dependent upon those elements of my new life. Judy Scott-Fox, who was living with us in St Mark's Place, introduced me to two friends of hers, Nathan and Caroline Silver; he was a snappy, amusing Jewish New York architect and she a horsy English-woman, with the voice to match, who worked for a publishing house. They took us to see what was by now a cult movie by John Cassavetes. It was called *Shadows* and it concerned racial issues, but had an anarchic jazz theme. The hand-held camera technique was highly unusual then; it made low-budget films a possibility and certainly gave Hollywood a bit of competition. Even today this film feels fresh and, apart from some of the street dialogue, it has not really dated. One particularly outstanding and beautiful performance came from Benito Carruthers, an actor straight from the method school of acting. He played the younger brother in a family with faces of varying hues. I was mesmerized by his expression, by the way he moved and by his unblinking gaze. So when Nathan told us that Benito Carruthers was 'between jobs' and working as a waiter at The Second City, the Greenwich Village branch of the famous Chicago nightclub, I said, 'Let's go!'

The Second City, based in The Royale Theater for a season, had spawned the talents of Alan Alda, Mike Nichols and Elaine May, and, like The Strollers, had its own group of performers who wrote their own material. Alan Arkin, best known as Yossarian in the film version of Joseph Heller's *Catch 22*, was one of their leading players. The show was brilliantly executed and took place in a large, darkened room, with a stage and tables and a long American bar such as you see in westerns. Behind the bar was the unmistakable figure of Ben Carruthers. He had a most beautiful sculpted head, like a native American, covered with tight curls. He was lanky, with a slight stoop in the shoulders – although I suspect this was part of the method look. I couldn't believe it when it turned out he was our designated waiter. 'Hi, Ben,' said Nathan and introduced Judy and myself. It really was one of those moments when the world stood still. We eyed each other, smiled and instantly knew something – something that communicated itself in every bodily cell.

Nathan, Judy, Caroline and I stayed a long time that night.

The show finished and the clientele left and Ben came to sit down and had a drink with us – a Budweiser. He was full of Negro jazz musicians' jargon: everything was 'cool, man', 'crazy, man', 'hip' or 'way out' – the first time I'd heard these expressions. He was funny, intelligent and had the most wonderfully mobile face. Half-Mexican, he was the very antithesis of the public school Englishman I was engaged to. Apparently Ben made a habit of marrying his leading ladies. His female lead in *Shadows* had been Leila Goldoni. Having divorced Leila, Ben went on to marry his next leading lady, the black actress Argos. I was later to learn that they had a son and that Argos was pregnant again, but for some reason at this point Ben was mostly living with Rick, another out-of-work actor/writer who was also working as a waiter at The Second City. I should have heeded the warning signs.

The American poet and lyricist Fran Landesman, who – together with her husband Jay – became a good friend back in London, also knew Benito. She remembers him once coming into a room, looking around, and saying: 'Which one of you girls would like to fuck me?'

'I am sure very often there were girls who volunteered,' says Fran. 'Who wouldn't want to? He was one of the dishiest guys.'

The Second City became a special haunt for Judy and me; she had forged a romantic link with Ben's friend, the acne-scarred Rick, with his deep, resonating voice. They made an unusual pair, but I was happy for her. Her English accent and 'jolly hockey sticks' cheerfulness were indeed an attraction to those Americans. I got to know Ben better and felt a great warmth flowing from him. We would walk in Central Park together or go to museums. I felt I was being shown New York by a real New Yorker. Peter didn't seem to notice much, although he'd been to The Second City and met Ben. I told him quite openly about our cultural meetings. Perhaps I'd hoped to make him a little jealous, as our own relationship didn't seem to be going anywhere. We were supposed to be engaged, but what about marriage? Would it ever happen? I was rather ambivalent about this next step. Life had escalated in an unimaginable way since that commitment we had made during the Edinburgh Festival and deep down part of me felt somewhat uneasy about all this glamour and overwhelming adulation. I could see through most of it, I felt, probably because I was an onlooker. Nevertheless there was a part of me that was seduced by it all too.

But now something unexpected was happening – I was very attracted to Ben Carruthers and in time we started an affair. He was an amazing lover; tender, romantic, attentive and thoughtful, though, come to think of it, not very thoughtful at all towards the other commitments he'd taken on in life. The fact that I managed to allow myself to become involved with a married man, with all my religious ideals of not so long ago, is difficult to countenance now. But romance was in the air we breathed, the pull of sharing oneself with another. Often it was the post-coital conversation that was so amazing, just lying there in each other's arms.

I still have a love letter he wrote to me at this time. Full of 'beat talk', it is very passionate too and, in places, poetic. One line reads: 'There are many a thing a man'll do to catch a woman's eye. He'll wear tight pants and act cold and have a tooth pulled for a tooth of gold. Baby I've got to get to you . . .' It sounds like a song lyric, but not one I knew: just the fruit of a fertile mind and a roving eye, I think.

Jay Landesman remembers Benito as a talented yet unfocused man, someone who always 'had projects by the bed they were "going to do"'. Much like Peter, Jay says, Ben was a great conversational improviser. 'Ben could do that very well too. He could spin out a thing.'

Our affair went on into the spring. I felt sure Peter must know. I wasn't doing much to hide it, but he was so self-absorbed that, as long as I ran the house well and kept the larder full, it seemed his attention was elsewhere. Then Ben confronted me about it all one day; he wanted us to go away together. We sat in a coffee shop; he looking pale and drawn, his face framed in the manner of a monk's cowl by a woollen hat and scarf. Tears ran down his cheeks as he professed his love for me. What a defining moment in my life! I had not expected this at all, although I too was by now involved on many levels – it was certainly no longer just lust. What was I to do? I was distraught. I went to see his wife and children and realized I couldn't take a father away from them. I felt real shame about what I had entered into so blindly. I decided I had to make a clean breast of it to Peter.

Whether he had suspected or not, the news clearly came as a wake-up call. Yet, like Mr Spiggott in his Tarzan sketch, Peter did not have a leg to stand on when it came to morality. Realizing he actually did love and value me, and that he didn't want to lose me, in a moment of statesman-like clarity he suggested I should go back to England, away from both him and Ben, to think about the situation and choose between them.

So I returned to London, visited my parents and friends and tried to put some perspective on the situation. Peter and I had become pretty reliant on each other and somehow I couldn't see a future without him. At the same time there were by now breaches of trust, on his part made worse, I felt, by his lack of honesty. My strategy, for better or for worse, was to try to be honest in all my dealings, but it didn't always pay off. We had been together for nearly four years and I knew that in my body and soul there was a strong desire to start having children.

It was good to get away from the New York scene. It all

seemed rather unreal, living a night-time life (and in a tent at that) – but I was optimistic enough to think our relationship could change, could deepen and mature. It's a tragedy that, back then, we were not taught anything about important things like relationships, loving, eroticism and parenting. Most people learn about life by example, from observing role models. Although my quarrelsome parents had stayed together, they were not ideally suited so I did not have a particularly good template upon which to base my own life. Peter was the opposite. His family were not really there; he didn't even meet his father properly until he was seven years old. So neither of us had a particularly good understanding of how marriages work.

While pondering these questions back home, a little light entertainment came my way, in the form of Gerry Mulligan who was visiting London and playing at Ronnie Scott's in Soho. I had met him that summer in America at the Newport Jazz Festival and he had invited me along to hear him play, dedicating a set to me, which was very flattering. He was an extraordinary talent and good-looking too. I showed my appreciation and for a while allowed him to become something of an emotional bridge for me between London and New York, a city that was already calling me back. But was the decision about what to do next only mine to make? There seemed to be no future with Ben, with all his familial encumbrances: I felt he just wanted to escape those responsibilities. Peter and I had something quite solid and powerful, though it certainly did not match up to the idea of courtly love that my heart pined for. But, my goodness, it was a rare and unusual relationship and, what was more, Peter had woken up to my importance in his life. I thought our love might blossom with time.

It was a special reunion in New York and I took a good look at Peter. You know how sometimes you forget how someone you know intimately really looks? He had, if only briefly, shown a crack in his vulnerability and it was this little crack that allowed me to love him in a deeper way. It is hard, after all, to love someone properly when he is always defending his castle by slipping into the guise of one of a myriad walk-on characters. It is confusing too to communicate with that person when he is always putting on funny voices. But I made my choice. Peter was clearly relieved and we entered a new epoch in our relationship. I think this pleased not only us, but also our friends who were happy about our new commitment.

Peter took me off for a weekend on Fire Island, a holiday destination favoured mostly by New York gays. We rented a cabin and I cooked freshly caught fish. It really was a special weekend, with all other distractions banished. The sun, the sea, the stars, and the boardwalk which we strolled down, barefoot, to bathe, gave us the space we had so long been missing. Peter even desisted from reading all the newspapers for two whole days! We made love in a relaxed way and I knew that we had connected with the being of our future child. I knew I would become pregnant and that this was what I had been longing for.

Summer was now on its way and most sensible people would soon be leaving New York. Alex Cohen owned a large house with a swimming pool out in Connecticut and he offered it to the four *Beyond the Fringe*-ers, along with a car and chauffeur to ferry them back and forth from the city. Everyone seemed to think this was a good way to cope with the city heat. Moving out of the Village also made the break between myself and Ben more decisive – not necessarily any less painful, but it reduced the temptation to see each other. In the end we were both trying to do the best for the people who had been affected by our brief liaison: that meant stopping seeing each other.

So the cast was installed in this comfortable wood-built summer house and I got involved with the cooking, which I really loved, although I'm sure that others helped. Judy Scott-Fox and I would commandeer the car, chauffeured by a black guy with several gold teeth and an immaculate Brylcremed bouffant hairdo, and go shopping at the local supermarket. We would stock up on beer and crunchy salads and lovely, summery ingredients. We would often have The Strollers team to spend the weekend with us – hilarious times. Alan made a wonderful paper hat out of newspaper that made him look like a bishop as he watered the roses in his bathing costume. Caroline and Nathan Silver visited frequently too. Nathan recently recounted the impression the four English Oxbridge stars made on him then.

'Caroline and I had been introduced to the other three before, but this was the first time we had the opportunity of spending a few days with them and we realised they were just the same as their stage personas. They were absolutely walking-talking replicas of what they did on stage.

'This would make a lot of sense, of course, because the show would have to reflect their personalities, but you don't necessarily assume this is the case. And that certainly was the case; Alan was this quizzical person, who was donnish. Dudley was this insecure, charming guy. I liked Jonathan too and wanted to get to know him, but he was so busy.'

Nathan, who stayed friendly with Dudley, has a clear memory of realizing he had a hidden disability. 'I first saw his shrivelled leg in Connecticut. I didn't know about it until I saw him get into the pool. I was very touched, as one is, and surprised because he had made no mention of it.'

His impression of Peter at this time was of a man who had developed a comedic style as a way of keeping people away.

'I did the same when I was at school,' he says. 'What made Peter unique though was, first of all, that he did it a lot better

Jeremy Geidt and Jonathan Miller by the pool escaping from the Manhattan heat.

Alan Bennett in his impromptu paper sun hat with the camera-weilding John Bird at our Connecticut hideaway.

than anybody else and, secondly, that there was a danger-
ousness. He certainly was never restrained by being tactful.'

I should mention here that our time in Connecticut has gone
down in posterity for one event which we could never have
foreseen gaining such widespread currency. This was where,
so history records, David Frost nearly drowned and Peter leapt
to his rescue. Jonathan was there and he remembers it, so it
must be true. Nathan was there and he remembers it too. The
incident was piquant because, not content with taking on much
of Peter's stage persona back in Britain, David was now starring in a satirical television show similar to one that Peter
himself had hoped to make. Called *That Was the Week That
Was*, or *TW3* for short, Frost's programme had quickly become
required viewing. Alan Bennett says the success of this show
had bugged Peter even as he and the others were busy taking
Broadway by storm. 'Peter would be on the phone at the stage
door on the Saturday night being told what *TW3* had done
that week, because, what with the time difference, they had
already finished going out. A lot of it was stuff he had written
himself, or co-written. He wasn't benign about this at the time,'
says Alan. Peter subsequently claimed the act of saving David
from sinking to the bottom of our pool was his only regret in
life. The fact is, though, that even if I was there too, I still
doubt it happened. I may have been making lunch but I can't
believe that something as dramatic as a near drowning could
have passed by without a bit more of fuss. Surely David can
swim.

Another great mystery from this period concerned the disappearing chauffeur-driven limo we had been loaned: driver
and vehicle vanished the same week. There was a great deal of
embarrassment about this incident. Nathan Silver recalls Judy
telling him at the time that we didn't want to report it to the
police because the missing man was black and we Brits were

afraid he would suffer unduly at the hands of the American cops. Nathan says he phoned up Jonathan Miller about it to reassure him the police would not shoot someone for taking a car. The drama was resolved without gunfire, I seem to recall, when it became clear that the chauffeur had gone off on an illicit jaunt with the maid at the Connecticut house.

Back in Manhattan, Judy and I would often go into the John Golden Theatre with the boys to watch their show. Every night they would come up with impromptu lines they hoped would 'corpse' the others. They usually succeeded. On one celebrated occasion Tom Miller, Jonathan and Rachel's new baby boy, was brought on from the wings to put his father off his stride. Jonathan recalls Alan coming to his rescue: 'Tom was born just six weeks before we came to America and so Rachel came and stood in the wings with the baby. Peter grabbed Tom and came on stage with him while Alan and I were doing a sketch and said, "Your wife has just had a baby." Alan said, "Put it in the fridge."'

We should remember that these were not trained thespians who had developed the stamina to recite the same lines night after night. What's more they had been doing this show, on and off, for over three years. Jonathan and Alan were now particularly impatient to get back to their own lives. I am told there was a great deal of bickering offstage, but I have to say I don't remember it being like that. They always seemed irrepressible, but it must have been a strain, night after night. Only Peter and Dudley were, as it were, born entertainers, actually unable to survive without a constant audience, and therefore more able to cope with the demanding routine of performance. According to Alan, rows flared up now and then between Jonathan and Dudley: 'They didn't get on. But it wasn't constant: it just occasionally blew up,' he says. 'They didn't get on because Jonathan, if he didn't like the audience or they didn't respond immediately, wrote them off and didn't work at it. Dudley was much more of a trouper. He would go out and try to win the audience over; he would mug away and do all sorts of outrageous things, while Jonathan couldn't be bothered.'

Alan too could be a trifle difficult, according to Jonathan Miller, and Alan himself admits that one of the cast threw a tea tray at him on one occasion: 'I hope one would behave better now, except I wouldn't want to be cooped up again with three other comedians.'

At The Strollers we had our regulars, of course, as well as some intriguing occasional visitors. Salvador Dali made ostentatious appearances with his silver-topped cane. I met Laurence Olivier and Joan Plowright in the club, and Rex Harrison and his wife Rachel Roberts. Kirk Douglas came in too – which was a real thrill, although I was disappointed that he was so short. In fact the Hollywood star was reportedly rather unhappy with a sketch that made fun of small actors, or so says Roddy Maude-Roxby, who was in the show. 'He didn't stand up when he met me afterwards,' he remembers.

Peter had brought Roddy and the rest of the team out, arranging for work visas wherever he could. Roddy got a Green Card eventually. Peter had apparently told him to fly out as a visitor, but Roddy was caught out by immigration: 'Next day there was a message from the embassy saying to let me in. I got a Green Card through Peter's manipulations later too and I kept it alive by going back to the States every so often.'

While John Bird and his team were out in New York entertaining at The Strollers, Frankie Howerd was given a run at the London club. It revived his career. Peter Bellwood and Roddy Maude-Roxby came over as part of The Establishment second team, joining American Alexandra Berlin, and did some new writing with Peter.

SHOWCARD

THE ESTABLISHMENT

Strollers Theatre-Club

The New York incarnation of The Establishment Cabaret: starring Peter Billwood, Francis Bethencauld, Roddy Maude-Roxley, Alexandra Boni and Carde Simpson.

'I could ad-lib,' says Roddy, 'and so Peter said to do some of my own lines as well as his. When he saw the show, he would then give me other sentences to say. I actually got a Comedy of the Year award and that would have been largely due to using a script that was written by Peter.'

The new theatre going up next to the club on The Strollers premises was also the venue for a production of Mike Nicols' play *The Knack*, in which Roddy also starred, alongside George Segal. It emerged that Segal was keen to meet Elizabeth Taylor and so Mike Nicols invited her along, without warning, to watch a rehearsal in the half-decorated new theatre. The panic this invitation caused is still etched on Roddy's memory: 'George Segal collapsed with stomach cramps, Alex Berlin started crying and the prompt boy "on the book" said: "I have had a nervous breakdown before and I need attention."' Eventually Taylor arrived, escorted by Roddy McDowell and Michael Wilding, in other words, with an ex-husband and a childhood sweetheart. She sat down and watched the show amid the drying paint and ladders. She didn't seem to mind the rough and ready state of the production, and pronounced *The Knack* a success.

'Miles Davis was the other enormous star who came to the club,' Roddy recalls, 'and Georgia Brown came too with Jack Nicholson. I told him I hadn't heard of him and he gave me a snarling grin.'

Roddy also remembers a row about the use of the word 'nigger' in a sketch about Welsh miners. He says all the black musicians walked out and had to be negotiated back in. Jackie Kennedy's sister, Lee Radziwill, also protested one night about the crucifixion sketch by John Bird. Roddy is still proud of telling her rather rudely: 'Peter Cook is always interested in what the public think.'

A pregnancy test now proved that my intuition about our

holiday on Fire Island had been right. Our baby would be due in May 1964. Peter appeared really happy about this and now we had something to plan for and a way, hopefully, to mend broken fences. I was really joyful, wanting so much to be a mother.

Bells Are Ringing

We began to plan our wedding, which was to take place in October. Peter's American agent, Janet Roberts, was a member of the congregation at St Luke's Episcopalian Church in the Village and she made an appointment for us to visit the pastor, Rev. Wilbur C. Leach. We felt quite chastened in his presence. He had been told of the forthcoming baby and warned: 'I must impress upon you as a couple I am not prepared to marry you just to give this child a name. You must understand that marriage is for life.' It reminded us of the seriousness of our undertaking. With Peter there was little that was serious; there was much to be mocked, and, for myself, the moorings of my faith had been somewhat loosened. A long silence ensued as we tried to digest the apparent enormity of our future commitment. Few people could have reduced Peter to a spirit of such deference, but this pastor was a real man of God and I certainly wanted a Christian wedding, so for once we needed to be clear about what we were stepping into. I was actually grateful for these words, though I must admit it was not without some trepidation that we both said we understood his meaning. There followed a series of meetings with him which were helpful. For the twenty-five-year-old Peter I think it was a formality, but at twenty-three I was a child in many ways and unprepared for the life that was about to unfold.

Soon the excitement of planning the wedding took over. I loved having events to organize and plan for. The reception was to be in The Strollers and would be a lunchtime affair. I planned to do a lot of the catering with the help of some of the staff. I found an Austrian baker who knew how to make a proper wedding cake, with all the tiers. I wasn't having any of the fluffy, sponge-cake jobs Americans seemed to favour. Having decided that a white wedding would be unsuitable in my condition, I designed an outfit and chose some deep blue crepe silk for an empire line dress and a sleeveless coat. We went to buy an elegant navy suit for Peter, then I chose a turquoise felt hat to go with my outfit. I organized the flowers for the room and hired some Hungarian violinists to play background music, along with a white-gloved butler to welcome the guests.

Sadly, my parents would not be able to come at such short notice, but we would have a party with them in London as some compensation. Peter's parents could come out for a week, and we promised to whistle them around New York and show them the sights. Sybil Burton, the estranged wife of Richard Burton, who had just suffered the excessive publicity generated by his affair with Elizabeth Taylor, now became very engaged with The Strollers and with the new theatre going up on the site. Sybil also helped me and Judy to organize the wedding and the guest list. She was an amazingly warm, strong and dynamic Welsh woman who carried herself with enduring dignity, despite the constant presence of the paparazzi. The press found it easier to hound Sybil than the two reclusive megastars playing out their real-life Anthony and Cleopatra romance.

Peter and I were still living in St Mark's Place, but had found a much more appropriate apartment, still in the Village, on West 9th Street. It was on the first floor of an old brownstone, with large rooms and windows and great Regency mirrors. Living our subterranean life in a tent on St Mark's Place had been fun but it had begun to feel oppressive and was not the right environment in which to grow a baby.

The wedding day, 28 October 1963, came up fast. Margaret and Alec Cook flew in and were safely installed in a nearby hotel. Dudley agreed to play the organ for the service. A dashing friend from Cambridge, and now part of The Strollers team, Peter Bellwood, was to be best man; Nathan Silver, as a solid academic, seemed an appropriate stand-in for my absent father and was to give me away. Nathan says now he was honoured by this selection: 'I took it so seriously and I thought it was amazing. I wrote a little speech.'

When they arrived, Peter and I did the tourist bit with Alec and Margaret Cook. It was cold, I remember, but we took them down to the Hudson on the Staten Island ferry. We visited the Guggenheim and had the great luck to secure tickets to the Metropolitan Opera House. We dined at the Four Seasons too, so, all in all, it was a very hectic build-up to our big day.

Elizabeth has one of the clearest memories of the wedding, although she wasn't even there! A schoolgirl at Sherborne at the time, she missed out on the trip because Alec and Margaret could not afford to bring out their daughters too. Distraught, she tried to stop them going. 'I said: "You can't go, because I have chicken pox", but they said, "Yes, we can", and they put me into school as a spotty boarder.'

She says Peter and I wrote nice letters in consolation, and so, apparently, did Dudley, with whom she was rather smitten. More welcome still were the presents we sent her to mark the occasion. She received, she says, a red velvet dress from Bloomingdale's and a hat with pompoms and a white velvet muff which she has now passed on to her own goddaughter.

I spent the eve of our wedding day putting the finishing touches to the wedding feast with the cooks from The Strollers, arranging flowers and making sure, with Sybil Burton's help, that all details were covered. I was staying with Nathan and Caroline so as to come to church from a different address to Peter and it was only when I got to their house that I noticed I was covered head to toe in a bright red rash. Horrors! What was I to do? I bathed in chamomile infusions, reckoning that the rash was a reaction to all the tomatoes I had been eating – my only pregnancy craving. Peter came to check me out before his little stag party and found me spotty and in tears. He tried to soothe me, but was never much good at playing the doctor. I said a little prayer, then fell into a sleep plagued by strange dreams. I awoke to find that the dreaded rash had disappeared as quickly as it had come. I wondered what it was trying to tell me.

I also awoke in a state of excitement that Monday morning, although deep down there was a note of melancholy which I quickly pushed away. It was our special day. Clouds scudded across the sun, promising intermittent rain – a weather forecast for our lives ahead, perhaps. I was brought breakfast in bed, but was too excited to eat much. I drank the freshly squeezed orange juice while eyeing my wedding outfit with the empire line I'd chosen to help disguise the growing bump of my tummy. I had luckily been free of morning sickness and still felt energetic, yet when I think back over what I managed to do in terms of cooking and organization for a big party like that I am amazed.

Caroline helped me dress. I had a simple bouquet of gardenias, one of my favourite flowers. Nathan looked dashing as did Caroline, in an amazing ostrich feather hat. As the three of us travelled together to St Luke's in a black limousine I began to feel nervous. There were crowds of people waiting at the church and lots of press taking photos. Judy Scott-Fox was my maid-of-honour, in a marvellous hat which made her look as if she were being attacked by a swarm of bees. Peter

Bellwood was best man and Dudley was already ensconced and playing the organ. When Handel's Wedding March began I almost levitated down the aisle on Nathan's arm. Among the smiling faces all around were John Bird, John Fortune, Jeremy Geidt, Sybil Burton, Jonathan and Rachel Miller, Alan Bennett, Margaret and Alec Cook, David and Cleo Balding and many others. The two Peters, both handsome and dashing, were like magnets drawing me up to the altar. The church was filled with freesias, gardenias, white roses and Madonna lilies. Peter looked very splendid with a white gardenia in the buttonhole of his navy wool suit. I was so happy and suddenly understood why people need to marry. It is a community affair in which friends bear witness to the commitment you make.

Many of these guests were new friends, friends made since we had arrived in New York. Americans were pretty easy to fall in with – generous and hospitable – but then we were in special circumstances. Peter was in the remarkable position of being part of a hit show on Broadway and the entrepreneur behind a highly successful nightclub, all at the tender age of twenty-five. It was good that we had some friends from Cambridge there, too. I wasn't too upset about my own parents not being present in the end. Since they had never been out of the United Kingdom I think it would have been overwhelming.

The ring was solemnly given: we had found it in an antique jewellers already inscribed with the date October 1863 – one hundred years earlier someone had married with this very ring. I loved that notion. It was old gold, very thin and engraved with a leaf design around the outside. In hindsight I wondered how good an idea it had been to wear somebody else's ring, infused with their years of marriage, sad or happy. Gold is very malleable. The vows were made – 'Till death do us part': is there only one kind of death, I wonder? But I was stepping out onto my path and on that day there was nothing but joy to be expressed. Emerging into Greenwich Village in a burst of sunlight and confetti, Peter and I embraced and posed for photos.

We were driven off to The Strollers. On the threshold stood an elegant butler wearing white gloves. In his most commanding voice, he announced us. Many guests had already arrived, as there hadn't been room in the little church for everybody, so there was cheering and clapping which was quite overwhelming. The room looked lovely, with the white flower motif picked up all round. Tables were groaning with whole salmon, the English roast beef, caviar and blinis, canapés, creamy mousses. The cake looked stunning with its three tiers and white-rosebud decoration. There was lots of champagne and that wonderful Hungarian gypsy music. Speeches were made by Peter's father and Nathan, who spoke hilariously as a stand-in for my father, throwing in some Yiddish jokes to boot. Peter Bellwood was witty too and made up all sorts of stories about Peter's and my childhood and our time in Cambridge.

The press had a good number of people to be interested in that day: Sybil Burton, in particular, was getting a lot of attention, along with a young, glamorous starlet called Pamela Tiffin, who appeared in *Come Fly with Me* that year. Guests danced to the music of the Hungarian trio and the party carried on into the evening. We had no plans for a honeymoon because of the performance of *Beyond the Fringe* the next day. Instead, we spent our 'honeymoon' in Times Square watching Ray Milland in *The Man with X-Ray Eyes* in a double bill. It may have been a cult movie, but what an extraordinary thing to do on your wedding day. Nathan's view of this feature of the day is rather jaded: 'You and Peter and Jonathan and Caroline and me, and two or three others, went and we sat through this dull, crappy film and I thought, "What an amazing thing to do." I think the idea was to be cool, but I don't think it quite came off, because it was a crappy film. Maybe we were wearing 3D glasses or something.'

It wasn't until the small hours that Peter and I arrived back at our 'tent', too exhausted to make love.

It would have been nice to have gone away, if only for a short time, but the show had to go on and we had only a week to finish decorating and furnishing our new apartment before Christmas would be upon us. Over the next few months America proved itself to be a country of extremes: we would witness both the ecstatic welcome given to the Beatles, and the assassination of John F. Kennedy, the youngest and the first Catholic President of the United States.

Everyone has their own story, I know, but on 22 November 1963 I was walking in the streets of Greenwich Village when I passed a huddle of people talking excitedly. Some of them were crying. 'What on earth has happened?' I asked one of them. 'President Kennedy has been assassinated,' she replied, 'in Dallas, Texas.' Everyone was devastated. How could this young man, in whom so many people had invested their hopes and dreams of a new America, be shot down as he toured in an open cavalcade? I somehow managed to get hold of Peter and he came straight home. We watched the TV newsreels and saw the grief of Jackie Kennedy and the children, the hasty swearing in of Lyndon Johnson and the capture of Lee Harvey Oswald with a great black eye, looking totally bewildered.

Roddy Maude-Roxby was told what had happened by Peter after making a journey similar to mine through streets full of people in tears. 'It was as if there had been a plague or something. I didn't know what had happened,' he says.

The Strollers was shut as a mark of respect. Then came the subsequent shooting of Oswald himself by Jack Ruby. The whole thing was so totally unreal. Kennedy had only led the United States for 1017 days, but what an impact he had made. We went to talk to many of our friends and acquaintances, including Norman Mailer, who seemed to be particularly affected, along with Jules Ffeiffer and Joe Heller. Their initial reaction was to want to leave the States. An emotional wave swept the nation; everybody had a different conspiracy theory. I felt anything was possible in such a vast country so full of contradictions: such wealth, such poverty.

Back in Britain, *That Was The Week That Was*, by now a national entertainment phenomenon, changed plans at the last minute in reaction to Kennedy's death and staged an impromptu tribute that has itself gone down in television history. Christopher Booker was one of the chief movers behind the tribute. 'We had only two days before the show,' he says. 'And everyone thought, "What the hell are we going to do?" I said: "Either the show is stopped or we do something different." I rooted for the idea we should do a positive tribute to him and I wrote most of it. There were individual tributes from each of the actors and songs and then from Bernard Levin. I did it all on my own and my heart was in it because I really admired JFK. I was really proud of it. But the actors had no idea how to do these sorts of lines. I could see them getting more and more and embarrassed. If you look again at a recording of the show, you can see it. The actors were allowed to do a bit of changing the script: Willie Rushton did an awful bit of changing and Lance Percival was so ill at ease he almost corpsed. He was nervously twitching as he read his piece.' Nevertheless, the tribute show was a huge hit in America, as well as in Britain. It was broadcast several times on NBC and even read into the congressional record by Vice President Hubert Humphrey. An LP was rushed out within a week or two and sold tens of thousands of copies. 'We all made a lot of money out of it,' says Christopher.

Peter and the *Fringe* boys were also pretty shattered by the Kennedy assassination. Jonathan wrote a controversial piece about it all in *Time-Life*. It was some weeks before anyone could face the idea of Christmas, but I was pregnant and the stores were full of festive decorations and gifts as usual. What was more, our friends Anneke and Michael Gough would be arriving during the run-up to Christmas.

Michael was touring America in *The Hollow Crown*, John Barton's Royal Shakespeare Company hit about the Kings and Queens of England, and they were to be in New York for a week. They came bearing, among other things, a Beatles album and some lacy, patterned tights of the kind that were fashionable in London at the time. Anneke was modelling some too, wearing long boots and a high-necked, ivory, wool coat with an astrakhan necktie – she looked gorgeous. Both gifts were very welcome and put us ahead of the New York crowd. We sat together with the Goughs in our new apartment watching the Beatles being interviewed on *The Ed Sullivan Show*. It was as if a barrel-load of monkeys had been released into the studio. Their humour and lack of subservience, together with their great music, were so refreshing. Anneke had also smuggled me out a can of Guinness, difficult to get hold of in New York at that time, so that I could finish my Christmas puddings.

Dudley joined us for Christmas Day itself, as seemed natural by this stage. He and Peter became obsessed, I remember, with the Dead Sea Scrolls. It was a flight of fancy typical of the way they now behaved together and they had us in stitches with talk of bones and relics and fishes and Jesus with his disciples. The Christmas meal was a great success and we sang carols, although Peter was not known for his tunefulness. Anneke still remembers the festive atmosphere: 'There was a huge Christmas tree and I had never seen so many presents. The pile was eight foot high. We spent Christmas Day with you and I remember some outrageous jokes about Jesus. It really pushed my boundaries back. I laughed so much I had no control and wet my knickers. I was cross because I was wearing a nice dress. I have never laughed so much, ever, as when Peter and Dudley were at it. It snowed around all the brownstone houses and it looked like something out of a book. It was so pretty.'

It was lovely to be visited by friends from England in our new home, tricked out in items of Americana I'd unearthed in various junk stores. I had a good eye for something that needed restoring. An old carriage wheel gave a bit of movement to the large main room. There were lovely, old American wooden chests, a few Victorian chamber pots, brimming with flowers and plants, and a couple of comfy sofas. A large Casa Pupo rug made it a warm and welcoming if somewhat 'junky pad' (as Ben would have called it). My present to Anneke was several pairs of knee-length Bloomingdale's long johns with a lace and velvet ribbon trim and a little rosebud – the trim just visible beneath the miniskirts that were then so fashionable. We both became rather keen on these bloomers, which ended up earning Anneke the nickname 'Knickers'.

Peter knew I had coveted a certain Tiffany lamp we had seen and he arranged a surprise trip to go and buy it as my Christmas present. It was a wonderful Christmas altogether and at New Year we went to a glamorous party at which Anneke recalls being jostled by Salvador Dali in the corridor, then making her way into a great chandeliered room where Dudley sat in the centre, playing a magnificent grand piano. Anneke went to sit by him on the stool, as she had so many times before in The Establishment Club.

'We also went to somebody's apartment who was very rich,' says Anneke, 'and we went up in a lift which opened up into their flat. I hadn't seen this before. And they had this beautiful tree with white, glass birds all lit up over it. It was very chic.'

During Anneke and Michael's visit we decided, against all advice from our New York friends, to pay a visit to Harlem for a concert. My friend Gaye Brown came along too. Everyone told us we'd get mugged, but Peter and Mick Gough were not to be deterred, so we took a cab to the Apollo Theatre where we were the only white people in the whole place. The concert featured Little Richard and Gladys Knight and the Pips and the energy of the show was quite amazing. It was a memorable evening, but we were quite relieved afterwards to find a cab to drive us out from Harlem. The atmosphere had been slightly menacing we felt, but then this could have been our projection. In the cab Anneke made a remark which Gaye Brown remembers to this day. Apparently she said: 'Everyone wants to be black, these days, including Alma Cogan.' For some reason there were quite a few Alma Cogan jokes in our repertoire at this time and apparently this was one for the record. Our friends were amazed we had been able to make this Harlem trek and return unscathed.

Anneke says her impression of the visit, shared at the time with Michael Gough, was that Peter and I had become somewhat different. 'We felt you had gone off into the upper echelons of success, with those wonderful parties with everyone there,' she says. 'I remember you had all the money. You could go into an antique shop and buy whatever you wanted there and, of course, that hit me because I couldn't afford to pay the bills. You were so monetarily successful, but the more that happened, the sadder you got. Although in my journal I wrote down: "Wendy seems better", because we felt that the relationship between you and Peter, now you were pregnant with your first, was getting a bit more grounded.'

A new year and the end of our time in America was in view as *Beyond the Fringe* approached the close of its run. By now I had a beautifully growing bump and I discovered that, while

192

Above The aspiring impresario outside the strip club that was to become The Establishment, 1962.

Above The beginning of a new era of live satirical comedy. The poster in the window shows an advertisement for Lenny Bruce, whose sets were so controversial that he was eventually banned from the UK.

Above The team behind The Establishment, photographed in the Spartan room above the club. On the top row, left to right: John Fortune, Bruce Copp, Peter, Nick Luard, Alan Bennett, David Walsh. On the bottom row, left to right: Hazel Wright, Dudley.

Above Members of The Strollers and *Beyond the Fringe* in the Connecticut summer house. John Bird is in the centre, Alan and Dudley are on the far right.

Above Peter and I having fun in the sun. Connecticut, 1963.

Above Alan Bennett watering the roses in the sunhat he made himself.

Above Eleanor Bron, Wendy and Bob Silver.

Above Hi-jinks with Alan and Dudley in Connecticut, 1963.

Above Peter and a pregnant me in New York, October 1963.

Above Is he going to make a mess of it? Peter cutting our wedding cake at the reception, held in The Strollers Club, October 1963.

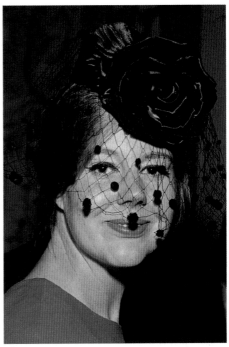

Above The wonderful Judy Scott Fox, Peter's PA and my Matron of Honour.

Above Sybil Burton, Richard's first wife.

Below Our wedding day in Manhattan with Margaret and Alec Cook.

Right Me with the
newborn Daisy
Clementine at
No. 17 Church Row,
Hampstead.

Below Peter, baby
Lucy and me on a
picnic at Lyme Regis.

practically everyone we met in New York had their own shrink, when it came to finding out about natural childbirth the city was way behind. Childbirth had been turned into an illness there that only doctors could deal with; midwives were more or less marginalized as far as I could tell. So I had to cope with the pregnancy on my own. Helpfully Jonathan Miller put me in touch with Professor Norman Morris, head of gynaecology at Charing Cross Hospital back in London, so I would have a place there for the birth, but since I would be arriving late, taking the last possible opportunity to fly home, there would not be much time left for natural childbirth classes. I learned, however, that the renowned Erna Wright ran classes at Charing Cross and I enrolled for a few. Erna, who died in 2004, was famous for the Lamaze method of childbirth, which trained pregnant women to know what to do at each stage of labour.

The main thing, however, was that the baby was healthy and I loved being pregnant. It was time to let my parents share this news with us, so after the holidays I picked up my pen. When I read the letter now I wince a little at the passages in which the tone is a touch self-important. But I was still young.

Now before I go into anything else I must tell you the great news before you either read it in the newspapers or hear it from some wayfarer . . . i.e. I'm going to have a baby!!!!! So you'd better all get knitting, 'cause I'm hopeless. Isn't that great? You really will all have to write to me now in congratulations . . . Peter is delighted at the prospect of being a Dad and is a marvellous husband so all is well with the Cooks. I only realized today that my initials are W.C. . . . A poor exchange for the rather elegant and distinguished name of Snowden I feel, but then you can't have everything, can you?

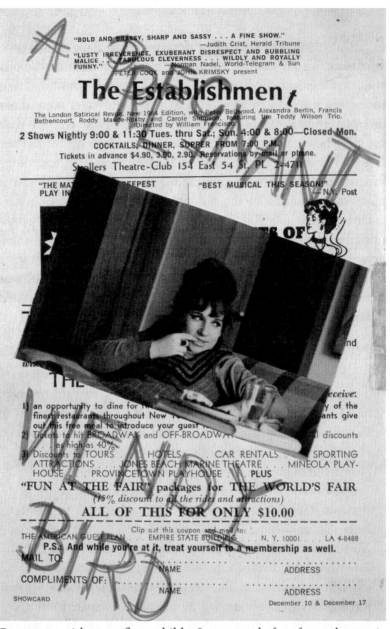

*Pregnant with my first child, Lucy, and far from home in
New York.*

Expressing sadness about the prospect of leaving New York later that year, I go on in this letter to sum up my feelings about the city and about the fate apparently befalling the 'satire boom' in England. After sweeping through the nation and then right across the Atlantic, some critics were now arguing that the fresh tide of satire had lost some of its vigour:

> Also, and this may sound strange to you, there is almost an air of 'old fashionedness' about New York, with a few exceptions the buildings look very dated somehow, and people aren't very smart on the whole, or if they are, they are always about five years behind the fashions . . . all of which is rather lovable and endearing and makes one feel rather secure, whereas in London there is an air of desperation about being in the fashion, not clothes alone . . . take 'satire' for instance, which *Beyond the Fringe* had most influence in bringing about. They played in London for a year and left the shores, so in popped a series of unsuccessful revues, all madly trying to be topical, but without the same wit . . . and then David Frost and his colleagues with their programme . . . brought satire to the majority of English homes, so it wasn't just for the privileged theatre-going public and did things which probably initially shocked a great many people, but in such a concentrated period of time that people's feelings were eventually blunted and exorcised, until they couldn't be shocked any more . . . and it seems that the whole thing was made into an industry, exploited in every way and then thrown to the winds, exhausted and finished . . . so when one enquires about The Establishment company's return to England with truly the best, cleverest and most outspoken show they have ever done, even the 'hippest of the hippies' old moralist Bernard Levin and his ilk tend to shake their heads and say, 'Satire, ducky, it's a thing of the past', and refuse to give it any more consideration.

Warming to my theme, I admit I am worried how Peter will be received back in Britain after the success of David Frost:

> Peter and Dudley and Co. have fantasies about being prematurely-aged, rather poor English gentlemen, clutching at piles of yellowing press cuttings, and trying to remind people of their success way back in 1960! . . . But I know that Peter is talented enough never to be out of work, in fact if he accepted half of the movie offers, to write and star in, that have been presented to him since we've been here, he'd make enough money to live on for the next ten years. But he's extremely choosy and will only do the right thing and things that really interest him, which is good and the only way to keep young and have a happy life!

Finally, after recommending the new films *Billy Liar* and *Tom Jones*, I enclosed a couple of magazine and newspaper articles about us for my parents to examine.

Various journalists had come to write up features on our home, with all its second-hand furniture, and were interested in my cookery ideas. One enthusiastic article described me as 'a little person, rounded like a hazelnut', with 'competent hands'. Much more flatteringly it went on to detail my typically sixties look: 'She peers out from under half-inch eyelashes with the look of a woman child, the sort of regard that melts men's hearts down to a jelly. She also has an unusually mobile mouth, embellished with a stylishly pale-coloured lipstick which some-how manages to give all her utterances the effect of curling upward into the atmosphere like tiny wisps of smoke. Com-bined with her natural British accent, it makes her a quite fascinating conversationalist.' Eventually the article got around to my recipe for roast duck with a black cherry sauce. I was beginning to have thoughts that one day I might even write a cookery page. Although by now a disciple of Elizabeth David, sometimes I tried out my own ideas on my friends.

Early that new year we visited Michael Bawtree, Peter's old Radley friend, who had set up a drama academy in Toronto. Michael and Anneke were also on tour there and Richard Burton was appearing in *Hamlet*. The whole Burton–Taylor romance was still front-page news and while we were in Toronto we learned that Richard had secretly married Liz that very morning in the city. By the end of the performance that night, which we were watching, news had leaked out and Burton came to the footlights and said, 'I would like to restate one of Hamlet's lines from the play: "There shall be *no* more marriages!"' It brought the house down – so actorly – but for me it has always served as a lesson in just how we tempt fate, particularly by making public statements of resounding import.

We were asked to go backstage to help celebrate the happy nuptials – and what an invitation! Richard Burton, with the lovely green eyes, was smoking a cigarette and drinking champagne from a plastic cup. His hands were shaking, I don't know whether from the impact of his performance, the drama of his romance with this Hollywood megastar or as the result of a lifetime of heavy drinking. We all drank champagne with him, an intimate group, while Elizabeth, giggling like a schoolgirl, was being stitched into a lavender tulle gown by her dresser. She had either just put on weight or lost it; I'm not sure. She had flowers in her hair and a long plait anchored into her hairdo, the effect being more Hawaiian maiden than Cleopatra. She flirted with Peter, flashing her famous violet-blue eyes. We did feel special to be included in such an informal and cosy little occasion; but, knowing Sybil Burton as I did, and what she had been through during this affair, my sympathies and loyalties were still definitely with her.

Shortly after our return there was a visit to New York from

the entire team of *That Was The Week That Was,* including the show's producer Ned Sherrin, who were to reprise their Kennedy tribute in front of an invited audience. We went along against our better judgement.

It is not one of Christopher Booker's proudest memories: 'We performed it for the Jewish Ladies Philanthropic League of New York at Madison Square Garden. There were 50,000 of them out there. It was a complete farrago as there were Mexican pianists and dancers from the Philippines on before us – international artists suitable for a very schmaltzy audience. Then the lights dimmed and Ned Sherrin came out and said, "We want to recreate for you what we did that night, but first of all here is a taste of what the show is normally like."'

So, rather oddly, the team performed sketches which included David Frost doing the sinking of the royal barge piece, which had originally been written by Peter. The reheated, sober tribute then followed.

'I thought, "This is the most embarrassing thing I have ever been involved with in my life",' says Christopher. 'A few months later I met an American lady in London at a business meeting. She kept on looking at me and she said, "I am sure I have seen you before. I know who you are; you were sitting there at the back of Madison Square Garden that night with your head in your hands."'

My own appalled reaction to this phony event is recorded forever in one of the most scathing letters I have surely ever have written. The restaging was, as far as I was concerned, 'the most nauseating, revolting display that is ever likely to happen in the history of mankind'. I was obviously very affronted by the whole thing – probably on Peter's behalf because of the material used that night that was closely derived from his own sketches. The incredible fuss made around the show was also a reminder to us of just how quickly Peter's

anointed role as Britain's premiere satirist had been usurped
by David Frost.

> David Frost, made up to the nines, glycerine tears asparkle
> [I wrote to my parents]. Poor old Roy Kinnear (who I love
> dearly), an honest thesp., dried and fumbled for his notes,
> Bernard Levin delivered with clinical accuracy the dissertation
> about Johnson, citing him as one of the chief figures to bring
> about the fall of McCarthy . . . Poor Willie Rushton, who had
> been staying with us and whom we had tried to persuade not to
> be a part of this travesty, without any success, spat out his
> pieces about peanut-butter sandwiches with as little emotion as
> possible and then collapsed into his chair sweating feverishly.
> Chris Booker, up there on the platform as chief author of the
> entire lucrative travesty buried his head in his hands in an effort
> to conceal his identity . . . Peter and I went along because we
> couldn't really believe that they were really going to restage the
> whole thing and we thought we might have a giggle. We sank
> through our seats with horrified embarrassment because not
> only did they do it all, but they interspersed it with sketches
> from old *TW3s*.

The rest of this angry letter home details how Peter had tried to
dissuade David Frost from using 'The Hilton Hotel Number',
because it was a sketch already being used in The Establishment show. 'Frost offered Peter $500 for the sketch, but Peter
refused and then it was used anyway with the hotel name
merely changed from London Hilton to Honolulu Hotel.' I
was not pleased. 'He really is a farce, but a seemingly successful
and well-heeled one!'

Christopher Booker remembers Frost as being obsessed by
two things during his New York stay: getting the first BBC
interview with Lyndon Johnson over Robin Day's head and

the phenomenon of the American chat show: 'It was the first time he had been introduced to chat shows, like Johnny Carson's, and he couldn't stop talking about it. I thought, "That is where Frostie's career is going". It was quite obvious for the first time he had seen where he wanted to go. You can never hate him, but he is just such an extraordinary piece of marshmallow. He was the commercial version of what Peter did.'

The *Beyond the Fringe* boys had to stay in the States until the end of April to avoid paying taxes there as well as in Britain, so I was sent ahead, with the intrepid Judy Scott-Fox by my side, to find us a home, get a layette together and do all the things one has to do to welcome a new baby. Winding down from our lives in New York was strange. There had been so many new experiences, but I would be glad to get back to London to have our baby. New York was not a place in which to bring up children.

Early April was consumed with packing up. Our personal belongings were stored or sent to England by ship. I was now faced with the question of what to do with our two blue Persian cats. We loved them so much, but how stupid to have taken animals on! It is time to tell the story of what befell one of them, Pyewhacket.

I had somehow conceived a ludicrous plan to smuggle out Pyewhacket in the plane with me. I found an obliging vet who agreed to give me some sedatives for the animal, which we administered before getting into our cab. Pyewhacket was put inside a holdall with adequate ventilation, but while we were waiting in the checking-in queue at the airport the holdall, placed beside us on the ground, started to move. Pyewhacket had woken up. A powerful 'Miaou!' issued from our hand luggage. Luckily Peter was still waiting to wave us off and had to take the poor creature back home and bequeath him to the incoming tenants. I was devastated, but thank goodness he woke up then rather than later. God knows what ghastliness might have ensued. I was so sad, but on this occasion not very sensible. How ever had I cajoled Peter, the vet and Judy into being accomplices? All of us quite dotty. Success would have required keeping the animal drugged for more than six hours!

The Family Cook

On our return to London we were to stay at Nick and Elizabeth Luard's flat in Hyde Park Square, at least until after the baby was born. The flat was vacant because Nick and Elizabeth were away building a house in Spain and it was a convenient and comfortable place to begin searching for somewhere else. In recent years the Luard flat had served as a sort of bolt hole for floating satirists and writers, with Lenny Bruce, Anneke, Jeffrey Bernard, John Fortune and Venetia Mooreshead all passing through. Fenella Fielding lived in the flat above and she and I would meet on the stairs and flutter our heavy lashes at each other (false eyelashes and lots of hair in beehives now being *de rigueur*). Once I had moved in, I had quickly to buy a cot and nappies and the baby's layette and try to squeeze in a few childbirth classes too. I visited Professor Morris who pronounced everything in order. The baby, I was told, would be due in the first week of May.

The London we came back to was still seen as the centre of the satire boom, as a contemporary piece in the *Observer* makes clear. Written by their Daylight team of reporters, it attempted to pull all the strands together and draw up a kind of family tree for the satire industry. Noting the sudden popularity of *Private Eye*, it points out that the new television show

TW3 and the exported *Beyond the Fringe* and Establishment shows were all part of the same movement.

'How to explain the speed with which the epidemic has spread? The obvious difference between our men and other countries' satirists is that ours are still essentially amateurs – undergraduates, in fact. Brechtian satire may be theatrically more interesting and Mort Sahl's school may be slicker and sexier; our hard-bitten twenty-four-year-olds have a triumphantly unprofessional freshness,' the piece argues, before going on to chronicle the rise of Peter Cook, his meeting with the other three *Fringe*-ers and the birth of the Luard/Cook empire. It joins the dots with the *Private Eye* team and then finally, inevitably, hails the arrival of David Frost. 'At twenty-three he is being talked of in the same breath as Richard Dimbleby; not since Beverley Nichols has an undergraduate risen to fame so fast.'

In theory, this was the situation that Peter flew back to that April 1964. But the picture was not quite so rosy for us. With no work in view, it was also clear The Establishment was going down the tube. Elizabeth Luard watched it all happen at close quarters while we partied in New York. Raymond Nash, a tough Lebanese entrepreneur with, as she recalls, 'a smooth smile, sharp teeth and a hunger for legitimacy', was to get his hands on the club. 'It was one of the few straight enterprises in Soho – and anyway, he could see it attracted a better class of client which might be useful. The club was vulnerable. Neither Peter nor Nicholas knew the first thing about stock control. At least half the goods moved out of the back door as fast as they came in the front. Cheques began to bounce. A holding operation was mounted – actually, more of a letting-go, since I, just married to the co-proprietor, took a pair of rather pretty diamond brooches, a legacy of my grand-mother, down to a Bond Street jeweller and exchanged them for a cheque, as I remember, for £1200 – the price of a couple of brand-new Minis. It wasn't enough.'

To make matters worse, *Scene*, Nick's arts magazine, and a forerunner of *Time Out*, went into receivership. To Elizabeth this still seems unfair: 'Never mind that it carried the first national article on the Beatles, flagged up the Stones and employed a young Tom Stoppard as theatre critic.'

What a different scenario London offered us, compared with what we had left in New York. There we had been courted to the last; here Peter had no particular project lined up. Once the country had accepted the dawning of a new satirical age, it was suddenly on the way out, much as I had predicted in my pessimistic letter home.

This unhappy series of events for Peter and Nick is etched on Elizabeth Luard's memory: 'What the papers had dubbed "the empire of satire" began to unravel. *Private Eye*, feeling its own financial position threatened, announced that unless Nicholas removed himself as proprietor, the editorial board would walk. Meanwhile, at the insistence of its creditors (mostly the bank) Cook and Luard Productions went into receivership and Raymond Nash took over the running of the club. I remember Peter dancing round the office in the final days, waving a financial document and mimicking the new chief operative's thickly accented English: "What is these? Em-ma Mouse? Who is-a Dee Duck?" Silly Disney signatures validating important transactions were typical of the kind of thing Nash encountered.

'The collapse of the enterprise was sudden. Peter and Nicholas never, to my knowledge, discussed it – still less apportioned blame. Certainly Nicholas blamed himself; and perhaps Peter knew that he'd left his friend up the creek without a paddle.'

Under the club's new management, Jean Hart was asked to wear a dress showing more cleavage when she sang and Venetia Mooreshead, returning from a long stay in Mexico, was shocked to find the club much changed: 'The Establishment used to have an audience that was louche intelligentsia, until Nash took it over. It was a great moment and it had had its moment. I think it was destined not to go on.'

The huge popularity of *TW3* somehow made all this harder for Peter to swallow. Christopher Booker was now the main political scriptwriter for the new TV show and, together with Frost he wrote the main sketch.

'I saw the whole *TW3* thing from inside,' he says. 'Tim Birdsall and I were the only two people who were in complete agreement about what an incredible farce and piece of charlatanry *TW3* was. I went out on Saturdays to White City and I used to sit in Frostie's changing room, because I was meant to be thinking up last-minute gags that Frostie could dispense live each Saturday night.

'I was sitting there at my typewriter and there would be a knock at the door and it would be Tim, clutching a script, which we only got when we arrived at the studio. And we would look at each other and say, "How can we put this stuff out? It is terrible."'

What Christopher found hard to handle was the sudden division between the writers, or satirists, and the performers on the studio floor. 'Suddenly we had this ersatz thing where there were the scriptwriters, anonymous behind the scenes, and then there were these actors who had been hired to act out the sketches; Lance Percival and Ken Cope, say. Then, when the show became a huge success, the press and the media hailed them as satirists. I liked the chaps, but there was no way they were satirists. Actually, if you look at *TW3*, the content of most of it was pretty terrible, so I don't know how it became

DAVID FROST

requests the pleasure of the company of

Peter Twent

at an End-of-Series Party on January 5th
in the Great Hall Alexandra Palace
from 10.30 p.m.

BLACK TIE OR INFORMAL   R. S. V. P. 46 EGERTON CRESCENT. LONDON S.W.3

A relic: our invitation to celebrate David's success at the end of his series.

so successful. The one person on it who was really successful was Millie Martin.'

The show went out for fifty minutes at the end of the evening and had become a huge hit almost overnight. The impact on David Frost was immediate, according to Christopher.

'Within weeks of that Frostie visibly broadened and grew. What I was struck by was how quickly he picked up the nature of television and, week after week, there was a trick he would do. The rehearsal would go on through the day and we would be a quarter of an hour rehearsing one sketch and then on to something else. Whenever Frostie had to be at the desk to do his introduction, Ned Sherrin, the producer, would be up there in the gallery and would announce "Moving on to number 15. David. Cue David". And David would be nowhere to be seen. "Cue David. Cue David. David, where are you? Cue David." And he would be outside the studio, holding back, so that there would be an air of expectation. I saw him standing there with a little smile on his face, with this Tannoy booming out. Then he would appear with "Hellooo. Here I am. Sorry I am late."'

The fact that Peter had come back to tread water in London was a surprise to Christopher. 'He was, without question, the supreme star of all that generation. For those of us who were at Cambridge it was such a shock and it must have been awful for Peter.'

But if The Establishment was beyond saving, the cash-strapped *Private Eye* presented a worthwhile cause, and Peter, already financially backing the magazine, now had the time to get involved with its content. As Venetia Mooreshead puts it: 'The world was ready for it. *Private Eye* may no longer seem novel, because the world has changed so much, but it took the gamble of printing things which no other newspaper would.'

Private Eye had grown out of the school magazine set up by Richard Ingrams, Willie Rushton, Paul Foot and Christopher Booker at Shrewsbury. It was a real 'chaps' affair', although there were pretty women like Liz Luard and Venetia Mooreshead around. They were also very bright, but their intellectual contributions were rarely invited. The 'cigars and port' audience was definitely cultivated. The magazine came out every fortnight mainly, as Christopher admits, because Willie and he could not face the thought of doing the whole thing every week.

Before we went to New York Peter had come up with the idea of using speech bubbles on the cover, something which, in Christopher's words, was 'the beginning of the most recognizable brand identification *Private Eye* has ever had'. After a period of booming circulation, when it reached the heady heights of 90,000 copies a year, our return to London had coincided with plummeting sales figures. According to

Christopher, Peter put in more money, but then, when the circulation had fallen to 25,000 the next year, he actually saved it from closure by going around various friends and asking for money. Paul McCartney remembers being touched for cash in this way and one wonders whether the current editors of the magazine bear this in mind when they occasionally poke fun at him.

A young Oxford graduate named Tariq Ali was also making his way as a young firebrand and a freelance contributor to *Private Eye* at this time, devouring each issue as it came out. He regarded it as the best thing he had seen since arriving in Britain from Pakistan to attend university.

'The Tories were in power and you had this slightly ghoulish Prime Minister, Sir Alec Douglas-Home, and Oxford was then not a very radical place,' he says. 'There were only about thirty or forty people on "the Left", and there was a benign social democratic consensus about between Labour and Conservatives. People who wanted to go into politics were really just deciding which party to join. So *Private Eye* was just manna from heaven. There was a whole group of us at college who used to wait for each issue and try and work out who was who. And that was my first introduction to this whole gang.'

Once Tariq was contributing and visiting the *Eye*'s London offices he began to observe Peter's powerful personality at work: 'Peter was very influential on all of them. It wasn't just the fact that he was the funniest, which there is no dispute about; he could just extemporize at the drop of a hat. Just being with him was so funny.'

Closeted in Nick and Elizabeth's flat, I was completely absorbed in approaching motherhood and nest-making. I knew it was also important to reconnect with some of our old friends, though, such as Nick and Harriet Garland. It was a good job I did, because they kindly looked after me during a false alarm when it appeared my contractions had begun. In fact, the baby wasn't to arrive for another two weeks. Despite believing that I was some Earth Mother archetype, I was totally ignorant of the complexities of childbirth and did not know what to expect. Peter said he'd like to be present at the birth, although this was then only just beginning to be a possibility. Peter knew even less about it than I did, but did manage to attend one fathers' class, where he was taught about 'effleurage', a kind of light massage on the mother's belly, and then shown how to moisten the labouring mother's lips with a wet sponge.

On 3 May the contractions started in earnest; everything was ready, the layette and the pink Moses basket were waiting. I had somehow intuited it would be a girl, so there was a fair bit of pink in the wardrobe. Peter took me to Charing Cross Hospital in a cab. I still felt quite calm as the nurses received me and ushered Peter off somewhere. I was shaved, which I don't think they do any more, but which was then just part of the procedure that led to birthing in the 'stranded beetle' position. This may work for doctors but gives you no help from gravity. I was all dressed up in a nightie covered with red poppies and my false eyelashes were in place, but I was not prepared for twenty-four hours of labour. The shock of it all made me tense and everything more painful. When the contractions really got going I screamed and shouted a lot and Peter sat glued to his seat, paralysed and not at all sure what to do. I told him to go away in the end, as his baleful gaze was not helping. He seemed to have forgotten about the effleurage. He didn't seem able to leave though. When the contractions got really strong I marvelled at my body, performing like a traction engine all of its own accord. As the baby's head was emerging I looked at Peter, all gowned up, and thought he looked incredibly funny, except that I was not in a laughing mood. Professor Morris himself arrived in time to do the honours.

She was there! My baby, in my arms, belly down. I noticed she had the most amazing golden down on her lower back and sensible, strong-looking hands and arms. Nothing can describe the poignancy of those first minutes, meeting the little, live being, tiny and covered with moss. Of course, Peter was thrilled, but it was the early hours of the morning so he went home to get some sleep. My eyelashes had survived the lengthy ordeal. What a tribute to the adhesive!

Next day Peter arrived with champagne, flowers and smoked salmon and I ate a hearty breakfast. We were so very proud, and my pain and our exhaustion were forgotten. This was the biggest miracle of all creation. Nothing – but nothing – can prepare you for what such a scrap of humanity will bring into your life. A newborn calf will get up and run within minutes of its birth, but a child is so vulnerable; it can only lie there, dependent on its carers for months.

I stayed in hospital for several days, as was the practice in those days, making sure breastfeeding had been established. I would look at this tiny baby, sleeping soundly; there seemed to be a wonderful quality of light surrounding her. Then, with Peter's approval, she was named: Lucy-Anne (Lucia being 'the light-bearer'). It seemed so appropriate. Nothing I'd experienced before had ever filled me with this tender, protective, compassionate love, quite different from the love for a man.

Congratulatory telegrams and bouquets from friends in Britain and New York started arriving as we returned to our temporary nest in Hyde Park Square and placed Lucy-Anne in her Moses cradle. Her sleeping spirit filled the whole apartment with a special atmosphere, usually one of peace and tranquillity, though of course she did cry too. As a young mother I had to learn to distinguish the different sorts of crying – of hunger, loneliness, discomfort, indicating a dirty nappy: each had a different tone. I tried to get her into some kind of rhythm, but nights were often disturbed. Sometimes we drove her in her Moses basket around London to lull her to sleep, in deference to Fenella Fielding above us. The sleeping baby would often awaken again just as we got back home. In the end we divided the task. Although Peter was a doting father, he never volunteered to change a nappy and when he was working he expected a decent night's sleep. I wanted so much to be a perfect wife and mother and thought this quite normal.

Jonathan and Alan seemed to have no difficulty adapting to life without *Beyond the Fringe*. In fact, says Alan, he was grateful to be out. The old academic life had somehow lost its charm, though. 'When I came back from New York my supervisor, who had inspired me, died and my heart went out of it really, so I started writing monologues. They were very brief ones. Peter had much, much more self-confidence than I did then, or have now, probably. I remember saying to him in New York, "When I go back I am going to see whether I can do these monologues on the Third Programme on the radio. I don't know whether they will take them." And he said, "Of course they will take them. Don't be so stupid." He was right, of course.

'It took me a time to recover from *Beyond the Fringe* and get going on my own account, but when I came out there was a tremendous relief to be actually working on my own. I thought it was wonderful not to be beholden to anybody else and for people to not think that you were the sidekick. That is after all what Dudley would complain about for half his life – even though he was a big Hollywood star.'

The Luards would soon return to London and we had to find another interim place to rent while I started house hunting. Through Anneke and Mick Gough we found a place in Ovington Square in Knightsbridge. It was not the most wonderful flat. The bedroom, as I remember, had been painted black and the bathroom was pokey, so Lucy had her night-time bath in the kitchen sink. Such a contrast to our life in New York. Peter was incredibly restless when he didn't have several projects to immerse himself in, so I suggested he take up Goethe's Faustian theme for a film script; he had intermittently been fascinated by the idea of the struggle between good and evil, conscience and temptation, ever since Cambridge days. But the timing was not right. Living a nomadic life was not conducive to creative concentration and Peter seemed to work best when bouncing ideas off others.

The black bedroom depressed me, or maybe it was postnatal depression. Nevertheless, around my birthday in January, after a celebratory dinner Peter and I made love and I felt once more an incoming presence. Put it down to feminine intuition. I was pregnant again.

Peter scuttled about seeing people – radio, television producers, *Private Eye* – and saw quite a bit of Dudley too. As a result, despite delighting in my new role as a mother, I started to feel a little lonely. I was relieved and delighted when Jonathan and Rachel Miller, blessed by the presence of their housekeeper, beautiful Beatrice from Jamaica, declared that one of her many nieces had hopes of coming to England. This was Patsy, the eldest of thirteen children, who wanted to work as a mother's help and to study. Would we consider taking her in? We thought it a good idea and made arrangements for her flight.

So, in the autumn of 1964, we went to Heathrow to meet Patsy, a shy girl wearing a pink hat shaped like an upside-down flowerpot rammed onto her exuberant Afro hair and a pink tulle dress spilling from underneath an overcoat that had clearly been lent to her for the expected chill of autumnal England. What an adventure for this seventeen-year-old and how different from her life in Jamaica. In time I kitted her out with more suitable clothes and arranged afternoon 'O'-level studies. She was good with Lucy, who was by now taking solids and formula milk. As the eldest of such a large family of children, Patsy had had plenty of practice with her siblings. Often I would take Patsy and Lucy to Jonathan's house where Patsy could socialize with Beatrice and help to make her introduction to London less overwhelming.

Now I could start to house hunt with a vengeance. I was set on living in Hampstead, which we had enjoyed in the early days. In principle, Peter seemed to agree but was, as usual, happy to let me get on with the looking; anything desirable I would take him to see.

If Peter and I had mixed feelings about coming back to what was to become Harold Wilson's Britain, we were among the very few who needed to be persuaded. London in 1964 was regarded as the centre of the 'happening' world. The haircuts and the clothes were as revolutionary as the politics, from Mary Quant's miniskirts to Vidal Sassoon's bob. Emma Peel was leaping around the television screen in *The Avengers* and even Christine Keeler, the call girl at the centre of the Profumo affair of the previous year, had a certain panache (so much so that at one point she was to have been the subject of a film Peter wanted to make with Nick Garland). An article in the weekend *Daily Telegraph* of April 1965 hailed London as 'the most exciting city', stating: 'It began in this period that youth captured this island and took command in a country where youth had always before been kept properly in its place. Suddenly the young own the town.'

Fran Landesman, who came to live in London at this time with her husband Jay, was immediately smitten with the place. 'People used to call it Swinging London and now they say that it was a myth. It was not a myth,' she argues. 'Well, maybe it was not the right word for it, but whatever was happening in those days was wonderful. Just wonderful. We went to Rome and we meant to fly back to the States until someone said to us, "You must go to London. You wouldn't believe what is happening there. Those people are partying there like there is no tomorrow." It was because they had finally shaken off all the dreariness of the post-war period and so people danced like only black people danced in America. We all believed we were just about to make a good world for everybody.'

It was true. When we returned to London there was a new optimism around and Harold Wilson tried to harness some of this 'can do' spirit by meeting up with the Beatles in March 1964, just before he was elected. Paul McCartney himself says now that he never really felt part of any crusade, or even believed that things were about to get permanently 'better'. 'We would meet people who would say the world was going to change and we would say, "Oh really? That is not what we're doing." People placed too much faith in the movement. I think I just thought that, well, this is now's attempt, and we will have to keep on trying: inch by inch we will claw our way towards perfection. But this idea in the sixties that it was around the corner, I never saw. I think it was a bit of a misapprehension. But I suppose if I hadn't been with the Beatles I would have bought this stuff we did, these albums, and thought *All You Need Is Love* – that will have a great effect. I don't mean to denigrate it all, but I never felt it was going to change everything next year.

'What the whole movement, the whole Establishment crowd, led us towards was this feeling that we can beat it.'

Christopher Booker suggests that, having got through the war, our generation experienced a wonderful feeling of liberation: 'We were exactly the right age to be part of that amazing explosion of rock and roll and *Look Back in Anger* and the rest of it. We were part of that and it was very exhilarating.

What was coming to birth at that time was the world as it is today. My kids grew up in a mental universe in the nineties that was essentially formed between 1956 and 1963, using the same language and the same attitudes. Of course, there are lots of variations within that, but basically we are now still living, fifty years on, in a world created then. And we are the generation that was on the crest of that wave.'

For a newcomer to British society such as the young Tariq Ali the push against the old restrictions of tradition was clear to see: 'What you have to understand about the explosion of the sixties is that the fifties had been an incredibly tight-laced era; stuffy, oppressive. The sixties were a farewell to all that: to the hypocrisy and the bullshit.' Tariq reminds me that not only was D. H. Lawrence's *Lady Chatterley's Lover* actually banned in England, but the Lord Chamberlain had to clear the script of every play or revue put into the West End. In fact, this official notoriously intervened to alter a phrase in a *Beyond the Fringe* sketch, insisting that the stage direction 'Enter three outrageous old queens' should read 'Enter three aesthetic young men'. People generally didn't swear so much in those days either, Tariq remembers. 'Whether the fact that lots of people didn't swear in public was due to the deference that people had been taught, I don't know. It was a very deferential society and that is where *Beyond the Fringe* and The Establishment Club became incredibly vital – just to puncture and deflate the hypocrisy and the lies. That was the popularity and the attraction. "These guys don't care a damn", people thought, "They just say it as it is."'

Perhaps I was beginning to look for ways to retreat from the whirligig of London, but at this time Peter and I often accepted weekend invitations to stay with Harriet and Nick Garland at Harriet's parents' beautiful country home, Park Hall, in Essex. Here I learned more about hostessing, cooking, good wine and flower arranging. Harriet's mother, Ariel, was an artist who had trained at the Slade and she had created such an elegant home. The guest rooms were graced with the most interesting and exquisite flower arrangements and her cooking was excellent too. She used fresh fruit and her vegetables and salads came from the kitchen garden. An *omelette fines herbes* she used to make, in particular, was luscious, packed with finely chopped fresh herbs again from the garden. Mealtimes were extended, the conversation witty and provocative. Peter and Nick Garland showed off on the tennis court while Harriet and I played with Lucy by the lake and enjoyed 'girlie' talk. Nick was especially lovely with Lucy, which was poignant as he and Harriet were trying, so far unsuccessfully, to have a baby themselves. With some difficulty, I broke the news to them that I was pregnant again. We spent a great holiday with the Garlands in Brittany too, during which time our evening conversations were particularly fertile: it was here that Peter developed some of his best comic creations, from Starborgling, to the *New Stoatsman* and the *Private Eye* cartoon character Barry McKenzie, the uncouth Australian wanderer who Nick worked with Barry Humphries to bring to life on the page once we got home.

We spent that Christmas at Knollside with Peter's family. As a present to his parents, he had had central heating installed in their house: it was always chilly there. Regardless of that, however, the heating remained at blood temperature. The English are fond of depriving themselves of warmth, comfort and expansiveness. Peter would secretly go around turning the radiators up during our visits and I was amused by these little games. While with my own family you always knew when there was trouble about (something would go flying and you had to duck), in Peter's home there were 'atmospheres'. Here, the disguised barbs aimed by Alec at Margaret, I saw, could be just as eroding to the confidence as the occasional flying plate. I recognized in Peter's father the sarcasm which Peter had developed to a high art – pity the poor recipient. It was interesting he should share this trait, considering how little he had been exposed to his father in childhood. Although Elizabeth Cook, as the baby of the family, has lots of happy memories of time spent with her father, she was conscious of the biting edge of his moods and the effect on all three children.

'I think Dad was touchy and insecure and we all suffered from his sarcasm as children,' she says. 'It is hard to remember it, because after someone dies you remember the good things. But I do think that we all winced a lot and hated the sarcasm and the sniping. There was quite a lot of sniping and we all inherited the capacity to do it. We all hated it, but we all can do it. There wasn't a lot of overt anger, but there was a lot of ill humour.' I later came to see these behaviour patterns repeated in Peter, although he was not the same with everyone, of course. Elizabeth's relationship with her big brother, in childhood and adulthood, seems happily to have lacked these tensions.

'I felt perfectly free with him. I adored him. I wasn't frightened of him, I just found him terribly glamorous. I could be very irritating, I am sure; I remember trickling glitter on to his head one Christmas and him getting really, really annoyed and saying he wouldn't give me my Christmas present, but I still went on, so I don't think I was intimidated by him.'

Christmas that year in Uplyme was a time for goodwill though, and for thimbles of sherry, visiting neighbours and singing carols round the piano. And, indeed, a time for going to church, which I always enjoyed. It snowed that Christmas, unusual for the mild west country, and created the perfect mood. Peter's parents adored Lucy and it was special to have her there with them on her first Christmas. We watched her face light up at the firelight and candles and saw her amazement as the snowflakes disappeared in her tiny hands. She was a cuddly and affectionate baby, interested in all that was going on, and Peter started amusing his new recruit at an early age. Carving and serving the turkey was Alec's job. Who wanted dark or white meat? By the time the last person had been served their vegetables it was a wonder anything was still hot.

In time, though, once I grew accustomed to their social niceties, I became fond of Peter's parents. It was a household in which I learned much by observing and listening. Sometimes, for instance, a conversation might veer off in a controversial or unacceptable direction, or questions might be asked (usually by me) which perhaps should not have been asked, and then there'd be a painful silence, or the subject would abruptly be changed. I have pondered these taboos for years. Whatever people may say about the erosion of the British class system, it is still in place. It thrives on innuendo, silences and on the tyranny of politeness. I also wondered about the provenance of these taboos and realized that Peter, although complicit while a guest in his parents' home, was determined to tear down, parody or destroy many of their hidden agendas. Nevertheless, he was inculcated with some of these social prejudices himself, though you needed to be a sleuth to uncover them. Finding this upper-middle-class family so different from mine, I took time to understand it and fit in. As a new mother, for instance, I wondered how Margaret Cook could possibly have torn herself away from seven-month-old Peter for long periods of time – months, years – in the name of duty to her husband in Nigeria. It must have involved a tremendous amount of repression of her emotions. They were always such a polite family and would often greet Peter almost as though meeting for the first time. Saying the right thing was an ingrained habit, but for me it took a bit of work.

The three Cook children had been born at seven-year intervals, making each rather like an only child. Elizabeth was therefore fourteen years younger than her big brother and in many ways had the best deal, in that she lived with her parents for some time. (Elizabeth too, as we have seen, was eventually sent away to join her sister Sarah at Sherborne, although, to her credit, she ran away towards the end of her time there, having found it utterly suffocating.) It was with her that I forged the most heart-felt contact. She was such an imaginative child, always creating exhibitions at the garden gate for passers-by to admire. One summer a 'fish museum' was erected, consisting of fish skeletons and hermit crab shells and assorted aquatic paraphernalia.

For Margaret, working behind the scenes in the kitchen providing meals appeared quite a challenge. In Africa she had employed a cook and maids and so simply had not learned how to cook. It was a source of bewilderment to me that such a basic thing could be left out of a woman's education. In Devon a part-time factotum would come and leave dishes prepared for reheating in the Aga. There were, however, always lovely raspberries and strawberries in the garden in summer, which I loved picking with Sarah and Elizabeth. They would be served with thick Devon cream and sprinkled with caster sugar.

A persistent problem on my visits to Knollside was what to call my mother-in-law, who had never suggested I use her Christian name. I baulked at calling her 'Mama' or 'Mother' – she just didn't fit that bill for me. As a result, we spent these years with me not finding the right way to address her. I simply avoided calling her anything, but it was a source of discomfort for me. When Peter and I divorced Margaret signed her occasional letter to me 'ex-mama-in-law'!

The Folks Who Live on the Hill

By January 1965 it really was time to return to house hunting in London. My second pregnancy gave me the motivation to find somewhere suitable and the job really was left to me. At this stage Dudley's claim on Peter's time was at least equal to my own and their growing professional and personal relationship had already led to a television commission. Dudley had been offered his own show, but he wanted Peter in on the act and so, early that year, the first seven shows of *Not Only . . . But Also* went out on the BBC, directed by Joe McGrath. There was a muted response to the first programme, but by the end of the series the plaudits were raining down on Peter and Dudley once more and impressive and wide-ranging fan mail had come into the BBC from, as one might put it, 'Not only Joyce Grenfell, But also Graham Greene'. A new series was commissioned for the following year, this time to be produced by Dick Clement, who was already an established name after the success of *The Likely Lads*.

I had my own success too on the domestic front. I had found it. Unbelievable! A five-storey Georgian house in Church Row, one of the most architecturally perfect streets in London. A former home of H. G. Wells, it was now owned by two elderly Catholic sisters; when one died the other found herself too frail to manage such a large property on her own. It was up for auction. The whole episode provided one of my first experiences of the power of intentionality – I willed my family into that house.

I used to lurk around it, trying to put my spell on it. I was completely smitten, although much work would be needed to make it comfortable. Peter was also keen and would not let me go to the auction as he said I would send the price rocketing with my obvious enthusiasm. He was probably right. By now I had many ideas about how to renovate the house, which already had exposed pine panelling in the hall and on the landing. There was even an old-fashioned dumb waiter, in perfect working condition, between the kitchen and the dining/sitting room.

The day of the auction arrived and I hadn't been able to sleep. I took Patsy and Lucy to the zoo to distract myself. When I got home there was Peter wearing a grave demeanour. My heart sank. 'We didn't get it?' I enquired tremulously. He couldn't keep the act up any longer and broke into a huge self-congratulatory smile: 'Yes, we've got it, and for twenty-four thousand pounds!' I could hardly contain my happiness. We danced around, with Lucy looking quizzically on from her high chair, as if we'd gone totally mad. Then Peter filled me in on the details of his steely strategy at the auction. He was a past master at remaining poker-faced and it had worked. We invited Dudley round for dinner to celebrate. Champagne flowed. It would not be too long either before Dudley and his new bride, Suzy Kendall, would be living round the corner as our neighbours in Hampstead. Alan Bennett says he still recalls the wallpaper and the exorbitant price we had paid, or so it seemed to him then. 'I remember thinking what a wonderful house it was, with the panelling in all the rooms. Twenty-four thousand; I thought, "It is insane. You will never make your money back." ' I recently spotted an identical house in the row on the market at £3 million.

While exchange of contracts was taking place, Peter – at Suzy's suggestion – arranged a holiday in the Bahamas for the five of us, including Lucy. How wonderful it was to leave cold, grey London for white beaches and coconut palms. Lucy was just about walking and it was lovely for her to be able to explore the warm water, naked and free. Dudley and Peter were supposed to be working on a film script together. I don't remember much work being done, yet a good number of new characters emerged during this carefree time. It was how they worked best. The symbiotic comic partnership really began here, relying as it did on the irreverent, but usually affectionate,

Peter on holiday in Caribbean: he always tanned quickly.

Peter goose stepping the strand.

trawling of surreal details about old aunts, ex-girlfriends, retired colonels, and, of course, bees and ravens. These unruly characters inhabited the recesses of Peter and Dudley's minds, to burst out in ever-burgeoning, fantastical stories and in reams of ludicrously unrelated facts. The holiday was preserved for posterity in national newspapers back home. One photograph showed Suzy and me on the beach, rubbing sun oil into the backs of our men; another showed Dudley and Suzy posing, nose to nose, in the sea.

Suzy and I got on well together too. She was a feisty and unpretentious girl from Belper, albeit an increasingly successful and glamorous film actress. She and Dudley doted on each other and I hoped he had now decided to settle down and temper his Casanova ways. He must have been thirty, which seemed like a ripe old age to us. Surely he would start having children with Suzy?

Back in London, all bronzed and me with a bump showing once again, our happiness at being new houseowners was compounded by the news that Harriet had also become pregnant, probably during our holiday in Brittany.

I threw myself into the house renovations with gusto, finding old tiled friezes for the en suite bathroom. I was in my element improving our new home. It all had to be done at record speed because we wanted to be in for the birth of our second baby, due in mid-September. (I wanted to go for natural childbirth again and so was back at the Erna Wright classes at Charing Cross Hospital. Peter came along a few times too.) The workmen in Hampstead had exposed original William Morris wallpapers, but sadly they were too damaged to retain. Such a pity; it was a beautiful Bacchanalian design of bunches of grapes on a petrol-blue background. I matched it as closely as possible with some modern William Morris reproductions and I picked out the petrol blue for fitted carpets. Lots of pine-faced wardrobes lined the walls of the dressing room/bathroom, with its sunken bath and turquoise art nouveau washbasin, found in the Portobello Road. It was the beginning of the craze for Victoriana and bargains could still be found there, as well as in Islington and the King's Road. The drawing room was decorated with pale green and cream chrysanthemum William Morris wallpaper. (Until recently this was still in place in the house, whenever I peered in.) The floors were sanded and varnished, then covered with cream and pale green Casa Pupo rugs. Cotton-satin curtains set off the bay window with its seat that overlooked the narrow, walled garden and its pear, fig and almond trees. We found a beautiful early English oak dresser upon which the Tiffany lamp looked wonderful. In between the comfortable chesterfield sofas stood a green leather Windsor chair: Peter's chair, from which he was to entertain so many dinner guests.

The kitchen was in the basement and we dined here, around a large scrubbed pine table. Victorian tiles made a colourful recess for the business of cooking, copper saucepans garnished the chimneypiece and a hanging Victorian oil lamp gave out a beautiful light, diffused on our warm yellow ochre walls. Altogether, it was a dream kitchen for me. The nursery was on the third floor with a room for a nanny or au pair, and on the fourth floor was the attic room, the study where Peter and Dudley would spend hours together in hysterics, improvising with the help of an impressive, state-of-the-art recording machine. If only we had kept those tapes. An intercom was installed and this proved invaluable since it was such a long way from the kitchen in the basement to the study at the top. This attic was where the relationship that came to be known as 'Pete and Dud' first flourished. In contrast to the way these two friends have often been portrayed since their deaths, they were affectionate and trusting. The comic rhythm between them may appear, especially latterly, to have relied upon humiliating Dudley, but this was only ever possible because Dudley was, in fact, much more confident, or 'grounded' as Suzy Kendall now puts it, than his hapless stage persona.

'He was very strong,' she says. 'He just played that part, but Dudley was not shoved around by anybody. He just knew what he wanted, knew what he could do and was very ambitious. It was never any surprise to me that Dudley became a film star. As much as Peter had this amazing wit, Dudley was very grounded. And he also had a great respect for Peter's wit.'

A few months before the baby was due we were invited to dinner with the film director Bryan Forbes and his wife Nanette Newman. After being wined and dined and flattered a great deal, Peter was invited to take on a considerable role in a film Bryan would be making, starring Michael Caine, Ralph Richardson and Nanette herself. *The Wrong Box* was to be filmed in Bath in a few months' time, precisely when our baby was due. Peter barely hesitated before agreeing; it would be his first film and I could hardly have expected otherwise. My heart sank, though, to think he might well be absent for the birth. Bryan Forbes tried to console me, promising to stop all scenes with Peter in them at the earliest hint of labour. By now I was aware of the persuasiveness of showbiz people when they want something.

The film was to be based on a Robert Louis Stevenson story about a murderous competition to inherit a fortune. It eventually starred Sir John Mills, Ralph Richardson and Peter Sellers, along with Peter and Dudley, and one scene required the casting of a hundred or so cats. One newspaper carried a story about Peter supposedly 'auditioning' cats at the Mermaid Theatre over the weekend. It described us as a family that had moved into 'big-time public eminence', next to a picture of Peter covered in cats.

To compensate me for losing him to filming later on, Peter suggested we should have a quick jaunt to Corsica. This wild island had been recommended to him by Billy Cotton Jr and Frank Muir, who both had homes there. Christopher Logue, always good company, was invited too, and Dudley and Suzy were to join us for the second half of the holiday. I was glad to go. It was a good time to take a break. Christopher, however, hated flying and we watched him trying to hide his agitation as we took off. The fact that he was reading his book upside down was a clue.

We stayed at the Hotel Napoleon Bonaparte in Ile Rousse, a wonderfully baroque edifice, with chandeliers and footmen and splendid French food and wine. And the footman didn't blink an eye as he helped us into the battered old Citroën Deux Chevaux Christopher had rented for our stay. He insisted on driving while wearing his Cuban, Fidelista-style peaked hat. The journey was Christopher's revenge for not having been in charge of the flight controls on the plane; he swerved dangerously around precipitous mountain roads, throwing up clouds of dust and laughing gustily. At the best of times I am a poor passenger and I thought I was going to have a miscarriage. These days Christopher blames the rough ride on the Corsican roads. He was, in fact, a good driver. It just looked dangerous as the Deux Chevaux bounced around. Peter comforted me with the thought that the French made very good cars. The scenery was breathtaking, however, and the people somewhat piratical. It was election time and the villages and towns were full of the kind of excitement that seemed to involve firing guns in the air, just to make a point. Frank Muir assured us it was perfectly common practice and no harm would befall us. He was right. The only harm that did befall me one night was my own fault. In a fit of pique I left the party to walk back to the hotel alone and I stumbled into a cactus bush. I was like a pincushion and had to tweezer the prickles out for most of the next day. My poor growing baby!

It was a colourful and memorable holiday and good to be with Dudley and Suzy. Looking at the photographs together recently Suzy reminded me how shy Dudley was then about taking off his clothes on the beach. She regards this holiday in Corsica as something of a triumph because she at last managed to persuade Dudley to remove his shirt and trousers when sunbathing. He was usually reluctant to reveal his club foot. 'He would sit on the beach with all his clothes on,' she recalls. 'So I said if you won't, I won't. I got him to do it by sitting there with my clothes on too. He did it finally because of that, and because he wasn't in England.'

On the way home Christopher, this time in a Mexican hat, naughtily used my pregnancy as an excuse to get us all better seats. 'We were in very uncomfortable seats and so I complained to the steward. I said you were pregnant and that "This is no way to treat the wife of this distinguished English comedian!" And they upgraded us. I felt so pleased with myself.'

How much I had missed Lucy! She had been happily absorbed into the Miller household with Patsy, though, and probably didn't miss us at all. What a joyful reunion we all had. Lucy seemed to have grown a lot in such a short time and discovered some new words.

It was now July and the move to Hampstead was arranged. We had decided to employ a trained nanny for the first month of the new baby's life, to help get her into a rhythm and to allow her father, now committed to unpredictable hours of filming, to get a good night's sleep. Patsy would come with us for the first six weeks too, but would then take up full-time studies in September. She had really applied herself and made amazing progress in several subjects. Like me, Peter had a very soft spot for Patsy, admiring her simplicity and vulnerability. Later she was to meet and marry a young flautist, Stephen Preston, who played in a chamber trio of talented young musicians with whom I became friends in the seventies. After producing two beautiful children with Stephen, Patsy went on to become a militant black feminist. It just shows what education and exposure to new ideas can do.

The move went smoothly and the house looked ravishing, but it needed to become a home: Peter, always quite untidy, and the children would soon see to that. I was incredibly house-proud and enjoyed polishing furniture and copper, as we had done in my childhood, and making wild, overblown flower arrangements. Lucy liked her room with Patsy next door, and us below. She soon adapted, though the whole place felt vast compared to the flat in Ovington Square. Going down for a glass of water in the middle of the night was a great trek. I had been longing to do some serious gardening, but it was difficult with the bump, so I had to wait. I contented myself with planting bulbs for spring.

Peter was disappearing frequently now, being measured up for costumes and going to rehearsals, so I concentrated on settling in, on the childbirth classes and on catching up with friends. Harriet and Nick lived nearby in Primrose Hill and it was Harriet who came with me to Charing Cross Hospital when the contractions began. Peter was in Bath filming *The Wrong Box* and a part of me was relieved there would be no repetition of the first labour, during which he had sat trans-fixed, unable to go or stay, while I was shouting my head off. The rest of me definitely wanted him there as soon as possible, to share the experience. It was early afternoon and the con-tractions were still weak. I felt so much calmer and more in control than I had before and I practised integrated breathing.

Word had gone out to Peter; Harriet told me he was on his way.

He arrived at eleven o'clock and the baby – clearly a well-mannered little thing – held on until Daddy was within earshot. The contractions then came thick and fast. Norman Morris was there again, begowned and ready to snip me (I wish he hadn't). Peter was also dressed up like a TV doctor, an old hand this time, as the baby popped out. What a difference the breathing had made. Or maybe it was not trying to keep a pair of false eyelashes in place this time around. Whatever the reason, it was such a different experience. Peter bought me an antique gold pocket watch to commemorate the birth of his second daughter.

The proud parents christened their new baby Daisy Clementine, because she looked so fresh and open and, because of the song 'Darling Clementine'. Peter had a brief break from filming, just long enough for 'happy family' pictures for the press. Our new neighbours, who included Sir Frank Soskice, then Home Secretary, and the local vicar, the Rev. Hall, tendered their congratulations. Flowers and telegrams flooded in. Our new nanny was installed and, ill-advised, I made the decision not to breast-feed Daisy. I took pills to dry up my breast milk and nanny administered bottles of made-up formula during the night. It is with real remorse that I recount this, knowing what I now know about the importance of breast-feeding; not only because breast milk is of prime importance for the development of the child, but for the bonding that occurs in those intimate moments. Bottle-feeding was so 'convenient', but, like many convenient things, it disdained the intelligence of nature.

Our two little girls were adorable together. Lucy seemed to love her baby sister right from the start and clearly recognized her role as 'big sister', though there was not much more than fifteen months between them. From the beginning their distinct personalities were clear. Lucy was reliable and supportive and very protective of her little sister, who was even then the more sensitive and impulsive of the two. Peter was concerned that Daisy, upon whom he doted, had inherited his wonky ears, so for some time she wore a little corrective bonnet at night that was always falling off. Eight weeks after the birth I was the subject of a national newspaper feature about child-rearing. Apparently I wanted two more children and believed in intuition rather than instruction. What does it matter, I say, if Lucy is a late developer who only walks a little, and then only if nobody is looking? From the sidelines Peter comments facetiously: 'I don't see why people should walk really – crawling is so much better.'

Life with Peter was more and more socially demanding, but I too was guilty of creating extra social events for us because of my increasing love of cooking and hostessing for friends and new acquaintances. These dinner parties became my creative outreach and, of course, they were also a helpful backdrop for Peter's professional life, which depended a great deal on contacts, goodwill and on putting people together who would stimulate each other, with the help of good food, good wine and good conversation. This, for me, is true alchemy. After one dinner I discussed the wonders of the digestive system in some detail with Peter and then later noticed much of our conversation transposed into E. L. Wisty's oft-quoted monologue about the extraordinary length of the human intestine. It is hard to even write that last phrase without hearing Wisty's drawl in my head. After travelling for more than three miles, food, he reasons, is actually far from fresh when it arrives.

Peter's study was well used. Dudley and Suzy had moved into their Hampstead home, around the corner, a Georgian house that Suzy proceeded to decorate with William Morris

Our beautiful Church Row family home.

(yes, more of the green and cream chrysanthemum design) and stripped-pine floors and furniture. It must have been the 100th Monkey Syndrome – suddenly everyone started to imitate each other. So now Dudley had only a five-minute journey to our house and he made it regularly. Daisy has very early memories of being pushed about by Dudley in a whicker shopping basket on wheels: 'Lucy and I couldn't pronounce his name. He was Cuddly Dudley, just this funny lovely man,' she says. Sue Newling-Ward, the young nanny we later employed, says she too always enjoyed Dudley's visits: 'I used to love it when Dudley came to the house. It was jolly exciting and I used to try to be the one to open the door to him. He would always say, "Is the master upstairs?" and we would go through this *Upstairs, Downstairs* bit. Then you would hear these guffaws from them both in the attic.'

Our cleaner, Mrs Hickey, was cleaning downstairs in the kitchen one morning, in one of her Irish reveries, when she saw a horribly distorted face at the window. She screamed and ran upstairs to find Peter, who came running down to meet her, reassuring her with the words 'Oh, Mrs Hickey, 'tis only the wee Dudley trying to frighten ye!' Dudley had squashed his face, fixed with a grimace, against the kitchen window and given the dear woman a shock she remembers to this day.

I would often take up a tray of coffee and home-made biscuits to Peter and Dudley later and stay to watch. The only word for what went on is 'hilarity'. Being with them was like being a bubble dancing around the surface of a glass of champagne. Their style of improvising was to replace gaps in thought, supposedly left by a disordered memory, with an imaginary experience. One outrageous event would be topped by another, in a crescendo of make-believe, usually ending in the trademark exclamation 'Funny!' Their view from the window of that study was inspiring too, looking out as it did over Highgate and beyond. 'I remember the loft well,' says my daughter Lucy. 'It had a long window and a long desk along it where Dad would write. He would go up there with Dudley and we would go and visit him up there while he was writing.' Much was created in that attic that later came to the nation's screens and is still regularly quoted today.

One afternoon I went up to get them to tell me the meaning of a word that I had come across: it had a sound I enjoyed: 'shibboleth'. They liked the sound of it too, and Peter claimed it was a secret password from the Old Testament, used by the Gileadites to test the Ephraimites, because the Ephraimites could not pronounce the sound 'sh'.

In the late summer of 1966 Peter and Dudley were to take a break from filming the next series of *Not Only . . . But Also* and Peter suggested he and I should go on a two-week gastronomic holiday in Provence that September. He loved good food, but the holiday was also arranged in appreciation of my own growing devotion to Elizabeth David, in particular, and to French cookery in general. Our little girls would go with their nanny to see their grandparents at Lyme Regis and Peter and I would have some time alone, to recapture some of the innocent fun of our student days. Those carefree times seemed a distant memory as the increasing obligations that went with his success took their toll, so I was very happy at his suggestion.

We flew to Nice, kicking off our holiday in grand style by visiting David Niven at his villa in Monaco. David, ever the charming Englishman, offered us 'shampoo', a cold bottle of excellent champagne, which we drank on the vine-covered patio, listening to stories of his adventures with the swashbuckling Errol Flynn. I could hardly believe the setting, with the boats bobbing up and down below on the sparkling Mediterranean. Here I was being entertained by one of my mother's heartthrobs! After an extended lunch we meandered back to our hotel in the rented open-topped car and planned our itinerary. Following this dazzling introduction to the South of France we spent a morning on the crowded beach at St Tropez. You had to pay to go on the beach, which outraged us, and, no, there was no glimpse of La Bardot either. (Peter was later to turn down an opportunity to make a movie with her; he said he kicked himself about it afterwards, but I suspect he was scared.) Our idea was to stay in little *pensions* and eat in some Relais routiers, where the lorry drivers usually eat, and which – unlike British transport cafés – have remarkably good, home-cooked fresh food.

We went first to Grasse, a town famous for its perfumes and where the cooks Julia Child and Simone Beck lived in the countryside. The heady perfume of the distilling flowers, mingled with the spicy aroma of wild Provençal herbs, rosemary, thyme, savory and marjoram, assaulted the senses delightfully. That evening we found a small *pension* where you could dine out on the terrace under the stars and where we were served the most unforgettable dish of sautéed potatoes with garlic and rosemary. Of course, there were other dishes, but that is the one I've tried ever since to emulate. Nothing ever matches that experience: the place, the company, the ingredients – and all so cheap! We drove on through the magnificent scenery of Carpentras and Orange, visiting Roman ruins where Peter got caught up in a fantasy of his own devising about the character of one of Caesar's less successful concubines, who met an untimely death from the sting of a giant scorpion.

We wandered about the Camargue. I loved the open spaces, white horses, rice paddies and reeds, and the salt wind and big skies. It was here we went to see a version of bullfighting known as 'bull-running', a much less bloody event than the bullfighting I had seen in Andalusia. This sport involves about twenty very fit men dressed in white vests and trousers, carrying in their right hands a ring with a sharp, curved hook. The quarry is a frisky black bull, bred on the plains of the Camargue, with rosettes tied to its horns. The idea is to jump over the bull and hook off the rosettes from the horns. It is extremely dangerous and probably has its roots in the bull-running cults of Minoan Crete. Bets are placed on the various participants and the odds are continuously relayed on a loudspeaker. Of course, this sport went down well with Peter, who never lost an opportunity to place a bet. He came away in high spirits with a fistful of francs. It seemed a fairer sport to me, with no loss of life (to the bull, at any rate).

We bought French cowboy hats, fancying ourselves as gauchos riding those wild, white horses over the plains of the Camargue and herding up the great black bulls. Instead, we drove the car, roof down, to attend a concert by Manitas de Plata, a gypsy guitarist of the Camargue, which I found rekindled the gypsy passion in my soul. There was something so proud and haunting in this music and in the story of the Romany gypsies, their lives and rituals.

I loved too the slightly salty rosé wine of the Camargue. Each area of this part of France seemed to be a different country with its unique landscape and regional dishes. Now we carried on through the great limestone hills to Les Baux, towards what turned out to be the apogee of our tour – a five-star hotel high among the crags. A uniformed bellboy showed us to our room, which seemed to be a grander version of our tented flat on St Mark's Place in New York. We unpacked and revelled in the luxury of an en suite sunken bath and having our clothes pressed. So, having cleaned off the white sand of the Camargue, Peter and I emerged, tanned and elegant, to saunter down to the terrace for a pre-prandial 'sundowner', to peruse the menu

Peter in cowboy hat

and take in the monolithic limestone peaks that rose protect-
ively around the basin in which the hotel nestled.

We had already rung home to check that all was well and
were able to enjoy the anticipation of the feast that lay ahead.
For starters I chose the pâté maison and Peter chose quail (caille
en croute), followed by lamb cutlets and sautéed potatoes. It
seemed hours before we were called to our table, but eventually
I was served and Peter's dish came ten minutes later. We both
froze as we saw a tiny little head and neck dangling dolefully
out of a pillow of puff pastry – the poor quail. I shall never
forget Peter's face, his horror, because he really did have a love
of tiny creatures. However, he gave it his best. My pâté was
good, but the sautéed potatoes were not a patch on those of
the Grasse *pension*. A good bottle of wine made up for what
turned out to be a rather disappointing meal and then it was
time for bed. Neither of us slept much that night, I remember,
not entirely due to high jinks in the nuptial couch, but more
to the presence of rats wearing high-heeled shoes and doing
the samba in the tent-like drapery. (Once again, shades of our
New York basement.) Added to which, there was an eerie and
stifling air of melancholy about the place. I wasn't alone in
sensing this; Peter also admitted feeling apprehensive. I learned
later that thousands of Cathars had been slaughtered in that
very area. We vowed we would stick to *pensions* if we came
to this part again. Needless to say, the bill was monumental.

Although I couldn't wait to be reunited with Lucy and Daisy,
part of me baulked at returning to our glamorous London life.
The sun and sea and wild limestone mountains had enraptured
me, not to mention the food and the gypsy music.

We collected our little family, who had been well-behaved.
They, too, looked tanned and healthy and were full of stories
of the beach at Lyme, of starfish and paddling. Peter gave his
parents some bottles of good wine and we made off back to

Me in one of the roguish Citroëns we loved.

London in the capacious old Citroën that rose up on its
haunches like a great toad when the ignition was switched on.
We taught the children some French songs on the way back.
Mrs Hickey had got the place spanking clean for us. The cat
had not been run over and Alma and Ivan, the two chameleons,
had refrained from eating each other and stuck to their juicy
mealworms. The flowers in the garden were nearly finished for
the year, though I knew I could now dry some of the beautiful
blue heads of hydrangeas.

Our first Christmas at Church Row was like a fairy tale.

The house lent itself so readily to being traditionally decorated with branches of fir, ivy and holly. In the sitting room we had a tree covered with candles and little gold-wrapped presents. Lucy was excited. Daisy was too little to know quite what was going on, but chuckled with pleasure. On Christmas Eve, after spending most of the day preparing for the Christmas feast, I arranged for a small group of choirboys, dressed in their cassocks and accompanied by their choirmaster, to sing carols outside our house. Lucy was particularly thrilled, especially when they came in for a cup of tea and mince pies; she looked at them as if they were angels. She hung up her stocking on the corner of her Victorian bed and we posted the letter up the chimney for Father Christmas, leaving carrots in one of Peter's old shoes for the reindeer.

And Father Christmas had a surprise in store for Peter on Christmas Day. The character Spotty Muldoon was by now one of Peter's chief alter egos. He had just written and recorded the song that went 'Spotty Muldoon, Spotty Muldoon, he's got spots all over his face'. Peter's own adolescent acne problem had somehow morphed into a 45 rpm single. In response to this I organized someone to make a life-size figure of Spotty Muldoon for his Christmas present. It looked rather like E. L. Wisty, with a flat cap and a moustache, but it had a recording device in its innards that played a tape of the song.

The first Christmas morning in our new home: breakfast, presents and church. And then, to everyone's surprise, Spotty was delivered. He went down well with Peter, although Lucy looked a little disturbed by this rather eerie, Madame Tussaud-style figure. He was relegated to the study thereafter.

Dudley and Suzy were coming over for a late lunch, along with John Bird and his American wife Annie, Paul Jones and Sheila MacCleod, and Christopher Garmony, a young writer friend, so after breakfast I sent Peter and the girls out for a walk on Hampstead Heath while I prepared a Christmas feast: smoked salmon with a colourful salad for the starter, followed by turkey stuffed with wild rice, apricots, chestnuts, spices and herbs – a recipe which I use to this day – served with cranberry and orange sauce, pommes dauphinoises, spiced red cabbage, Brussels sprouts and bread sauce, wine gravy, and followed by home-made Christmas pudding, complete with silver sixpences and threepenny pieces.

After the meal, which lasted hours, Dudley played his setting of a medley of Christmas songs with his own words and Peter added a few too, singing with great gusto. Sally Bullock, our mother's help, had managed to get the exhausted children to bed, but we continued into the wee hours, bringing out some old cognac and chocolates with the coffee. I wonder now about the people who drove themselves home after such evenings. Still, there were no breathalyzers back then and the police were not so Draconian. Let's hope they all took cabs.

The next morning was taken up with washing up and clearing away, after all the drinking, dancing and smoking. (Most people smoked in those days and Peter indulged occasionally, but I don't think Dudley ever did. He was fairly abstemious and Suzy tells me he would only ever have one glass of wine.) Peter never seemed to be part of the washing-up team. Having bought a dishwasher, he exempted himself thereafter; I don't think I ever expected anything different. When it was done, we wrapped up warmly and went for a long walk with pushchairs on the heath to blow away the cobwebs. We felt pretty upbeat – as a family we had so much to be grateful for.

The *Not Only . . . But Also* programmes were recorded in front of a live audience, so we always invited lots of friends along. The programmes were brilliant, and used many prerecorded filmed excerpts, like the famous 'leaping nuns' or the footage of the lads being lowered into the Thames dressed in tie and tails and playing a grand piano. Of course, ad libs crept in on both sides, leading to the now familiar corpsing in several sketches, something that was certainly encouraged by an audience peppered with friends. Gay Gottlieb, the wife of one of Peter's best friends, the psychiatrist Sidney Gottlieb, recalls a real sense of occasion as we all turned up to support Peter and Dudley: 'There were often about twenty of us. I must have seen most of them recorded and we all got dressed up to the nines. We were in competition, I suppose. I remember one occasion, when the white Courrege boots and macs had just come in, and three of us turned up to the recordings in the same macs. Some of us looked like twins anyway because of the fashions then, and the back-combed hair and false eyelashes.' On those nights Peter and Dudley performed some of their most inspired material. What a tragedy that much of it was needlessly destroyed later by the BBC. After the show, friends would often join us at Le Celier du Midi, a wonderfully authentic French restaurant in the basement of a house on Church Row.

Came 19 January and another celebration was in order, this time for my twenty-sixth. Peter suggested we all go out to Boulestin's in Covent Garden, another favourite restaurant: Nick and Harriet, Paul McCartney and Gavin Young were among those invited. It was a wonderful evening and Peter and Nick Garland amused everyone by drawing cartoons in a Coutts chequebook that I still have. It must have been in the early stages of Nick's career as a cartoonist. Harriet, who was now heavily pregnant, felt a little faint in the heat of the basement room and the gallant Paul McCartney came to her aid. 'Paul helped me to get upstairs,' she remembers, 'and I said to him, "I can't make it. I must lie down." And I just lay down near the stairs. I remember Paul saying to everyone who

*Nick Garland's doodles for Peter on a Coutts cheque book late one
evening in a London restaurant.*

passed by, "She is having a baby. Not now, but she is having a baby."'

When Harriet was restored to us it was time to wind up the evening and the bill was presented. It sat there, between Paul and Peter, who were sitting opposite each other. There followed an unendurable resounding pause before Peter made a move to pick up the tab. I think he was waiting to see if Paul would offer, which was very embarrassing for me as we were the hosts and Peter had invited everyone – about a dozen guests. Eventually, much relieved, I watched him stretch out laconically to examine the damage. This was not unknown behaviour in Peter, who, like many well-known comics, sometimes had a deep-seated reluctance to part with his money. Utility bills, for instance, were frequently left to the last minute before they were paid. In public, he would often appear generous, particularly with his humour, but his attitude to money was complex, to say the least! Quite often he would not carry any cash with him. In contrast I may have appeared extravagant to him, but I was fairly good at budgeting and knew how to make a little go a long way.

Around this time Peter and I went to see *Charade*, an extremely well-designed thriller starring Cary Grant and Audrey Hepburn and directed by Stanley Donen, who had also directed *Singin' in the Rain*. I loved the look of it. As Peter was still working away in his spare time at his Faustian film script, once we got home I told him he had to get this director for his film. If he and Dudley were to make that leap from television to the cinema, they needed someone like Stanley Donen who could do it with visual imagination.

By chance it was only a matter of weeks before we received a dinner invitation from Dirk Bogarde and, when we arrived, to our amazement there was Stanley Donen. The other two guests for this intimate soirée were David Niven and his

Swedish wife Hjordis. Peter and Stanley got on like a house on fire. Dirk Bogarde and David Niven were delightful, but I remember I fell foul of Niven's wife when I laid into her for boasting that she had had to engage another suite of rooms at Claridge's just to house her Christmas presents. I thought this too decadent, and said so. Luckily, Peter came to my rescue and we all parted as friends. A week or so later Stanley Donen came to dinner with us and it was then that he was persuaded to direct *Bedazzled*.

This film, which now has something of a cult following and in 2000 was remade with Elizabeth Hurley in Peter's role of the Devil, tells the story of Stanley Moon, a short order chef at a Wimpy bar, played by Dudley, and of the satanic compact he makes in an attempt to satisfy his unrequited passion for a waitress. At this stage Peter, who wrote the screenplay himself, was still fine-tuning the story.

Early spring: snowdrops appeared in the garden and what a cheerful sight they were. But something was happening which wasn't such good news: dear little Daisy was developing eczema. Peter had also suffered from this as an infant. Our local GP gave us a cortisone cream to put on the affected places. I didn't know then that this cream often 'thins' the skin. It had limited success, but many a night poor Daisy woke herself up with the scratching. How miserable! The itching was an early sign of health problems that were to change our lives in due course. Peter, although sympathetic, was convinced the doctors would sort her out and was now at one of the busiest and most creative points in his meteoric career. The show had to go on and so on it went; in such a helter-skelter of events that I now have difficulty unravelling it all.

It seemed to me that suddenly anything, particularly anything treasured or sacrosanct, was now a target for parody. The orthodox rituals upon which our lives had been built were being exposed. The 'new' was welcome, whether it was needed or not. By the end of the decade the Lord Chamberlain's powers of theatrical censorship had been abolished and little was considered too extreme or offensive to be shown on TV or cinema screens. Although I was firmly ensconced in my domestic bliss, I kept up to date with all this, and with the great dramas playing out on the world stage, through Peter. Whatever was happening, it would be subjected to my husband's scrutiny each morning as he waded through the newspapers. I would then be made aware of developments, which were usually relayed to me in the meandering tones of E. L. Wisty.

It was during these early months at Church Row that I was introduced to a talented young fashion designer, Hylan Booker, from the Royal College of Art. Hylan was a black ex-GI married to an Englishwoman and with a young daughter. I had noticed his work at an end-of-year show and thought his designs outstanding. For the past three years I had been well served by a wonderful dressmaker off the Portobello Road, who had been able to translate my drawings into some lovely, wearable dresses, but now it was time to seek a bit more elegance and move away from the dolly bird look. I suggested to Peter that we might support Hylan and help him to establish a small fashion house. Peter was happy enough to let me explore this initiative. We invested £500 and I found some premises for a very reasonable rent, just behind Liberty and near the new Cranks health food restaurant, which was becoming increasingly popular. Hylan created beautiful garments and I was his guinea pig: I loved going to Liberty's fabric department and having bolts of wild silks and colourful crepes unrolled and draped about me. Hylan designed and made me stunning first-night ensembles. His small collections were always well received for their classical cut, excellent fabrics and simple elegance. Eventually he was head-hunted by another fashion house, the House of Worth, and I was delighted for him. (He later went on to have a relationship with the journalist and broadcaster Dee Wells, married to Professor A. J. 'Freddie' Ayer, and these days he designs clothes for the stars in Los Angeles.) At this point in London the jeans-with-everything, cool, casual, Julie Christie look had not quite come to prevail in women's fashions; this would follow as women became more militantly feminist in the seventies. I still wore dresses in the mid-sixties, even with little children crawling all over me.

Peter, of course, could not be left out of this fashion consciousness of mine. As a birthday present I got the trendy tailor Dougie Hayward, later married to my friend Glenys Roberts, to create a wonderful suit for him of charcoal wool with a wide pinstripe and lined with maroon silk. It looked good, although I had to admit he really was becoming vainer and vainer and was often to be caught preening in the mirror. As well as the Dougie Haywood outfit, I had a grand plan to organize some sky-writing for Peter, spelling out the words 'I love you, P. Cook'. Unfortunately the plan was squashed by the authorities. I was really sad about that.

Determined not to be bossed any longer by despotic nannies, I advertised for somebody new to help me with the girls. The search netted Sue Newling-Ward, a chirpy nineteen-year-old who, despite her youth, had a natural authority with children. I paid her eight quid a week, with time off that allowed her a weekend every month to visit her parents, and informed her firmly that she was to take her guidelines from me and Peter and was to call me Mrs Cook to boot. I did want to bring up my own children and Sue was someone I reckoned would not try to take over the job, or undermine me, while still allowing me some time to have a life of my own. On Sue's part, she says she was astonished to have landed what she regarded as a plumb position. 'I saw the ad in the *Telegraph*. It said contact "Mrs Peter Cook", so I rang up and you said, "Could you come next week?" I was amazed, because I thought I would have to wait weeks for an interview.'

When Sue arrived in Hampstead, things were not as she expected. 'I found my way to Church Row and you answered the door, looking like a dolly bird. You used to wear those high-waisted empire dresses or very colourful tops. I said, "Is Mrs Cook here?" and you said, "I am Mrs Cook". You didn't look like a mum: your make-up, your hairpieces and your skinny tops. All that.'

My heavy eye make-up, in particular, intrigued Sue: 'You did the most beautiful lines and then a bit up at the side, then a whitish bit and you always had a dark socket.'

Cooking really took hold of me now: I loved going to the markets in Portobello Road or Covent Garden and returning with armfuls of flowers and baskets overflowing with fruit, vegetables and salads. At an early age Lucy helped in the kitchen too, enjoying unpacking the produce or making bread. I would often give her dough to play with, while I wallowed in Elizabeth David's cookbooks, reading them like novels. She had travelled and lived a romantic gastronome's life in Egypt, Greece, Italy and France over ten years, and although most of the ingredients she wrote about were hard to find in the fifties, by the sixties they were becoming much more available. People's taste in food was changing. When it came to herbs, David found a keen student in me:

Once you have become a basil addict it is hard to do without it. Mediterranean vegetables such as pimentos and aubergines, garlicky soups and wine-flavoured dishes of beef, salads dressed with the fruity olive oil of Provence or Liguria, and all the dishes with tomato sauces need basil as a fish needs water – and there is no substitute.

About rosemary, however, she was more cautious, writing: 'It is disagreeable to find those spiky little leaves in one's mouth.' Elizabeth Luard and I paid no heed and would giggle together, after some joint culinary event, as guests left picking their teeth.

Of course, Elizabeth David's books were also a key piece of social commentary. They marked the change in post-war attitudes just as clearly as Peter's satire or the new plays at the Royal Court. Until foreign travel and food writers had shaken things up there was little to enjoy in English cuisine.

So cooking became my creative endeavour. It suited my temperament, in those days somewhat choleric and a bit theatrical. It served my love of seasonal produce too, although as yet I could not grow it myself. I loved combining interesting ingredients and immersing myself in a world of process and transformation and alchemy. It was a social thing as well, in that, just as carefully as choosing the ingredients you had to choose the right combination of guests; and when you cooked you had to give your efforts away. Therefore, cooks needed to be generous by nature. I hope my nature was generous; I certainly enjoyed feeding my guests and putting different types together. To prove the point, here is a name-dropping list I have drawn up of some of the guests at our table in those days: Kenneth and Kathleen Tynan, Peter Ustinov, Malcolm Muggeridge, Paul McCartney and Jane Asher, Cynthia and John Lennon, Alan Bennett, Jonathan and Rachel Miller, Richard Ingrams, Christopher Booker, David Frost, Joan Collins, Nick and Harriet Garland, Adrian and Celia Mitchell, Paul and Sheila Jones, Alan Price, John Cleese, Terry Gilliam, Nick and Elizabeth Luard, John Bird and Annie, Sidney and Gay Gottlieb, Barrie Humphries, Jay and Fran Landesman,

Jean Hart and Bill Oddie, Stanley Donen, Joe and Shirley Heller . . . and sometimes the postman.

Alan Bennett, in his usual charming, self-deprecating way, says he was unsettled by these starry line-ups in our new house. 'When you were living in Church Row I remember coming to a party and the Beatles were there and I thought, "I am nothing really now".'

Our nanny Sue Newling-Ward has similar memories of the growing celebrity element in our lives. Testing the employment market one day, she rang up her agency to ask about another job: 'They said to me, "What are you doing looking for another job? You have got the best job in London." And it was true,' she says.

'It was so interesting. Every time I answered the phone I thought, "Oh my God!" It would often be David Frost in a taxi going around London with a phone – one of those things the size of a brick.'

Suzy Kendall now confesses she was a little jealous of the apparently sparkling world that Peter and I had created for ourselves. 'I was so envious of the wonderful life you and Peter had. Maybe I had rosy glasses on because I saw your life together as very happy. Such wonderful banter used to go on.'

Dudley and Suzy were among our 'regulars', our close friends who came all the time, people like the Garlands, Christopher Logue, the Gottliebs, Fran and Jay Landesman; people around whom we would build the group.

According to Christopher Logue, the competing attractions of Peter's sense of humour and my cooking sometimes caused tension among our guests. Peter's comic barrage was so relentless that it distracted from the food. 'In the end you were quite tired with laughing and you used to get terribly cross if Peter would just make us laugh all the time so we couldn't eat the food. As soon as I got a spoonful halfway to my mouth, Peter would make a joke. It must have been very frustrating for you.'

John Lennon and Peter had admired each other's work
for some time, so John was apparently chuffed to be invited
around one time to do a vignette in one of the *Not Only
. . . But Also* sketches. He played a top-hatted, brass-buttoned
commissionaire outside London's newest and most celebrated
nightclub, located in a gentlemen's lavatory. John arrived for
the filming with his son Julian, who was about the same age
as Lucy, and they played happily together while John and Peter
worked. The children produced some lovely drawings and
later John suggested the Lennon and McCartney song 'Lucy in
the Sky with Diamonds' was not about LSD, but rather the
title his son had given a drawing he had done while playing
with a little girl called Lucy. When asked what the picture
showed Julian had simply said it was a 'Lucy in the sky, with
diamonds'. I have always thought it might well have been our
Lucy. Who knows?

John and Peter were in high spirits when they returned from
filming. John retained his quasi-subservient lavatory attend-
ant's character and Peter took on the roles of a succession of
visiting American tourists. The sketch itself was a real success
and John and Cynthia were invited to dinner with us two
weeks later. I wanted to make something special and decided
to do filet de boeuf en croûte – fillet of beef smothered in pâté
de foie gras with truffles and wrapped in a jacket of puff pastry.
I made a special expedition down to the French butcher in
Soho who provided me with a fine fillet of beef, threaded
through with lardons. We would have a crisp chicory, lamb's
lettuce, watercress and orange salad to start and the beef would
be served with green beans and pommes dauphinoises. The
Lennons were invited for eight o'clock.

Dudley and Suzy, Nick and Harriet and the Landesmans
were all there on time. Eight-thirty came and went. I retrieved

On the set of Not Only . . . But Also *as John acts commissionaire to a trendy club in a gents' loo.*

the filet from the oven – it is the kind of thing that needs a quick blast in the oven and not to sit around after that. Nine p.m. and we got a phone call from Lennon's Rolls-Royce. Their driver was lost. It was nearer ten when they arrived. Our other guests had politely decided to wait until our special guests arrived before starting dinner and luckily there were copious amounts of *amuses guelles* and nibbles to keep them going, plus, of course, lots of good wine. But my special meal!

It eventually appeared, looking rather forlorn, and judging by the expression on John's face I might as well have opened a can of baked beans. He would have been just as happy. Luckily everyone was so well oiled that they didn't mind the lateness and, according to Cynthia, this meal offered them their first taste of garlic. The evening's badinage went on into the small hours. The occasion taught me a lesson: don't show off when planning a menu for dinner guests who are unknown quantities. It also made me realize that the age of deference had passed; good manners and punctuality had flown out of the window and people did whatever they pleased. Of course, the fact that a lot of people increasingly smoked dope and did other drugs interfered with any sense of time too.

In spite of this unfortunate overture we became friends with the Lennons for a while and were honoured with an invitation to dinner at their new home in Weybridge. In this case it was not the guests who were late, but the host.

Cynthia was such a gentle and soft-spoken girl, quite shy, but obviously a strong, gritty, Liverpudlian soul. She had survived the humiliation of being kept out of all the publicity in the years of the Beatles' sudden success. Their manager, Brian Epstein, thought the group would have optimum impact if they appeared to be four bachelors. I found her story of how she and baby Julian had to be hidden from sight heartbreaking, but it taught me a little more about what fame and success can do to a relationship.

Paul McCartney also visited us on several occasions. He and the other Beatles believed the title *Beyond the Fringe* had been a dig at their 'mop-top' haircuts. 'We felt it was associated with this whole fringe-haircut thing,' he says. Nice idea though this is, I don't think it possible since the Beatles' early hits came after that first Edinburgh revue. Today Paul says, jokingly, that he 'insinuated' his way into our group of friends so that he could 'party with Logue and the boys and Dudley and Pete'.

'I used to show up any old time, uninvited. I have the funniest memories of your place. The general wash is of having a great time with fun people and, of course, Peter being so funny and witty and talented. It was always a great pleasure.'

At this time Paul was living in the house of his girlfriend

Jane Asher's doctor parents in Wimpole Street and as a result he was more involved with London nightlife than the other three Beatles. 'It was just that I lived in London and they lived in Weybridge,' he explains, but he was also more able to adapt to upper-middle-class manners, including punctuality and keeping your elbows in at the table. He always showed a certain polish, at the same time as being cheeky and fun.

On one occasion, however, his naturally diplomacy was shelved for our benefit. Paul takes up the story: 'I was standing chatting to Christopher Logue and somebody came to your front door and whoever answered the door came back into the room a bit white, saying, "There's some ruffian out there who wants to come in."

'In this company I felt the hard man, so I said, "I'll deal with this", and wandered out to the door. There was some drunk there who said: "I wanna come in." I said, "You are fucking not, you know." He came swinging at me and I think I landed a rather light punch which put an end to him. So I was the pugilist hero that night. Everyone was very impressed, including me.'

Quite something to have a Beatle as a bouncer at your home.

Jane Asher, with her red hair, was stunning, intelligent and very *au courant* with what was going on, particularly in the theatre. Paul always gave her a chance to join in the conversation, something Peter often failed to do with women. In fact, thinking about it now, the female guests were nearly always playing a supporting role at those dinner parties.

Talking to Gay Gottlieb one day as we looked at an old photograph of us all sitting around my table, she commented on how the women all looked rather depressed. 'I think this was because they were the wives of famous husbands,' she explains. 'We were struggling with that, although we were all very capable people, many of whom eventually got very good jobs. We were just an accessory then though. We had to look good, of course, but the women were only there because they were wives or girlfriends.'

I am sure I always had plenty to talk about, however, and I was passionate about my views. I often arranged the supper table so that I'd have people who liked to discuss ideas sitting down at my end, while down at Peter's would be the courtiers who loved to be entertained. Needless to say, by the end of the evening we were all pretty much courtiers.

Adrian Mitchell is one of the few of our friends who saw Peter as a sensitive host, happy to listen to others. He disputes my memory of a husband who dominated the conversation. 'Everyone seemed to be witty,' he remembers. 'He didn't monopolize. He helped me be funny.' Peter's talent to amuse, Adrian felt, was extraordinary because it was so free-wheeling. 'A lot of funny people travel on the rails and know where they are going. Peter was off the rails nearly all the time. Completely wild.'

Peter's ability, or perhaps compulsion, to entertain his friends, never mind his audiences, is one of the hardest things to convey about him. Some of our friends found it difficult, while many celebrated it then, as now. For Jonathan Miller, as we have heard, he was something of a 'ventriloquist's dummy', inhabiting a series of funny personas. For Christopher Booker it was the 'beguiling yet compulsive production of a monologue'. 'I have never known anyone else come into a room and just dominate by force of personality,' says Christopher. I think there is a technical term in psychology – 'confabulating' – that describes what Peter did with ideas when he was on a roll, distorting them creatively in a way that was almost pathological.

Alan Bennett recognizes that this also made Peter difficult to spend any time alone with. 'He was quite shy, I think,' says Alan. 'And as John Bird has said, the constant stream of jokes was a defence. But because I was quite shy, it never occurred to me, but I never wanted to be alone in a room with Peter because he would then go on and on. It was always better to have three of you there.'

Sometimes at the end of one of these epic evenings there would be food left on the plates. I have always hated wasting food. The early experience of rationing had a lasting effect. If ever I commented on this waste to Peter he would respond sarcastically, 'Well, why don't you wrap it up and send it to the Chinese?' It was a joke, but our values were diverging.

In my recent meetings with old friends I have found that those Hampstead evenings, nearly forty years ago, are often etched in their memories too. They were special gatherings, when bonhomie and a sense of wellbeing pervaded.

'You were welcoming and full of fun. I can't remember better dinner parties than those,' says Adrian Mitchell. 'We drank so much wine we were blotto by the time we went home. And your kitchen was wonderful. We always wanted a kitchen like it, we aspired to all that, but we were trying to live on almost nothing.'

Tariq Ali recalls being coaxed over to our house one Christmas. 'Peter invited me round on Boxing Day saying, "My wife wants to meet you." There were a few other people and the children were there too. I was basically chatting you up and listening to your husband. I was sitting between the pair of you. A lot of nice red wine was consumed too. I walked back from Hampstead across the heath to Highgate. It was a cold night, but we were all quite warm by the time I left!'

Gay Gottlieb goes so far as to detail, off pat all these years later, the trendy décor I had so carefully put together: the wallpaper that inspired her to buy the same too, the big kitchen with its stripped-pine table, the converted gas lamps and, the *pièce de resistance*, the Tiffany lamp given to me that New York Christmas.

Our place, Gay adds, became famous among our friends for good food, for what she now calls my 'exotic' style, and for gatherings of influential people. In truth, however, part of the impact on our guests must have been that this was the era that marked the beginning of the modern, semi-formal, dinner party: now a middle-class institution.

'It never really struck me that you and Peter were snobby,' she says, 'but there was nobody there who was not well known or who was not at the top of their profession. I don't think you realized quite how central you were for us. Or, if you did eventually, you wanted to get away from it.'

Once more my enthusiastic hostessing was written up in the national press. One of the articles I have kept is accompanied by a photograph of me laden with a tray of champagne glasses. I was laying on a suckling pig for a dinner party given for a visiting American friend, Joseph Heller. I see that I did admit, however, to having bought it from Harrods, pre-stuffed and cooked, at 13/4d a pound, plus £2 5s for cooking. I go on to offer some helpful tips to would-be supper party-givers, including offering departing guests a baked jacket potato to take home with them on a cold night. A cup of tea should be served at 1.00 a.m., I also suggest.

Once Paul McCartney had moved nearer to us, to St John's Wood, he would walk his famous Old English sheepdog, Martha, up on Hampstead Heath. Sometimes he would pop in for breakfast or coffee, driving up in his mini with this vast Dulux dog somehow accommodated inside. In the days before Paul was a vegetarian, Sue Newling-Ward cooked him bacon and eggs one morning when she was making it for my girls. 'He would be up talking to Peter and then he would bring his great big dog down. He came for dinner on Christmas Eve one year and I stayed for Christmas because I wanted to see him!'

Sometimes I would go for a walk with Paul too. We were

Observer *article dinner table with roast suckling pig*

sitting in a clearing in the woods one day when he pulled out a packet of cigarettes and offered me one. But these were no ordinary cigarettes; they were perfectly rolled joints courtesy of Paul's roadies. I can't say I was ever keen on marijuana, but that occasion was rather special.

Other times Paul would come by and have jam sessions with my visiting sister Patsy and her husband Rod, who were both folk singers. They made some good sounds together. On the subject of musicians, I should also mention Paul Jones and his wife Sheila MacLeod who became close friends. Paul, then of Manfred Mann fame, and Sheila had met as students at Oxford and had two sons. Sheila, a melancholy person, was interesting and became a writer, latterly sharing her problems as an anorexic. Paul was friendly and good-natured and we had some great evenings together; I recall one with the Animals' Alan Price during which they improvised together. All this free entertainment was going on in our kitchen and sitting room.

When *The Wrong Box* was premiered – featuring as it did Peter and Dudley's first screen appearances – it did not land rave reviews, but then again it didn't do too badly either. Bryan Forbes gave a party at his home for the stars of the film, including Peter Sellers, together with the other great comic icon of our day, Spike Milligan. Sellers was married to Britt Ekland at the time and was clearly going through one of his mental health 'episodes'. He refused to come into the main room, where the party was in full swing, but stayed in the corridor, frequently poking his head round the door and demanding that Britt bring him a drink. It was strange behaviour. He would neither join nor leave; he just hovered. I enjoyed talking to Spike Milligan, though. He was dressed in his khaki army kit, including a shirt with epaulettes. His wife Paddy was with him and seemed warm and earthy.

One of Peter's public engagements was to take part in a

debate on 'Good and Evil and the Role of Lucifer' with the Rev. Joseph Needham in one of the big City churches. In the run-up he cursed me for encouraging him to take it on, but started reading the Bible in preparation. When he got to Genesis he got caught up with all the 'begatting' going on between Ishmael, Enosh and Ishbar. This was later to become a comic theme of his, culminating in the sketch where he rolls out a whole list of ridiculous names, all begatting each other, to a bemused 'Dud'. He concludes that the entire Book of Genesis is 'an allergy' of the human condition. Biblical pastiche of this sort during the debate had them rolling in the aisles and obliterated chances for serious discussion.

Another interesting episode at this time concerned Peter's connection with *Private Eye*. Together we attended the court proceedings of a libel case brought against the magazine by Lord Russell of Liverpool. It was the first of many court cases for the *Eye* and revolved around an accusation that Lord Russell's book *The Scourge of the Swastika* tastelessly revelled in details of Nazi atrocities. Peter spoke in court as a witness, but with no legal acumen he did not really help the case along. Watching the proceedings I became fascinated by how the juxtaposition of two words in a particular sentence could suddenly be termed 'libellous'. I began to see how language could be manipulated or used carelessly so as to constitute an unlawful act, punishable by huge fines. In the end the magazine lost the case and had to pay £5000 damages plus £3000 costs. Peter set about getting the money to meet this payment by putting together a gala evening on 1 May – 'The Rustle of Spring'. Performers including George Melly, Manfred Mann, Peter Sellers, Spike Milligan, Larry Adler and Bob Monkhouse all offered their services and a large sum was raised to bail out the *Eye*. At this period Peter also became very absorbed in the details of the James Hanratty A6 murder case, a *cause célèbre* in which many suspected a miscarriage of justice had taken place. DNA tests undertaken in the last few years suggest that the original verdict was sound, but Peter, along with Paul Foot and John Lennon, publicly questioned the outcome of the trial at the time.

While Peter's comedy with Dudley was growing increasingly surreal, his work behind the scenes at *Private Eye* satisfied his trouble-making, satirical urge and his interest in politics. It did, however, cause some problems with old friendships. Jonathan Miller, for one, was unhappy about the way things that were said between friends around a dinner table frequently appeared in the *Eye*'s columns. He was also directly satirized in its pages. '*Private Eye* began dumping on me – about which Peter didn't object at all, as an old friend. Week in and week out I was Dr Jonathan. I just thought, "Oh, God I can't really be friends with him any more."' Maybe Jonathan was right. Others, such as Tariq Ali, thought the importance of having the kind of political journal that was happy to upset the great and the good outweighed these personal considerations.

Much of the old order, old standards of behaviour included, was undergoing revolution in these years. On television our friend the critic Kenneth Tynan infamously said 'fuck' for the first time during a late-night discussion show, causing uproar. Christopher Logue remembers being at Ken's house that very night, after the offending show had been broadcast. He says that Ken's stutter had made the build-up to the word itself even more dramatic. 'Of course, he said "fffff—fuck", and he finally gets it out. Nobody remembers the stutter, which was funny because you could see it coming. Once it had happened there was all this stuff about how Ken had planned it. It is rubbish. Something annoyed him and he didn't care. He didn't give a toss.'

Ken hardly referred to the incident that evening at first,

according to Christopher, and then suddenly there were phone calls and photographers at the door of their flat.

Of course, Peter and Nick Luard must own some responsibility for introducing an acceptance of foul language into this country. Lenny Bruce's entire act at The Establishment was peppered with the strongest of language, especially the word 'fuck'. I think Peter was proud of this and I have often wondered what his parents made of all this 'filth'. It must have reached their ears somehow, but I had never heard either of them swear. I guess that, as with any other unpleasantness, Peter could rely on them not to mention it.

Peter's interest in living on the margins (he was becoming fascinated by all sorts of subcultures, from betting to brothels) now led us into the boxing world and an unusual but very genuine friendship that sprang up between us and Terry Downes, the British middleweight champion, and his wife Barbara. Terry was very good at jokes – cockney ones – and he and Peter had some impressive verbal sparring sessions. Terry was soon invited to be a guest on *Not Only ... But Also*, where he played himself. Barbara remembers meeting me in the ladies'. She was having trouble with her false eyelashes and asked me if I had any glue in my handbag. I had, and as a result we bonded, just like the lashes. Barbara and I were to have some great times together, including celebrating England's World Cup win in 1966 at the Hilton and going off on our own to hear Joan Sutherland sing at the Albert Hall. Barbara had a sharp tongue and I loved the fact that she and Terry were such good, old-fashioned parents to their lively family of four. Terry was almost Victorian in his authoritarian stance at the head of the family. You didn't mess with him and the children soon understood this, although they were not cowed by their pugilistic papa. All four turned out very spunky and resilient, and with good manners.

Peter, Barbara Downes, Wendy and Terry Downes at Danny La Rue's.

Terry and Barbara took us to a Mohammad Ali fight, for which we had ringside seats. It was the famous encounter with Henry Cooper at Highbury which Ali won and we met him afterwards, surrounded as he was by his entourage. We went on to Danny La Rue's with the Downeses for dinner and the show. I can't say it was especially my scene, but what a lot of contrasts – a kaleidoscope of people and places.

Ken Tynan was a regular dinner guest too, with his wife Kathleen, so beautiful and intelligent. Ken had rather cold eyes and was very intense and he would hold his cigarette un- usually between third and fourth fingers. Being exposed to Peter's sense of humour benefited him greatly. Bernard Levin was similarly intense; always immaculate and with very highly polished shoes. He seemed held together by nervous energy. I remember him sharing a story that has stayed with me. It was about an exercise they carried out at the London School of Economics. An incident was staged on the campus in which someone appeared to be shot and wounded – a put-up job, though the students didn't know that at the time. The eyewitnesses were all rounded up but no two accounts coincided, according to Bernard. It made me think about the way we all inhabit very subjective universes and see things totally differently, including apparently objective elements such as the colour of a woman's dress. I came to the conclusion that it is women who tend to be more interested in the details of their surroundings, and only artists who have been taught to look properly.

A Shrinking Marriage

Our social circle continued to expand feverishly, just as the time I spent alone with Peter diminished. Through his former assistant Judy Scott-Fox we had became friendly with Adrian Mitchell, the poet, and his wife Celia, and it was through them in turn that we met Dr Gerry Slattery and then the psychiatrist Sidney Gottlieb and his wife Gay. They all spent a lot of time together and Peter and I came to enjoy the company of this group very much. Before long Sidney had become one of Peter's closest friends.

Gerry Slattery was Judy's doctor and became mine too. He was a handsome, debonair and witty Irishman, with a complicated personal life, who felt that we'd all be better off if doctors could prescribe some good Irish malt whiskey rather than the plethora of allopathic drugs they were expected to dish out. He believed that many ailments were psychologically induced and that sorting out a patient's mental issues was often the key to restoring good health. I was beginning to acknowledge a certain tendency to depression in myself at this time, so I was especially interested. Up until then I had associated my feelings with postnatal depression and had been given some tranquillizers by my then GP, who, by the way, had made no proviso about not drinking, which we all did in those circles. I had found myself feeling very strange as a result.

Whatever was building up inside me reached a climax one winter's morning. The cleaning was being done by the cleaning lady and the nanny suggested I shouldn't be around during the children's mealtimes as it interfered with their eating habits. So I just went out and spent lots of money, about £100 (a great deal of money then). I returned with my shopping and went up to our bedroom feeling devastatingly empty. I had to acknowledge deep despair. How could I possibly be unhappy when I had absolutely everything that I – or any other woman on the planet – could dream of? A highly successful and hand-some husband, an exquisite house, two beautiful, adorable children, help with the housework and childcare, exciting friends, interesting holidays. How dare I be anything but deliri-ously happy? I had created a storybook castle and imprisoned myself in a dream. I recognized that, despite the family life Peter and I enjoyed on our lovely holidays, our physical love life was in a rut. We had both been so inexperienced when we met and Peter was never one for romantic talk or build-up, which I desperately needed. Our relationship, on many levels a strong one, was unusual in that somehow we had not ever become friends, at least not in the way that friends usually share intimacies and develop greater trust. I felt Peter's attitude was 'I've bought her this lovely house, given her two babies, what more can she want? I now have to give full throttle to my career'.

Two of the problems – easy to see in hindsight – were that I was not being artistically or intellectually challenged, so I had too much time on my hands. I also had a tendency to those cyclical depressions in wintertime, now known as SAD – seasonal affective disorder. Added to which, of course, was Daisy's deteriorating health; her eczema had now, worryingly, turned to asthma. Just like both her parents before her, Daisy now spent horrible nights struggling to breathe. 'I remember feeling frightened and very debilitated,' she says. 'Having a sick child must have been the most frightening thing too.'

I found it increasingly hard to live with someone who was seldom 'off-stage', on the one hand delightful, but on the other demanding and tense. Peter was bewildered by my depression. I generally managed to cover it up, but I would burst into tears periodically and was prone to obsessive fears and panic attacks that seemed to be linked to my childhood in the war and the claustrophobia induced by having to wear gas masks. Peter just didn't know how to cope with all this.

To Harriet Garland it was clear I was not content in the marriage: 'There were times when the children were a bit older, and you were drinking quite a lot and we would go off on our own and be very unhappy.'

I went to see Gerry Slattery and he suggested I should start seeing Sidney Gottlieb as a patient. I had already taken to Sidney, who saw many people from the theatre and jazz worlds. A Jewish South African, I thought him an incredibly interesting man with real insight. While living in New York it was impossible to be unaware of the number of friends who were in analysis. I had read books on psychology and was particularly impressed with R. D. Laing, the Scottish 'psychedelic' psychoanalyst, reading *The Divided Self* and *The Bird of Paradise*. At that time too I was something of a disciple of the New Psychology, which meant that for any psychiatrist to understand you they should know about your life, not simply through your perceptions, but through observing your actions in life and in relationships. Sidney fitted the bill. He, Gay, Peter and I spent a good deal of time in each other's homes. They would often come to the filming of *Not Only . . . But Also*, and Peter and Sidney went regularly to watch Spurs play at White Hart Lane on Saturday afternoons. So I started to work professionally with Sidney, and Peter was grateful for someone else to help him cope with 'my' problems. He eventually revealed to me that he was terrified of delving into his own psyche, probably for many reasons, but the one that he gave as his biggest fear was that, if he examined his genius his muse might dry up or disappear.

It certainly helped me to have someone to talk to about my doubts and fears. Our sessions were usually in Sidney's office in their large, comfortable mansion in Highgate, where Gay bred dogs and brought up five children. Sidney was shortish with a large frame, dark hair, and handsome in a swarthy way, with deep brown eyes. Most of all, he had passion and charisma. It was good to know I was not the only one to be suffering from depression; it was endemic to our times, Sidney assured me, but it usually heralded a much needed change in one's life and self-perception. He used a combination of seda-tives and hypnotherapy which left me in a rather drowsy state and in no condition to drive home, which I regularly did none-theless. It became clear to me in our sessions that I had tied myself to the cross of perfection, doing everything I could to be the ideal wife, mother and hostess. It was all a terrible strain. I had subjugated a great deal of my own authenticity, assuming that what Peter wanted was an upper-middle-class backdrop for his astonishing career. But, despite him visibly enjoying all this *mise-en-scène*, he did not have much clue himself about how upper-middle-class families lived because he had had so little experience of it. We were both making it up as we went along and making mistakes. Sidney said I must assert myself. What a powerful directive! He could never have guessed what it would lead to.

In response to Sidney's exhortations, I began to behave dif-ferently with Peter. Friends who looked on from the sidelines in this period claim they could spot signs of trouble. Nathan Silver tells me I was 'waspish' to Peter. 'You would run him down to his face. He was getting a lot of aggravation and you were feeling a lot of resentment.' To Nathan, who had given me away at the altar, I now appeared bitter. 'You inflicted emotional pain on him. I could see you doing it to yourselves privately, but also publicly. I understood you were unhappy, although I am not sure that I knew what was making you unhappy. I assumed there were reasons.'

The next messenger of change was my psychiatrist's wife, Gay Gottlieb, who said to me one day: 'I've met this interesting young man called Simon I'd like you to meet. I'm sure you'd enjoy each other.' She arranged a drinks party and Simon Gough and his mother Diana Graves, the actress and writer, were both there, among the guests. Simon was also an actor and writer; his father Michael Gough was already a dear friend of ours and married to Anneke now, but for some reason we had never met Simon. Special meetings come at particular times.

He had a mop of black hair, with Celtic blue eyes which met yours, and loads of passion and enthusiasm for books, poetry and theatre. Gay said much later, 'You spent practically the whole evening talking to each other, sitting on that circular carpet.' An enchanted ring. Usually at parties I had to queue up to speak to Peter, so to have the undivided attention of this vivid young man for a whole evening was a huge bouquet of flowers for me. I felt my spirits lifting.

Simon remembers talking on that carpet on the floor too, and that Peter was somewhere in the room. 'What I loved about you, apart from your warmth and kindness – and the fact you were very pretty,' he says now, 'was that you refused to accept anything but the truth, which could be wearing sometimes. This was possibly what drove Peter slightly round the bend. You were snapping at the heels of truth right from day one, right from that time on the carpet.'

Simon was invited to dinner with some other friends a couple of weeks later. He and Peter seemed to relate well. After that Simon and I would sometimes talk on the phone; I had confided in him about being depressed and having consultations with Sidney Gottlieb. His attitude to my problem was: 'You're a very intelligent young woman and you've not got enough challenges for your creativity. I reckon you should go back to school and finish off your 'A' level English Literature. It would give you practice at writing essays and you might find you have a talent.' This sounded a good idea and Simon went with me to enroll at Westminster Tutors. The tutors themselves were a wonderful body of scholastic women, dedicated to opening up young minds to the splendours of literature. My course covered Shakespeare, Wordsworth, Keats, Byron and Chaucer and Simon came with me on a book-buying trip. It was part-time, naturally, but it worked like a miracle. It stimulated a lot of curiosity and creativity in me and enabled me to pick up the threads of my unfinished grammar school education. (We always have to return to finish the unfinished.)

The satisfaction I gained from all this had a knock-on effect on my relationship with Peter and with everything else. I had much more self-confidence and the effects of Sidney's dynamic injunction, 'You must assert yourself', started to gain momentum. I think Peter was relieved, but a little taken aback when I started to give back as good as I got. For years he had used me as a congenial butt for a great deal of his jokes and eventually it had got to me. It was a progressive grinding down of my own self-esteem. My sense of myself, as I have recognized now, had always been shaky anyway, probably as a result of the mixed feedback I received from my parents as a child. And I am able to see Peter's perspective too. If I watch *Bedazzled* today the echoes in our own life are both plain and painful. In one scene the husband, played by Dudley, showers his wife with fur coats, eventually buying her the *Mona Lisa*, all of which are accepted but don't do the trick. His wife still prefers to spend her time with the music teacher.

I cannot deny that Simon was part of the equation. Three years younger than me, he became my close friend, providing something that was missing from my relationship with Peter. It was not that Peter lacked affectionate warmth, but he had such a steel-plated shield over his vulnerabilities, preventing any admission of sadness or fear, that one was put on guard against one's own deeper feelings, until they accumulated like volcanic lava and came spilling out. There was a certain inevitability that I would fall in love with Simon. (In fact, I think I loved 'falling in love'. I have done a lot of it throughout my life. I seem to want to share myself, or even give myself away. The burden of one's own life can be so onerous.) He was virtually penniless, a struggling writer and actor and not threatening like all those successful actors, journalists and writers that we knew. He was a free spirit who had grown up partly in Italy with bohemian artists like his mother. He had met lots of good actors and painters in his father's house and spent summers in the equally colourful household of his great-uncle, the poet Robert Graves, in Deya on the Balearic island of Mallorca. In the various permutations of relationships among his parents' friends he had witnessed many experimental ways of living. Threesomes, even foursomes, where people enjoyed a sanctioned sexual diversity.

Simon had quickly become a friend of my family, an extended member, delightful with the children. Sue Newling-Ward thought him 'gorgeous' and has an image of him arriving at the house in his big black cloak with a red lining. She used to hear classical music being played in the kitchen and wonder what we were up to. 'He phoned up a lot and came around a lot, but I never knew what your relationship was,' she says.

Speaking to Simon now, after a long absence, he tells me he felt great excitement in getting to know both Peter and me. He seems to have had an astonishing admiration for the older man, whom he describes as 'completely bewitching, very beautiful'. It is surprising I got a look in!

He says that when he came onto the scene Peter and I were surrounded 'nonstop' by famous people. 'I was the odd man out. Not only younger, a lot younger, and I had done nothing. I was there for what I was worth. And Peter was incredibly generous to me. He never, ever was rude; never pointed me out for what I was . . . a nobody. It was always almost a shared joke between us that this was his world, and I was welcome to it. I remember him saying to me once, "God I envy you, Simon", and I said, "What for? What could I possibly have that you envy?" Peter replied, "You are anonymous. You can go into any porn shop in Soho and nobody will know you." I completely understood him.'

Although Simon claims he had no desire for physical contact with Peter, his feelings for him back then were, it turns out, much more sensual than I could ever have supposed. 'I fancied his smell. He smelled extraordinary. It was a chemical ema-nation. It was nothing to do with Aramis, which was his scent, or with Vetiver, as it was later. But his scent was absolutely extraordinary. Quite befuddling. I loved him. He was extra-ordinary to me as a man. He wasn't this cold-hearted cynic that he made himself out to be. He could be cold: he could be cynical. It paid him to be cynical because it protected him, it kept him safe. If I ever had "a pash" on a man it would have been Peter. His magnetism was astonishing.'

Meanwhile, I was still seeing Sidney and sharing my personal awakening with him. He said there were incredible changes in me: a new kind of radiance and generosity. Maybe it was reading Romantic poets such as Keats and Byron, and Shakespeare's *Antony and Cleopatra*, that had rekindled something in me. Perhaps it was the tender love I felt for my daughters.

Simon read and commented on my essays and gave me something Peter had never given: his time. I often visited him in the little wooden house he had built in a friend's garden in Chelsea. 'I was a free man,' he says, 'living in my extraordinary converted washhouse in the garden at Oakleigh Gardens for one guinea a week. That funny house was four feet wide and twelve feet long.'

One night we became lovers, and he clearly knew how to make love. He was tender and passionate, but also sensitive to my shyness. I could not feel guilt; it was all too innocent and beautiful, a natural continuation of our friendship. I don't think either of us believed for a moment that I would leave Peter. I thought that in principle Peter would be grateful to Simon for providing me with what he was unable to supply. In truth, Peter was often completely puzzled by women during his life. He knew that on a certain level he needed WOMAN, but at the same time he had complex feelings about the opposite sex. Sometimes he even came over as misogynistic.

While I was preparing this book Simon wrote to me with astonishing clarity, all these years later, about what happened back then. It is a letter which, although off the cuff and intensely personal, says a lot about the way people are drawn into emotional treachery. Describing us as naive 'babes in the woods', Simon agrees our illicit relationship was based as much on our 'mind swaps', or soulful conversations, as it was on physical attraction. He goes on to analyse the marriage he was to have a hand in uncoupling. His first impression, he writes, was that Peter loved me in a 'contrary sort of way':

His love was not unmixed with possessiveness (you were his, although he seemed not necessarily to be yours), and your perpetual questioning of his motives was a constant source of irritation to him – understandably sometimes. But you had far more guts and character than any of the others gave you credit for, though Peter, to his credit, was occasionally moved to astonished laughter by your temerity, particularly when you had won a minor point at his expense and he could afford to be generous. Your thinking speed in those days was not as quick as his (few people's was) but you thought more deeply, which may have been part of the trouble, because while he thought fast, in fantasy most of the time, you thought more literally, a lightning conductor to his bolts of lightning, diffusing his power deep under the ground – the last thing one should do to a fantasist.

If not class, then at least attitudes to class, was part of the problem between us too, Simon suspects.

At the time when I first met Peter you yourself had become quite upper middle class, part of the New Elite, with nannies and charge cards and credit cards (quite rare in those days) and a lifestyle that had become quite different from your own 'bringing-up'. And yet you didn't seem either to flaunt or resent this – on the contrary, you enjoyed many of the trappings of fame – even while, at the same time, never losing sight of your own beginnings. You certainly weren't ashamed of them, despite Peter seeming to be ashamed of his . . .

His contempt for his beginnings seemed to drive him to re-invent himself every day, with new and ever more sarcastic common voices (Wisty to name but one), and unerring sniper-fire directed at every class but one – the artistic class to which he aspired, that one true classless stratum of society to which he belonged by right, and yet awed him because he didn't belong to it by birth. If only he had truly relaxed into it, things might have been easier for him, and yet if things had been easier for him he wouldn't have evolved into the Peter Cook that he was. He needed to hate and ridicule, lampoon, burst bubbles and bugger up the works of Comfortable Conservative or Smug Labour Thought, of gravy-trainers, whether they were civil servants or union activists. And his sniper-fire was almost always lethal.

Simon and I met at fairly discreet intervals; he was often a guest at our home. Peter was immersed in work. It was, strangely, an unusually happy and creative time, marred only by Daisy's asthma attacks. Simon also suffered from asthma, so was understanding. I was still seeing Sidney Gottlieb professionally and I had made him aware of the relationship with Simon and, though not necessarily condoning my actions, he seemed to have a real grasp of the situation. He could not have failed to be impressed by my flowering. (A woman becomes more beautiful when a man loves her.) I believed that Sidney would find an appropriate way to discuss the situation with Peter. I felt, as did Simon, that Sidney was acting as a discreet conduit between husband and wife, arranging some sort of modern, arm's length absolution for us. How very naive of me! It was my responsibility, of course. Never one to hide the truth for long, and, realizing Peter had chosen not to see what was happening, I decided he should be told. I needed to clear my conscience and, since his reaction to my affair with Ben Carruthers before our marriage had been so sensible and statesmanlike, I thought I had little to fear.

That night Peter had come in from some press function. He had been drinking, but I didn't think he was drunk. He went upstairs to his study to make some phone calls. I went up too and waited for him to give me his attention. I knew Simon might turn up that evening, but I wanted to get it off my chest. I began to explain, haltingly, as I watched Peter's eyes narrow.

By the time I had spoken, Peter had become violent. He hit me and kicked me down the stairs in a fit of rage. Gerry Slattery, who tended to me a few days later, said I looked as if the Irish rugby team had used me as a football.

As I arrived in a dishevelled state on the ground floor, the front door bell rang. It was Simon. Peter immediately, without a word, punched him in the jaw, breaking it in two places, and then said, 'If you come here again, I'll kill you!' Poor, poor Simon. I wanted to follow him, but knew I would be locked out of the house, away from my children. I sat on the front doorstep, sobbing. Luckily the girls slept through all of this. Peter telephoned Sidney, who arrived shortly afterwards. Simon's father Mick came for him. I think Sidney took me to his home. I was sedated for some time after that; the following days are a blur. I do know that Peter and Sidney, together and separately, tried to intimidate me into forgetting all about Simon. At some point Peter's attitude to the situation softened and he became remorseful. I now know that he even apologized to Mick Gough for hitting his son. Part of me still felt justified: my actions had been those of a neglected wife and were based on the admittedly unreliable assumption that Peter was 'in the picture'. The other part of me, however, felt I was in the wrong, although certainly not deserving of the brutal treatment I had received.

Back at our house the next morning Sue had thankfully carried on as normal with the children, getting their breakfast and taking them to playschool. At lunchtime I had phoned: 'You asked how the children were and I said they were absolutely fine – which they were,' she says.

The next evening she let herself into the house and found Peter sitting grimly in the living room, facing the door in his leather green chair. He asked her if she had seen me. She hadn't.

Simon's recollection of these violent events has not dimmed over the years either. 'I had expected a grown-up settlement of the matter, in the French or Roman style. Instead it was a moment of primal instinct and I came off the worse,' he remembers, still full of regrets. 'I was terribly sad because it was the end of a friendship. The end of what I regarded as a perfect friendship, because I was making love to his wife, but he knew, so it was all right. I thought Peter liked that because it took the pressure off him. It worked. Peter was happy. I have never seen him happier than when we were together.'

Barbara Downes also remembers this terrible period. She says she came to visit me one evening and went upstairs to my bedroom. 'All you had around you was a bath towel and you were black and blue,' she says. I suggested to Terry that he provide Peter with a boxer's punchball to exorcise his anger and it was delivered within days, taking a place in our dressing room. Such a light-hearted response was a symptom of an era when such violent incidents between married couples were dismissed by police as mere 'domestics'.

After my incarceration I decided to stay with my parents and I travelled there alone. They had always left the door open to me, despite a certain distance that had grown between us. In eight years I had followed a steep trajectory from a rural life in the cabbage fields of Bedfordshire to my extraordinary showbiz life with Peter. The apparently desirable world I had embraced had cut me off from my roots. Peter, perhaps, had been attracted to me because I was so different; yet at the same time we did share an intuitive capacity and a wish to penetrate hypocrisy. Peter's gaze, though, was usually extended out towards the world, so it seemed I had to do the inner searching for both of us. How sad that we could not speak openly and that he could not unburden his fears and misgivings.

I was shattered and bewildered and still sporting two black

eyes when I drove to my mother and father at St Neots. They had managed to buy their own house, a chocolate-box thatched cottage with a large garden in a hamlet, surrounded by lots of open countryside. I was able to reconnect with my love of nature as a healing force. My parents were understanding and protective towards me. The question had to be asked: could I ever share my life again with a man who could be so violent?

It had never been my intention to leave Peter. I was committed to what we had built together, and to the children. I was just exploring ways in which everyone might get what they needed. How foolish. For Peter it was his pride that was most bruised, despite him having had affairs during our engagement and then lying about them. He found my relationship with Simon threatening, while I had thought the fact they liked each other made it a shared love. But now the possibility of seeking a divorce began to emerge. The prospects were unthinkable either way. I would ring the children and end up in tears. Peter wanted to talk to me, but I couldn't bring myself to speak to him.

I went out on long walks into the countryside trying to find some clarity and guidance. One day I found myself in one of those open, perceptive states of mind, watching nature, very alert. I had a notepad with me and wrote what turned out to be a communication to Peter, a metaphor or allegory that unfolded before me:

I am sitting on the edge of a field, balancing my notepad on my knee. I wanted to be alone for I know that I have to find my own answers. Soaking in the peace of the countryside is balm to my tired mind and bruised body.

On the horizon are two dun-coloured creatures which could be rabbits, partridges or female pheasants. Rabbits would have been nice – furry, shy creatures – but these, as they came closer are pecking, female pheasants. I tried a few of my bird calls and to my astonishment many birds flew overhead and perched in a nearby tree with a flurry of cheerful and comforting chirruping. Some came very close, pecking fallen grain on the ground. A thrush sings very boldly and now a nightingale, as the light diminishes. The sun is setting very quickly.

The horizon is straight, interrupted only by a few apologetic bushes and one antlered oak tree. And all the time creeping up on my right-hand side is the male pheasant. He is curious, pretending not to be as he pecks about, but clearly coming in my direction. I wonder how near he will get before I have to leave.

Now the male pheasant is carefully picking his way towards me, but he's being so tentative he's left his womenfolk far behind. My hands and feet are so cold . . . and the light is going. If I stay here until he comes I'll be dead with cold and inactivity, if I whistle at him to come he will be frightened. Will he reach me in time? His progress is so slow. If he reaches me what am I going to tell him? We speak different languages, we are different species – and yet we are interested in each other.

I am going to have to go, because although there are pretty birds in the trees telling me to stay, the male pheasant comes forward three paces and then retreats two. The light is going, the warmth is going, I cannot go on playing games with this beautiful creature. Come night-time when nobody is around, when nobody else can see, he may come to me, but I will be frozen, numb.

It was one of those pieces of grace that I was able to write in allegorical form rather than justifying, rationalizing, accusing – all those things we tend to do when in a tight corner.

> Beyond ideas of right and wrong doing,
> There is a field, a singing field,
> I'll meet you there. *Rumi*

It certainly dissolved a great deal of the surface anger and punitive zeal in Peter. As I understood later, he wept upon receiving this letter. I had only once seen Peter shed a tear in our ten years together (and that was when we had to have the cat put down). Not that it was my aim to make Peter cry, but since I was an emotional person myself I longed to be able to share a mutual propensity for making mistakes, to feel that we were friends, as well as husband and wife. Was this wrong of me?

It had been healing to spend time with my parents, who remained surprisingly tactful (not easy for my mother). They didn't ask too many questions or judge. They were simply concerned for me, and for Lucy and Daisy. Over the years we had grown apart, I am ashamed to say partly because I felt they were unsophisticated and would not easily fit into my new life. In fact, of course, I had picked up some of their own snobbishness towards the country folk around them and taken it up another notch.

More walking in the country, accompanied by the family's long-haired dachshund, Fritz, helped put things into perspective. My father felt strongly that he should go and talk to Peter but I asked him to wait a while. I made an effort to catch up with my exam work for the literature course, since it had been such a lifeline. Viewing my privileged existence in Church Row from St Neots made me realize what a fantastic roller-coaster ride I had been on. It had alienated me from what had always supported and sustained me as a child – nature, and a sort of spiritual matrix upon which to base my judgements.

Carried along by laughter, fun, exciting events and opportunities; becoming a mother so young and still not knowing who I was at the age of twenty-nine – all of this had made me lose my moorings. I had forgotten to 'tether my camel'. Depression can arise from too great a split between our imagined selves and our real, authentic selves. What's more, we were all living in a time of accelerating change. I believe the speed at which this was happening was itself pathological. (Anthony Newley's musical *Stop the World, I Want to Get Off* was a real *cri de cœur*: the world seemed to be spinning out of control.) So when I thought I could carry off something unorthodox within a relationship – something everybody else was reportedly doing – I was actually visited with what seemed to be the punitive wrath of the Old Testament.

I realized now how economically vulnerable I was too. Peter owned the house; it was in his name. We did not share a bank account. I had little idea of how much he earned; he was always rather secretive about this. I did know that he had Swiss bank accounts, but he gave me adequate housekeeping money and I had accounts at a few stores. That was how it was and I had accepted it.

So now we were at a crossroads: Peter wanted me back, but I was frightened of him and also scared of a future without him. We had become such a habit and had two little girls we doted on. There was much that merited salvaging. I returned to Church Row feeling restored, but something of an exile from my own home, regardless of having poured so much of myself into making it a warm and friendly place. I agreed to put an end to my affair with Simon, but would not agree to eradicating our friendship altogether, the core of our encounters, our mosaic of shared interests. It was impossible for Peter to own my emotional life. We often try to do this to others, but it is futile; we can own nothing of another except what he or she chooses to give.

In fact, of course, Simon's part in our lives inevitably did fade from this moment, by his own admission. 'I realized that I was out of my depth, that I didn't quite grasp the new morality, and retired from the fray – to your relief, I think, in some ways. You had a final battle to fight with the father of your children, and I had no place in it.'

Nevertheless, it was not going to be easy for me to find a way forward. Sue Newling-Ward remembers me asking her opinion in blank desperation one evening: 'You were at the top of the stairs and you sat down near where I was in the utility room and you said, "Do you think I should get divorced?" And I said, "I just don't know."'

Island of Forgetfulness

As he escaped through the window, Nana had closed it quickly, too late to catch him, but his shadow had not had time to get out. Slam went to the window and snapped it off. Mrs Darling decided to roll the shadow up and put it carefully in a drawer until a fitting opportunity came for telling her husband.

It was Wendy who tried to stitch it back on: 'I shall sew it on for you, my little man.'

'How clever I am,' he crowed rapturously, on receiving his shadow back. 'Oh, the cleverness of me!'

It is humiliating to have to confess that this conceit of Peter's was one of his most fascinating qualities. To put it with brutal frankness, there never was a cockier boy. But for the moment his Wendy was shocked.

'You conceited boy!' she exclaimed, with frightful sarcasm. 'Of course, I did nothing!'

'You did a little,' Peter said carelessly and continued to dance.

'A little!' she replied with hauteur. 'If I am no use I can at least withdraw.'

'Wendy,' he said, 'don't withdraw. I can't help crowing when I'm pleased with myself.'

'Wendy,' he continued, in a voice that no woman has ever been able to resist, 'Wendy, one girl is more use than twenty boys.'

Extract from J. M. Barrie's *Peter Pan and Wendy*

Simon's parting gift to me was a gesture that furnished me with an important introduction to the next chapter in my life. He suggested I take a holiday with the girls, to recuperate, on the island of Mallorca and he gave me a letter of introduction to his great-uncle, the poet Robert Graves, author of *Goodbye to All That, The White Goddess* and *I, Claudius*. Peter would only go along with this if I was accompanied by my sister Patsy and her husband Roderick, and if Sue Newling-Ward joined the party too. I think he was suspicious that Simon might be out there waiting for me. But Simon simply hoped to find some way forward for me. It was typical of his imaginative nature to suggest something to heal the wounds.

In the run-up to Easter, I went home and, with relief, bonded once more with the girls, who were overjoyed to see me back and wouldn't let me out of their sight to begin with. I was determined to keep studying and take the exams. Was I trying to ignore the punching episode and carry on regardless? I felt, I think, that I had to make the best of it all. We are not taught enough in life about the really important things, such as how relationships change within marriage and the stresses of parenting. Only much later I learned from women friends that they too had experienced substantially reduced libido after bearing children.

It is important not to argue that what happened to me, and to lots of women like me, was simply the fault of an unenlightened husband. It was more complicated. Middle-class women wanted to hold onto some of the security that traditional values offered, just as much as we wanted our new freedoms.

'If wives were victims,' says Gay Gottlieb, 'we had made ourselves a victim because we felt that we were; that it was our place. We were brought up to do that, and men were brought up to think, "Have my tea on the table when I get home". However sophisticated we were, we were all still doing that.'

Patsy and Roderick had driven me back to London and stayed until the arrangements were made for Mallorca. Peter turned his charm on them, making them feel pretty important. He was making sure I would be properly monitored by my companions. Since he was financing the trip, they felt beholden to him, which brought out the choleric in me. I was not having anybody monitoring my movements and I made that pretty clear. Lucy and Daisy were innocently excited though. Now three and four and a half, they loved the sea.

Once we arrived on the island we were driven to the tourist resort of Paguera, fairly undeveloped at that time. The warmth and spring flowers were exquisite. The water was a little too cold to swim in, but the children paddled and we made sand-castles. Friendships sprung up with other children and with Luis who looked after the pedalboats, a particular favourite of Sue's. Patsy and Rod had brought a guitar with them and serenaded us on the terrace of our rented villa, while I grilled fresh fish on the fire outside.

There was a lemon tree in the garden and I found it a delight to be able to go and pick lemons to squeeze over the fish, and to make fresh lemonade. There was wild fennel by the roadside, which we used in our barbecues. How wonderful to live out-doors, breathing the wonderful air and not wearing many clothes. And how wonderful to be away from phones, flashing cameras, the front door bell forever ringing. Fantastic too to be away from people who were constantly trying to dazzle each other with their wit – effusive at one moment and barbed at the next. It was great to make contact with the locals. With the exception of our maid, who tried in all manner of ways to fleece us, the Mallorcans were hospitable and willing to share their island. Tourism was in its infancy at that time and the place was relatively undiscovered. Lucy and Daisy soon learned the word *helado* (ice cream) and Daisy's asthma disappeared for that brief time.

After some days I rented a car to drive to Deya to meet Robert Graves and to explore the island. I set off early one morning wearing a white lacy dress and open sandals. I was already more relaxed and hopeful – hopeful about the future, about finding a way to redeem the marriage and yet find my own voice. Getting used to driving on the right on those precipitous mountain roads was quite a challenge. As I drove along I could smell the asphodel; a slightly bitter, acrid smell that permeated the island in spring, from those tall pale pink spikes of lilies with sage-grey leaves. At one point I lost my way and stopped to have a *café con leche* and seek directions to Deya and the poet. 'Ah, señor Graves, la poeta,' exclaimed the proprietor of the café. He was clearly well known in the area. The proprietor pointed out a startling road, winding intrepidly along the side of the mountains; sheer drop on one side to the sparkling blue sea beneath. 'Heavens,' I thought, wondering how many literary pilgrims had made their way along this narrow road to seek audience with the great scholar. There were another ten kilometres of this breathtaking road, and sometimes lorries would come lurching from the opposite direction, usually in the middle of the road. You had to have some bravura to cope with this in the blinding heat of the day.

It was siesta time when I arrived at Canellun (The Far Away House). It nestled into the base of the mountain, with a broad terrace bearing fig and orange trees. They were expecting me, but Robert Graves was sleeping. He kept a well-ordered rhythm to his day, with which nobody should interfere. I was met by Juan, his youngest son, who offered me a cold beer. He was handsome and slender, a little shy; he could have been

Mallorcan, so bronzed and dark. I thought of Simon spending so many of his youthful holidays in this dramatic setting. He had been working on a Greek theatre in an olive grove overlooking the sea which belongs to Canellun; a special place, built of grey and silver limestone where plays and poetry have since been performed.

Juan was interesting to talk to, but I got the impression it was not altogether easy to be the youngest son of such an icon and to live as a foreigner in this tiny mountain village. Deya attracted many would-be poets and writers, however, drawn by the mythology surrounding Robert Graves, Gertrude Stein and other bohemian characters of the fifties and sixties who had lived there. Situated in the north of the island, the village nestles on a hill. A church stands on the summit, a neat row of cypresses leading up to it. The almost biblical atmosphere together with the lush tangle of fruit trees made it a real Garden of Eden, prompting the Spanish writer Santiago Rusiñol to write:

Among the branches of a fig tree appear clusters of grapes from a neighbouring vine. From the vine emerge the plums of a tree that embraces it, and the plum tree produces oranges lent to it by an orange tree that has no room to mature. The tones of green are so varied ... everything grows, blossoms and fructifies as if to relieve its heart of some burden in gifts to this little village, like a latter-day Bethlehem.

And this is how I felt, wanting to relieve my heart, longing to unburden it. I caught myself wishing Simon had been there to share this moment with me. But no, I must shield my heart against such feelings. That part of my life was over. Simon, though, had gifted me with this introduction to a special new place and people. Now it was up to me.

Quietly, but with palpable presence, the tall, striking figure of Robert Graves appeared on the terrace. What a beautiful head, with a high brow framed by unruly curls of white hair and a strong Roman nose. He was smoking a thin cigar and wearing a comfy old cardigan, darned at the elbows. 'Well, who do we have here?' he said, kissing me on both cheeks in the local fashion. I was a little overawed, but only briefly, as he was clearly another of those raconteurs who loved an audience. He asked after Simon and seemed to know something of our situation, but dismissed any hiccups as a storm in a teacup. Love was for the having, as essential to life as breathing, and it had to be as varied as a rainbow – many colours, many people. No one person could supply anybody else with all that they needed. This all seemed very simple and straightforward and, of course, from a man's point of view it was. I wondered whether Beryl, his wife, was allotted the same kind of freedoms. I didn't argue with him.

He took me to the end of his garden where there were many more olive trees and pointed up to the mountains soaring into jagged peaks at dizzying heights. 'See these mountains?' he said. 'They are full of iron ore and they set up a magnetic field that affects people here very strongly, some more than others. You have to be strong to live here, to withstand this powerful magnetic field.' I was a little bemused by this at the time and full of awe for this man and his insights. But I had a sense of how claustrophobic it could be to live on that narrow plateau, fringed by the great mountains on one side and the precipitous drop to the blue sea on the other. I was to learn later that what he had said was true: the magnetic pull of that field was known to interfere with shipping radar out at sea. It was true too that over the years to come I certainly did witness people behaving dramatically in that region, but maybe it was the vino and the dope!

Above Peter, Lucy and me on holiday in Barbados, 1964.

Right Dudley fully dressed, snoozing on the beach in Corsica.

Below Me relaxing in Corsica after picking out the cactus prickles.

Left Poor little fish! But Peter was proud.

Below Whilst I hauled up a nice 'Porgy'. Grenada, 1962.

Above Daisy is introduced
to the world while Dad
grows a moustache for
The Wrong Box.

Right Spotty Muldoon is
delivered on Christmas
Day, 1965. Lucy was not
too sure about him!

Above Christmas Dinner at No. 17 Church Row with Dudley and Suzy.

Below John and Annie Bird, Suzy and Dudley, and Christopher Garmony dancing in the background.

Right Peter 'butlering' at Park Hall with Harriet's mother, Ariel Crittall, and her brother, Charles Crittall.

Right The press photo showing Peter and me on the way to court during the Lord Russell libel case in 1966.

Left Lucky me, dressed in an original Hylan Booker design, standing with the great man himself.

Below Peter and Lucy in the heat of Mallorca.

Above Daisy's wedding day. From left to right: Mary Rose Hardy, Peter, Simon Hardy, Daisy, Dr Hugh Hardy and me.

Below Christmas in Mallorca, 2005. From left to right: Ben and Matthew Cawdery (Lucy's sons), Daisy, me, Benjy the dog and Lucy with Elle (Daisy's daughter).

Robert took me into his study, packed with extraordinary artefacts, talismans and figurines, many of which he handed to me to hold. I felt privileged, sensing he had connected with me and so was able to share things quite intimately. He obviously felt at liberty enough that day to recast for me some of the most important stories I had been brought up on. He offered me a more credible explanation, as he thought, of the story of the virgin birth of Christ to Mary: it was, he said, based on the ritual of a young Jewish man simply passing under the skirts of a virgin in order to be reborn. Well . . . maybe. He went on with a great flourish to state that Jesus Christ had survived the crucifixion and gone travelling. His grave, he said, was to be found in a remote corner of India. All this information had apparently come to him as a result of lengthy research into ancient documents. Then he took me to the other side of the terrace and, pointing out to sea, said, 'Out there lies the submerged continent of Atlantis!'

It was evening now and I was introduced to his very sensible wife, Beryl, without whom I think his life would have fallen to pieces. She was strong, firm, noneffusive and very much 'there'. Other people started emerging from behind the scenes too – Robert always seemed to have lots of acolytes, 'some terrible old sycophants who hung around' as Simon has since described it to me.

We were to go out to dine at his son William's restaurant. William had married a Catalan girl and together they ran a hotel in the village. Robert was rather dismissive about this development in his family. 'No member of my family, hitherto, has ever been a grocer!' he snorted. Nevertheless, their food and wine were good and, sitting next to Robert at the head of the table, I was treated to more wonderful stories. Better still, he sang lots of lusty ballads, getting everyone else to join in.

That night I stayed at William's hotel, having contacted my

family and Peter to let them know I was all right. It was strange to speak to Peter from such a different world and we didn't have much to say. Simon has pointed out to me since that there are some similarities between two such talented and charismatic men as Peter and Robert Graves. Having observed them both at close quarters he detected a special kind of self-possession they shared.

'It is confidence. Or arrogance; knowing you can pull it off. It is based on genius and . . . just fucking well knowing you can make it all right with the aura you give off. Robert had it totally, but it was less premeditated than with Peter.'

Soon it would be time to leave. I bought some fluffy ensaimadas, the turban-shaped breakfast buns which are a speciality of the islands, and shared breakfast with Robert before he shut himself in his study to write. His poems, he told me, generally involved an average of eleven rewritings. He was so meticulous, a craftsman and a true scholar. As we waved goodbye he said to me knowingly, 'You'll be back.' He wasn't wrong.

I decided to return to Paguera another way, taking a detour past a little town called Pollensa. Scanning the map, this name had leapt out at me. I cut through the mountain pass and at Lluc Monastery the road wound down through Caimari, with its exquisite terraces planted by the Moors centuries earlier. The gnarled and twisted forms of the silvery olive trees gave animation to the landscape. Along a little back road I came upon Pollensa, overshadowed by its 'pudding-basin-shaped' mountain and topped by the monastery of Santa Maria. The mountain's shape was echoed by a smaller hill known as the Calvario, reached by a flight of 365 steps which ran up through pencil-shaped cypresses to the chapel on the peak.

I parked and walked into the plaza. The streets were empty and soon I knew why, for the entire town seemed to be gathered in the central square. The silence there was broken only by people sobbing. Children had hastily gathered flowers from the wayside. Their attention was directed towards a funeral procession heading towards the church as the town band played a doleful requiem. Coffins were being carried: some large ones and some smaller ones, and some really tiny ones. I lost count of how many. The mood in the square was solemn and full of grief and I was very moved by this show of community solidarity at a time of loss. Later I found out that a whole family, three generations, all squeezed inside their tiny car, had come to grief in a collision with a large coach. All were killed. I turned quietly away, not wanting to appear a voyeur to such open and manifest suffering. Somehow, though, I did identify with them and I knew I had found a place with which I could have a long-term relationship. I drove back to Paguera in a thoughtful state, deeply impressed by the events of the past two days.

Arriving at our little villa, everybody seemed cheerful. Lucy and Daisy were deep golden all over and Sue's romance with Luis-of-the-Boats was flourishing. This meant everyone got free rides on the pedalos. All too quickly, however, it was time to pack up. The taxi came to take us to Palma, back into the unknown. But I had been captivated by the island, by its magic and its mystery – the Island of Calm, the Island of Forget-fulness.

Peter was delighted to see us back. He was not good at being alone and fending for himself and the house had a slightly forlorn air. But we soon put that right. He was trying to be very affectionate but I was still feeling inwardly bruised. It would take time to forgive, for both of us.

The screenplay for *Bedazzled* was now ready and a filming schedule in place. With Stanley Donen, the man who had made *Singin' in the Rain*, as producer/director the finances had come in. In film-making terms it was still a limited budget, around

$600,000, but Peter and Dudley were really chuffed about it all and so was I. Of course, I did not know then to what extent our various marital difficulties would be drawn upon, woven as they were into the comic Faustian struggle; in a pretty exaggerated way, of course.

Patsy and Roderick were off to Paris to participate in some folk music festival and I would miss their company. Although, as sisters, Patsy and I often had run-ins, she was larger than life and it had been good to reconnect during this holiday together. Lucy was attending a playgroup and my own new term was also due to begin, so we were drawn into a new rhythm that shaped the days. It was difficult, however, to find any rhythm in Peter's work: he was either at home reading all the newspapers, seeing Dudley, creating in the study, or, if filming, up at 5.00 or 6.00 a.m. and out till late. Such is showbiz, I know, but it was hard to weave a family life around such erratic schedules.

Our marriage began to knit together again, but Mallorca had struck such a deep chord in my soul that I wanted to return. I wanted Peter to come and experience the place too. He spoke passable Spanish and loved swimming and the heat too, so we planned a trip for the early summer, before filming began.

In the meantime, I had a new project – getting a young sculptor friend, Nathaniel, to design and build a Wendy house for Lucy and Daisy. It was a beautiful design that could be dismantled easily and was painted in gay colours. It was to afford the children many hours of magical play. They would gather leaves from the trees to use as pretend money and turn the house into a post office, a tea room, a hospital, or whatever. To this day they cherish their memories of that Wendy house. 'It was stunning, amazing, and very imaginatively done,' says Lucy, who had one day chanced upon it being built in the loft where her dad wrote. 'I saw this guy painting the door and I asked what he was doing. I was told he was just building a wardrobe.'

Anneke would come round often with her daughter Polly. By now she had also produced Jasper, her son by Mick Gough and an adorable blond child. Anneke and I would have sewing sessions, making wacky clothes for our children. She was sympathetic too to my situation, strange though it was to think she was Simon's stepmother! The children played happily together in the Wendy house. Harriet and her daughter Emily were also frequent visitors, Emily looking so much like Nick, with great brown eyes and a mischievous smile.

My English Literature exams were looming. By some miracle of will I had completed all my assignments, although the Old English in Chaucer was something of a challenge, but *Antony and Cleopatra*, Lord Byron and Wordsworth had all become bedfellows and I immersed myself in their imagery. The exam paper was a joy and I left the room feeling good.

The dinner parties started up again with a definite Mediterranean direction, inspired by the wonderful produce I had found in the markets of Mallorca. Judy Scott-Fox, now a freelance actor's agent, had taken on Alan Bates as a client and he came to dine with us. What a delightful man he was. Through Ken Tynan, who had become rather intimate friends with Princess Margaret and Tony Armstrong-Jones, Peter and I were invited to St James's Palace. Margaret Rose, as she was known, had expressed a desire to meet Peter and we were to join them for a light supper and then go on to the theatre to see the show *Hair*. This was upping the social stakes somewhat, especially in the light of the joyfully, disrespectful sketch 'Royal Box', performed by Peter and Dudley back in *Beyond the Fringe* days. In the sketch, Royal fan Dudley is asked by Peter if he really spends twelve and sixpence each night on a theatre ticket just on the off-chance of spotting a member of the Royal Family, to which Dudley replies: 'Well, they're not worth the fifteen shillings.'

Margaret, having married a commoner, now had her feet in the artistic, literary and theatre world as well as the monarchy, a difficult balancing act. She expected the curtsy and to be addressed as 'Ma'am', yet she also wanted a certain intimacy with the brilliant talent of the age. This made it confusing for her new companions in terms of etiquette.

Peter and Dudley were being measured for their costumes in *Bedazzled*, of which there would be many – from the uniforms of General Post Office telecommunications engineers to the habits of an order of leaping nuns. They were in high spirits about the film. In fact, it was hard now to be anything but cheerful around the two of them. Dudley then was so utterly lovable, despite or because of his love of women and song. The boy from Dagenham could hardly believe his luck when they signed up Raquel Welch for the role of Lust, one of the Seven Deadly Sins, while Peter had invited his old Cambridge and Establishment team chum Eleanor Bron to take the leading female role of the waitress whom Dudley adores. Eleanor was by this stage a comparative silver-screen veteran, having already appeared in *Help!* alongside the Beatles. She tells me now she didn't feel experienced at all at the time and had been terribly nervous on the set with the Beatles. 'I was very shy. I was too young and lacking in any kind of confidence. People hear about the glamour of this work but they very rarely hear about how frightened you are,' she says.

Working with Peter again was not quite so daunting, although Eleanor shares the consensus view that her old friend was no great actor.

'But he did come to be wonderful later, though. He was so wonderful in that episode of *One Foot in the Algarve*, for

Peter in Bedazzled

example. He wasn't an actor and yet the four things he did at the end on television with Clive Anderson were wonderful too.'

Deep down Peter still wanted to be a rock star, never mind an actor, and he was always eager to perform in such a role. In *Bedazzled* he compromised by speaking to the music of a hauntingly cruel, anti-love song, in which a cold and blankly aloof rock star asserts his hatred of a woman.

Among the things I found rather alien in Peter's life was a new obsession – the World Domination League, an idea Peter had been mulling over at the same time as he was developing the Faustian/Mephistophelian theme for his film script. In 1965 he employed one of several lovely secretaries from *Private Eye* to busy herself with publicity, effectively setting up a cottage industry to promote the League from our home. Postcards picturing Peter in two modes, first as his dashing, glamorous, besuited self, and second as the flat-capped E. L. Wisty, were sent out as a stamp of membership. Both E. L. Wisty and Spotty Muldoon were then to be set loose, hypothetically actually walking into people's living rooms with the simple, but surreal query, 'Excuse me, we are the World Domination League – may we dominate you?'

Among the aims of the League were:
1. Total domination of the world by 1965.
2. Domination of the astral spheres quite soon, too.
3. The finding of lovely ladies for Spotty Muldoon within the foreseeable future.
4. Stopping the government peering up the pipes at us and listening to all we say.
5. E. L. Wisty for God.

There was some seriousness embedded within all this. Not only was there a bit of genuine political satire intended, but also, in some unacknowledged way, I suspect Peter actually relished playing with the idea of wresting power and taking control of the country. I believe Peter, exposed increasingly to the world of celebrity, to uncritical attention and to money, underwent some deep personal changes. Despite all his protestations, his idealism was under threat. Having previously shown disdain for certain friends who had 'sold out' to join the ever-expanding world of advertising, to my surprise he agreed to do a series of E. L. Wisty sketches to sell Watney's beer in exchange for a considerable amount of money. He had, many times, categorically stated that fame could never change him, but this decision looked to me like the thin end of the wedge: he was losing some of his incorruptible principles, the most valuable thing he had inherited from his honest father.

The coiled spring I had always detected inside Peter now appeared to be fast uncoiling. While it was exciting to witness with him the demolition of all kinds of orthodox dogma in society at large, a kind of personal recklessness was creeping in. I wondered where it was all leading; as a parent I felt he and I should be building some new values. These concerns were behind my depression and were part of the reason I had gone to a psychiatrist. (In fact, I had by now stopped seeing Sidney Gottlieb professionally. It had all become too murky, especially as he had never submitted a bill, despite requests. My own attitude to the Gottliebs was rather cautious from here on, although Peter remained a close friend and shared happy holidays with them and Lucy and Daisy.) Having stood shoulder to shoulder with Peter in the front line of the firing squad as traditional values were gunned down, where could I now find some help? My continuing admiration for R. D. Laing's work now led me to seek him out in person. He approached the study of the mind in a liberated, intuitive way. One particular section of *The Divided Self* had made me hope he would understand a complex person like Peter. This passage seemed especially apt.

> His ideal was never to give himself away to others. That is, he was not simply and spontaneously himself. Consequently he practised the most tortuous equivocation towards others in the parts that he played.
>
> The outward appearance could not reveal that his 'personality' was no true self-expression but was largely a series of impersonations. The part he regarded himself as having been playing most of his schooldays was that of a rather precocious schoolboy with a sharp wit, but somewhat cold.

Here was a man who I thought could help me.

It was not so easy to get an appointment with Laing, of course. His revolutionary techniques had hit the headlines. I imagine I pulled a few strings, which, as the wife of a celebrity, I had learned you can do. I went along to see him with apprehension, having invested a lot in his writings. The room I was shown into was, as I remember, painted black. In it sat R. D. Laing looking like an Aubrey Beardsley drawing: hooded eyes, high cheekbones, thinning longish hair, dressed in black with a light scattering of dandruff across his shoulders. A curling sandwich sat on a plate on the arm of his chair. He pulled contemplatively on his pipe.

I cannot recall him saying a word to me, or smiling. I think he gestured to get me to start speaking about my situation and just sat there, listening. This made me nervous, so I probably babbled, spurting things out willy-nilly. Then there would be long pauses. Very disconcerting. Perhaps he was developing a new technique, but I found it most challenging and lacking in warmth. This 'technique', or whatever it was, was not for me! I decided I would stick to reading his books and I never returned, but sometimes we would come across him at gatherings of the 'successful ones', often in his cups. All in all, this psychiatry business was becoming a bit of a dead end, but it didn't stop me wanting to explore the complexities of human relationships.

Our friends Caroline and Nathan Silver had recently relocated to England, Nathan landing a teaching professorship at Cambridge School of Architecture. They too were experiencing some marital hiccups, so Caroline and I were able to confide in each other. But their problems didn't stop them throwing open their large Cambridge home at the weekends. Peter and I would go up from time to time. There were always a lot of G & Ts, nice food, elaborate parlour games and sometimes croquet too, weather permitting. One particular weekend we were introduced to Germaine Greer, who had just exploded onto the Cambridge scene accompanied by stories of how she had supposedly appeared for dinner at High Table wearing little beneath her academic gown. She was suitably outrageous, but I didn't really enjoy all that sharpened wit and harsh feminism. She was not good at listening to others. I think she and Nathan were involved, but this didn't stop her flirting with Peter (who, I believe, picked up the invitation at a later date). Dear Caroline, so trusting and perhaps a little naive, didn't seem to have homed in on this extra-curricular scenario.

Caroline and Nathan would also visit us in London and at one bibulous dinner Nathan and Peter got carried away with the idea of building a fantastic conservatory at the back of our house, and Nathan did go on to create a wonderful design with a bridge. Nathan says, however, that he had his doubts from the beginning about this glass castle in the air. 'You were actually getting on very badly at that point,' he says. 'I thought the pair of you were doomed and I wondered if this feathering of the nest was his idea or some component of something else or to make you happy.'

Didn't we have enough rooms in our house already? Yet Peter thought it would please me, so he commissioned the design, which never got built. And I wasn't sure, when I met Nathan recently, whether he ever got paid.

'I did have to nag him for the money. I did a lot of work. I did a design and a model. It was lovely. The roof was a kind of funnel that would catch rainwater and go into a pool in the middle. God knows whether we would have got planning permission.'

During this period, which was a rather uncomfortable one on some levels, my father kept his promise to come and have a 'man-to-man' talk with Peter. However, Peter instantly charmed him into his own camp, with an ease I could hardly believe, although I should have known from previous experience that this was often his strategy when in difficulties. He really should have gone into the Foreign Office! I had pictured my father taking up my cause, but there were to be no duels at dawn. Instead we invited Jonathan and Rachel Miller to supper and enjoyed a highly entertaining evening during which my father (on his own for once) was able to shine and converse, at last, with 'intellectuals', his abiding hope throughout his life, chained as he felt he had been to people 'with the intelligence of cabbages'. When the guests had gone, my father, admittedly with a tongue loosened by wine, exclaimed, 'Aren't we Jews intelligent!' I was astounded. My father could certainly have been taken for someone with Jewish origins; indeed, the odd person in our little Bedford village would whisper about this possibility, but he had always denied it. Now here he was, claiming he was one. There had always been something of a mystery about my father's parentage; I never knew my paternal grandfather, who was dead or had disappeared. I believe my father's mother had been widowed with one child, his sister Effie, and had then begun another relationship with a man of European Jewish origins. My father's piece of information, unsubstantiated though it was, somehow provided a restorative present to me. It somehow supplied a possible reason why I had felt different as a child. And it certainly might explain my love of feeding people! I promised myself to investigate further one day.

As I saw my father off at the station the next day he said to me, 'You'll be all right, Wendy. Peter loves you very much. He told me so.' What is love then? It has so many faces. We all search for it, but can we truly give it? Marriage for my parents' generation was for life; divorce was not a possibility for a wife and would have been economically disastrous. So did I now have choices? It was suddenly clear to me how very precarious my situation in this marriage was. Peter owned me, the house, the children. We were part of his goods and chattels on a certain level. For me, as a rather independent person, this was untenable. Apart from the emotional scars left by my interlude with Simon, it was proving difficult to build a trusting relationship with Peter again. But I was willing to try.

I had to adopt a strategy that would give me some personal security and independence. Only through parity of status could the freedom to love and respect be reconstituted somehow. Whether I worked this out rationally, or by instinct, I don't know, but I was moving towards something radical. Mallorca was the place that offered so much that we needed, primarily somewhere with the sun, sea and open spaces that had such a favourable influence on Daisy's health, indeed on all of us. Seeing the delight of those little girls in that environment had been marvellous. It was a society that adored children, treating them like little princes and princesses, but also giving them the stability to grow into confident adults. Seven years in a capital city for me, the country girl, was enough. I found it stultifying.

Of course, because of Peter's career there was no way I could expect him to relocate to a Mediterranean island, but the intention was that the family would enjoy special time with him, away from fans, phones and agents. Our life had become a circus in which I felt trapped. I had also begun to suspect hidden infidelities. It really wasn't my world any more and I couldn't bear the thought of our two children turning out like some of the precocious showbiz offspring that I'd met.

Some scientists say that after seven years each cell in our body has changed at least once, so perhaps it is the most natural thing to happen, to grow and to make changes. ('But, you're not the person I married!' comes the familiar cry.) We can't be petrified, held in one place. Somehow I managed to persuade Peter that buying a place in Mallorca was worth a try. He didn't want to lose us and was apparently bewildered by this turn of events. He had been so wrapped up in his own world that he hadn't noticed what was happening. We both felt betrayed. However, the children pulled us together. We would go as a family to Mallorca.

Peter and I had become acquainted with Nell Dunn (the author of the influential plays *Up the Junction* and *Poor Cow*) and her husband, Jeremy Sandford (best known for writing Ken Loach's powerful television drama about homelessness, *Cathy Come Home*). Nell, whose father, Sir Philip Dunn, lived in Mallorca, also had her own house on the island and she kindly lent it to us. Sue Newling-Ward came along and we had Peter's company for two whole weeks before he had to go back to start filming *Bedazzled*. It was a good time and he really relaxed, so that we could talk more deeply than ever before. We spent a fair amount of time in and around Pollensa and discovered a beautiful little beach with a fisherman's restaurant at Cala de San Vicente. We made friends with Tom and Laura Eastwood, he a composer, who had rented the old bullring in Pollensa in order to work on some music. Tom, an Old Etonian, and Peter struck up an amiable relationship and our children played happily together. It didn't take Peter long to see this island as a good place to have a hideaway.

So it was with a lighter heart than usual that I said goodbye to him and started looking around for a suitable property. As so often, there was a local person dedicated to finding properties on commission. In our case it was Juana Cabrer, an aristocratic looking Pollensan woman, who offered to drive me around the hidden parts of the countryside. I had so thrived on the restoration of Church Row that I wanted to find an old ruin or at least something unconverted. Part of my problem, I felt, was the need to be engaged with a project, and preferably nothing that arose from my husband's life.

I hoped for a property with land or an orchard where I could create a garden and grow vegetables. Eventually I found it: an unconverted traditional farmhouse with no electricity or piped water, just a cistern to hold rainwater. It had about three acres of *terra secana*, which meant it was planted with trees that needed no watering: figs, almonds and carobs. It was beautiful and had a provisional price of one million pesetas, then about £5000. It was cradled in the foothills of the mountain range, which framed it exquisitely, about three kilometres from the old Templar town of Pollensa and about eight kilometres from the cove of Cala de San Vicente. It was called La Sort de Cuxach (The Luck of the Valley of Cuxach).

Lucy and Daisy thought it great and had already started to play hide-and-seek in the empty rooms. Lucy managed to find the old brick bread oven and would have secreted herself there if I hadn't plucked her up in time. Daisy found a stick insect and observed it carefully in her own inimitable way. This promised to be a place where they could happily explore their environment to their hearts' content. That evening I sat in the telephone exchange in the port, waiting to put through a call to Peter. Any international telephoning had to be done this way and it sometimes took hours, and even then the connection was often crackly. Eventually I got through and Peter answered. 'I've found a wonderful small farm at a good price. Any chance you could come over and see it?' Peter sounded as excited as me: 'I think we're having a pause this weekend. I'll try to get a flight. I'll send you a telegram.'

He kept his word and we met him at the airport, the girls immediately telling him how lovely La Sort was and that Lucy was now swimming with armbands on! I couldn't resist driving by the farmhouse on the way back to Aucanada, where Nell's house was, although we had an appointment with Juana Cabrer the next day. Peter was suitably impressed, although he thought he would try to reduce the already low price. In 1967 there were limits to how much money could be moved out of Britain, and also limits on how much land foreigners could buy in Spain. We had dinner in the local *celler* with Tom and Laura and their children.

There were in those days only a few resident foreigners and you could meet them all in the Bar Juma and the Celler Font de Gall in one evening. We met Dick and Lisa Campiglio, an American painter and his heiress wife, with an assortment of children from different fathers. Then there was Pamela Brown, a very sedate English writer, author of *The Swish of the Curtain*, which I had enjoyed as a child. She was with her Spanish consort, the painter Rafael with his walrus moustache.

The Pollensa people were smiling and hospitable, but had known bad times. The Spanish Civil War had been horrendous for them. During that time some people lived on nettles and fled to the mountain caves, so now they were welcoming the prospect of foreign money coming in. Little did they realize this trickle would turn into a vast flood, bursting the banks of a once poor but balanced economy.

Almost overnight the peaceful environment worked on Peter, slowing him right down. He played with Lucy and Daisy in the sea, built sandcastles and ate grilled sardines in the fisherman's café. I cherished these idyllic moments. Came the cool of the evening and we met up with Juana to visit the owners of the property, a family who ran a bakery in Sa Pobla. We went into the kitchen where dough was rising in an old wooden trough. The husband and wife were busy kneading still more for the ensaimadas. Juana spoke to them in Mallorquin, an impenetrable sounding dialect of Catalan. Luckily she could also speak Castillian, which Peter could manage. My French filled in the gaps. The couple muttered to each other as they pummeled the rising dough. It was hard to tell which way the deal was going. Then the husband shrieked 'Pep!' and a fifteen-year-old boy appeared, shaking the flour off his hands. He was dispatched on an old rusty bicycle to find the deeds, in an attic in an old trunk somewhere in another property. Juana eventually informed us there was a slight problem because there were sitting tenants working the farm. Our faces fell. 'But,' she continued, 'they could be bought off with the price of installing a *pozo* [a well] on their *finca* in Sa Pobla.' Peter did some calculations and offered the full million, to include the *pozo* for the sitting tenants. A compromise was struck and by now the boy on the bike had returned triumphantly brandishing the dusty deeds. Agreement was reached, everybody shook hands and a bottle of Cava was brought in. (The ensaimadas were now curled into lovely spirals and proving.) We still had to meet the tenant farmers to make sure they were prepared to accept a new well as a bribe, but both Peter and I loved the drama of all this –

so much better than seeing some sterile estate agent in his office.

The sun was now setting: a wonderful vermilion and coral sky with streaks of turquoise set seal on a satisfying day's negotiations. Now we would need a lawyer. Peter had set things in motion for the funds to be released and Stanley Donen had offered to help with any currency problems. Meeting up with our friends the Eastwoods, who had taken Sue and our little girls to the beach, we began to feel part of the scene. The children danced and chased each other around the square, a place that would witness many contrasting celebrations and moods in years to come. Yes! This was a place I had come home to. Overshadowing the town was the mountain with the monastery perched on its summit, the focus of a yearly pilgrimage for the townspeople, and next to it the smaller sacred hill of Calvario. An old couple could be seen driving their mule cart up the narrow medieval streets. I cannot tell you how atmospheric I found this place.

The next morning Peter and I went to La Sort to meet the old peasant farmers. Two gnarled but beaming old people embraced us as the bringers of good fortune. They had waited a long time for the opportunity to prospect for water on their own little farm, where the soil was much richer than La Sort's. Everyone was happy. Next to arrive was Juan Salas, a *maestro de obres*, or master builder, who was to give us some ideas about renovation. He thought we should turn the stable into the kitchen and build a new master bedroom with bathroom en suite under a new flat roof, with balustrades and a balcony. He reckoned it would take nine months to a year to renovate. No JCBs or diggers back then; just donkeys and carts and a cement mixer.

So much had happened in one weekend. Peter stayed long enough to get the legalities going and then left for the airport with a big grin on his face. We both felt optimistic about a future together – but one with space.

Once I had lined up a house to rent at the end of the summer on the Calvario, I too returned to London, along with Sue and the children. But trying to resume normal family life while *Bedazzled* was at the nail-biting stage of assembly and final editing was something of a challenge. I added to the pressure by signing on for a month's intensive Spanish course. It is true that the more you do the more you can do, but only up to a point. Peter was home one minute and disappearing to the studios the next. It was hectic. As an antidote, a friend suggested yoga. I found a teacher who would take Daisy and Lucy too and we had private classes in his studio. It was a revelation; he was so gentle with little Daisy and her asthma was immensely helped by the special breathing he taught her.

I also took to the language course like a duck to water and within a month had grasped the basics of Spanish. Peter invited me to attend the rushes of *Bedazzled*, which I did with certain trepidation. It carried for me a rather onerous burden of expectations, like a long-awaited birth. I knew Peter had been drawing on our marital circumstances for material, but even then I was not prepared for some of the portrayals. Although funny, they were pretty close to the bone, and always caricatured so as to be favourable to the 'Peter' character. In one scene he dons an apron and gathers up the children so the wife can go out with her lover. Cathartic no doubt for Peter, but disturbing for me. The peevish tricks Peter's Lucifer character plays, like cheating old ladies of their savings and taking pleasure in seeing the pain and dismay of tender-hearted Dudley, got to me, although I knew it was 'pretend'. It did so, I think now, because it seemed to point to a buried seam of sadistic vengefulness in Peter's complex make-up. What I found so chilling was the ultimate rant of the Devil to God. Peter's voice thunders out

in anger, threatening the 'great git' above with endless chains
of fast food stores, airports, motorways, television, cars and
advertisements. He will, he warns God finally, make everything
so unpleasant, 'that even you'll be ashamed of yourself'.

This speech was delivered with such vituperative rage,
against the lacy background of the Kew Gardens Victorian
Plant House, that it seemed Peter was actually invoking all the
environmental degradation that has come to pass. No wonder
I wanted to return to the Garden of Eden that Mallorca
represented.

For his own part, Peter regarded the screenplay almost as a
way of exorcising his demons. After confessing that the writing
had cost him £50,000 in lost earnings, he told the *Daily
Express*:

> 'This was something I had to do. It reflects my ideas about the
> funny position we are all in, stuck between God and the Devil,
> and I won't have any regrets, even if it doesn't make a bean.' It
> is the Faust legend in which Cook plays the Devil and Moore is
> the man who sells his soul . . . 'I've always had great sympathy
> for the Devil. It seems so hard that he should be chucked out
> of Heaven for competing with God . . . He doesn't want this
> mouldy job of being in charge of all the sinners. My theory is
> that he would like to get back up there! . . . I would rather have
> taken the chance to do something I really want to do than work
> myself into a withered rag by the age of 40. I would rather go
> back to being a beach photographer; at least I'd be getting the
> fresh air.'

Since Peter had taken the job of writing the script entirely
upon his shoulders, it lacked the balancing levity that Dudley's
spontaneous feedback often bestowed upon their magical inter-
action. But this was big money, big business, big names and

nothing could be left to chance. That was the trouble. Stanley Donen, the experienced and highly professional producer/director, had them on a tight rein. They were not used to it and it showed in the rushes. I guess I was Peter's severest critic, which was difficult for both of us. On the one hand he valued my input, but at the same time disliked (as we all do) any whiff of criticism. He usually trusted my judgement because so many others in our circle were sycophantic, but could I now be trusted not to have been contaminated by hurt and malice, when our marital problems were being paraded in public? I cannot respond honestly to that question myself, even in hindsight.

I had to be in Mallorca for a crucial stage in the building procedure just when *Bedazzled* was to be premiered. In the past to have been away at such a moment would have been unthinkable, so my decision indicated a change in the way we worked as a team. However, I made sure Anneke would be around. She had been a huge help to Peter in learning his lines, great swathes of speech that he was not accustomed to delivering, so it was fitting she should accompany him on opening night. 'I came to see him diligently for quite a few weeks and showed him how to break the script down into beats and thoughts. This was a miracle for him because he didn't understand. And all of a sudden it changed it for Peter. He wasn't afraid. He was so grateful he sent me a big bunch of flowers.' On the night of the premiere they both turned up in brown velvet, Anneke in a trouser suit. 'We looked like twins because we both had fluffy white shirts on too. It was frightfully grand for me. We went on to a gambling club afterwards and I won ten quid and I was pleased about that because my velvet suit had cost me ten pounds to get made.'

Miles away, I was collecting pebbles from the beach in Mallorca to restore the ancient cobbled floors.

The critical response to *Bedazzled* was mixed: *Time* magazine said that Peter and Dudley had failed to grasp the basic difference between a four-minute sketch and a 107-minute feature film. It was true the film unfolded in a somewhat staccato and patchy way, despite the underpinning story of the seven wishes Stanley Moon (Dudley) is given to win his girlfriend's empty heart, and despite too Donen's undeniably professional pacing of the plot. Whatever the truth about this engagingly odd piece of work, the reviews did not in any way come up to Peter's hopes and expectations. Neither did it do well in the US, in spite of the appearance of Raquel Welch; it was judged too English and too learned to be a hit there. But it did better on the Continent and Peter took some consolation in hearing how beautiful his character's voice sounded dubbed into Italian. The reception was a real disappointment for him, although he would not admit it openly. Even co-star Barry Humphries, in the role of Envy, called him a bad actor.

In order to get more practice Peter threw himself into some supporting screen roles, one of them a cameo with Dudley in *Monte Carlo or Bust*, to be filmed in Rome. I went out with the girls and Sally, our au pair, to join him in a bleak hotel on one of Rome's nastier beaches. The thrill for me was meeting Tony Curtis (a teenage heart-throb of mine). For Lucy and Daisy it was meeting Terry-Thomas in the VIP airport lounge. He said in his inimitable voice, 'Hello, darlings, when did we last meet? Was it Henley or Cowes?' They were charmed. The rest of our visit was unremarkable, save for a special conversation with Dudley which has stayed with me all these years. It was about Jiddu Krishnamurti, the inspirational figure who emerged from the theosophical movement, whom we'd both discovered. His religiously inclusive ideas were based on the importance of meditation and solitude.

While Dudley proved himself 'on the boards', starring in

1970 in a West End production of Woody Allen's *Play it Again, Sam*, Peter had yet to show whether he could handle dialogue. Determined to learn, he took on a part in *A Dandy in Aspic*, a film starring Laurence Harvey and Mia Farrow. He returned from the set to tell me how like Mia Farrow I was. I never met her, but I guess he meant in personality rather than appearance. Peter had also appeared as the Mad Hatter in Jonathan Miller's BBC film version of *Alice in Wonderland* alongside Mick Gough as the March Hare and a long line-up of stars that included Peter Sellers, John Gielgud, Michael Redgrave and Malcolm Muggeridge. Unfortunately Federico Fellini, upon discovering that Peter was a Scorpio, had decided not to offer him a lead role in *Satyricon*. Perhaps this was just as well, since the character in question had to be naked and in bondage.

But what was really to occupy Peter's attention over the next months was a new film project backed by David Frost. Written by John Cleese and Graham Chapman, it told the story of an ambitious young politician and was to be called *The Rise and Rise of Michael Rimmer*. Peter was interested in how somebody unscrupulous could manipulate the increasingly reliance of focus groups and referendums in government – a prototypical spin doctor, before the term existed. He was to play the lead role, an ambitious character who bore a strong resemblance to one of the men behind the film: David Frost. The end result was not good, however, and I have a memory of walking out of the premiere in disgust. Not only was it flawed, it seemed to be parodying a sickening obsession with power and celebrity that I now felt I could see in Peter himself. It is not a film one hears much about these days.

I sought refuge in the still unspoilt spaces of Mallorca, although life on the Calvario could perhaps be compared to living in a kind of Coronation Street, with a Spanish twist. The neighbours were just as entertaining. There was toothless

Juana, the stocky old pinafored matron who lived next door and patrolled the street like a town marshal while her son, Jaume, repaired shoes and kept pigeons on the roof. It was said there was a husband too, but he must have been shackled in some back room among the swathes of home-made raffia rope, for we never saw him. Juana did a good job babysitting for 100 pesetas (a fortune in those days) and the children seemed to like her, teeth or no teeth.

Next door to Juana were the exotic Lisa and Dick Campiglio – he more often than not drunk beyond being upright. In this state he once tried to drive his car down the 365 steps of the Calvario. But he did turn out fine paintings from time to time and Lisa dealt with it all with an elegant phlegmatism, surrounded by her brood of assorted children. She was a great cook and taught me, among other things, the importance of adding a little curry powder to home-made mayonnaise, when serving it as a dip with artichokes.

At the pinnacle of the Calvario lived the American painter Margaret Stark, whose paintings and collages were exquisite, and next to her an Italian film producer. Below her were Gene and Francesca Raskin, Russian Jewish New Yorkers, songwriters and artistes, who wrote the song 'Those Were the Days', which was later discovered by Paul McCartney and recorded by the ethereal Mary Hopkin. Francesca sang this song with a Marlene Dietrich-type voice, full of the experience and pathos of a sixty-year-old Russian Jewess. What a contrast the two versions are.

By this point I was on my own with Lucy and Daisy. Sue Newling-Ward, our nanny, had been seduced by the spirit of the island. She was still so young and needed her freedom to go to discos and nightclubs. 'I felt it was all work and no play,' she says now. 'I wanted to get out there and play a bit.' Sue had been good at her job and kept things going through difficult times. Once I had adjusted to her loss, though, I was grateful to regain my authority with the children.

Lucy and Daisy attended the nuns' little school in the cloister at Pollensa, wearing white smocks. They were the only blonde heads among the black-haired, brown-skinned Mallorcans. It was so lovely to go to collect them and find them surrounded by a swarm of lively children, being made a fuss of because they were so different. They soon picked up a reasonable vocabulary and it was good to see them growing strong, healthy and more confident. We kept up the yoga and went to the beach whenever we could; going barefoot and naked was great for the little girls, as was eating lots of sun-ripened fresh fruit and vegetables, while I revelled in shopping visits to the markets.

Peter kept in touch by letter and obviously found separation from the girls difficult. 'I do miss you all so much,' he wrote one lonely Sunday, going on to regret the fact that I had made him tapes of Lucy and Daisy going through their song repertoire, because it made him so very sad to listen to it. He was living off tinned grapefruit juice, he wrote, alternated with eggs and a Swiss muesli he had misguidedly bought as part of a sudden health kick.

Bemoaning the grim British weather, he went on to describe in this letter how he had been spooked by the creepy noise of the wind as he sat in his bath the previous night. The footsteps on the stairs he had also detected were, it turned out, only those of Queenie the cat, hoping for another tin of food.

One morning a pretty young woman cycled down our drive. I noticed she had a slightly deformed arm. She introduced herself as Margarita, the daughter of the couple who ran the dairy. She had heard I was looking for some help in the house. Her real profession was that of seamstress, but work was in short supply. I took to her immediately. She was a great cleaner and cook, and was good with the children, longing to have one of her own. Her arm, I learned, had been broken and then badly set, but it didn't stop her doing anything. This apparent disadvantage had helped her develop incredible willpower. Her help, along with the introduction she provided to Mallorcan culture, was invaluable, particularly during that fraught year when our futures were so uncertain.

I was in Mallorca with the children, with odd intervals spent in London, for the best part of a year. I went daily to give a hand on the building site, or to bring treats to the two valiant builders. Unlike many other builders, who took a two-hour siesta, these two ate their lunch, had a half-hour snooze under a tree and then continued till almost dusk. It was a wonderful experience to have a master builder with so much knowledge about traditional buildings. We had no need of an architect. I would ask whether we could have an archway here, a round window there. Within minutes he had drawn a charcoal archway on the wall, a circular window on another and soon afterwards they had been expertly hacked out.

Marble was inexpensive so I had a lot in the kitchen and bathroom, but managed to keep the overall balance rustic. The byre was made into a feature, keeping the stonework and wooden separations, where we would keep vegetables and fruit as it would be so nice and cool. The carpentry was of wonderful quality, reusing old doors, one of which was turned into a dining table complete with keyhole. A large cistern for water storage was to be excavated using dynamite and then covered with a layer of pine branches. The intrepid builders lit the touchpaper, having warned us all to hide inside the house, and shouted the word *foc* (fire in Mallorquin) which sounded like something else to us and made us laugh. After several explosions they had blasted a pit the size of a decent swimming pool in the sandstone rock.

Under the baroque law for imported cars my little Triumph Herald had to be sealed up after six months, so I took the opportunity to return to Hampstead to avoid the hottest weeks of the Mallorcan summer. Upon arriving home I found to my dismay that the outside of the house had been redecorated, brightly painted and with neat little window boxes of geraniums installed on the front balconies. In the garden the luscious and carefully nurtured herbaceous borders had been purged and standard roses planted in most beds. I wept copiously over this intervention. Peter, not having consulted me, thought it would be a nice surprise. How little he understood me. Although I would have welcomed some interest in this area, ordering some landscape gardener to come in and reorganize the whole garden was extremely difficult for me to swallow. Gardens are the most personal things and the place had been my own artistic project. I expressed my dismay in a letter to a friend:

> I know it was all meant to please me, but one of the nightmares I'd had abroad was about coming back to find everything different. Maybe it is dotty and perverse of me, but I had liked our house being the grottiest on the outside, but the prettiest inside in the row, but now it is the showiest, richest, grandest looking house in the row, with very dinky window boxes and I liked the garden to be wild, I really hate everything to be 'bien en ordre'.

I also knew that Peter had phoned his secretary and got her to do all of it . . . and I'm afraid I reacted rather unfavourably and sat in a corner and cried. It is potty, I know, perhaps, and everybody said he had only done it to please me. This I knew, but as far as I was concerned it was like me taking some of his films and cutting out bits, or tampering with it and saying:

'Look I've made it better for you!' I recognized that in the past I would have pretended to be pleased, but now I couldn't, even though my lack of gratitude provoked a violent response from Peter.

I bounced back for the children's sake: they were not to bear the brunt of our differences. Yet however one might try to protect them, children are like blotting paper and soak up atmospheres. Daisy's asthma was always a barometer of tensions in the air. I did appreciate that Peter was making an effort, but the more obvious the effort, the more difficult it was to behave naturally.

On Peter's side, however, the socializing stakes were being upped once more. Lord Snowdon had visited to photograph Peter in the house for *Vogue* (before the garden makeover, thank goodness). When I asked later who had been muddling up the LPs, Peter replied casually, 'Oh, Margaret Rose was here last week.' Socialite Suna Portman was also a visitor and I believe Germaine Greer may have had what might be called 'a lot to discuss' about feminism with him. There were others, or so people hinted to me, but Peter was always so good at hiding things that it was not worth trying to find out what his life was like in our absence. There was, though, the odd placatory letter from him. These conciliatory moves, designed I think to try to keep the marriage together while allowing him to live like a single man, tended to be couched in clumsy sexual terms and I would be depressed by how unmoved I was by them. I was sure, all the same, that he missed us. He was not a natural enjoyer of his own company and once said in an interview that he could not imagine ever being unmarried.

The five-storey house came to life again with children's laughter and I cooked up a storm in the kitchen and put wild-flower arrangements in the rooms. Was I really hellbent on a course of destruction for our once apparently idyllic partnership? I thought, possibly misguidedly, that the house in Mallorca was a way – a distraction – to soak up some of my abounding energy. In all sincerity I believed that for our relationship to evolve we needed somewhere private and distant from the clamour of the media. Working on a farmhouse where even a phone call had to be planned brought many benefits. I had begun to wonder whether I had any intrinsic personal value other than as the wife and satellite of Peter Cook. It was a deep and unspoken fear. The only antidote to fear is love and so this was my justification for doing what I was doing. Learning to operate in a foreign culture boosted my self-confidence although the Mallorcan culture was, in some ways, less foreign to me than the fast-moving London life we had been swept up into.

The new series of *Not Only . . . But Also* had been poached by the competing commercial television company, ATV, thanks to the persuasive wallet of Lew Grade, and was now to be called *Goodbye Again*. Peter wrote to me of his efforts to make the show work. 'We start filming next week; we are doing all the shows from a different realistic setting so as to get away from the ghastly ITV light entertainment sets; the first will be from the maternity ward of a hospital, the second from a gymnasium etc.'

Several new sketches on the subjects of both psychiatry and marital infidelity seemed to me to be overtly flagging up our domestic situation. I did realize that Peter was being unfaithful, but such episodes were largely undisclosed. Several of the offending sketches now took place inside a set representing a smart London flat and featured sophisticated versions of the Pete and Dud characters. One revolved around an attempt to disguise an affair during a telephone call to a girlfriend or wife abroad, a 'Penny'. After the call, Dudley, playing the unfaithful man, complains that he thinks he sounds guilty on the phone.

'Pete and Dud' chat over one of their famous pints in Not Only . . . But Also

Peter then wonders, po-faced, whether this could have something to do with the fact that Dudley is actually guilty: 'Could those two be possibly linked together, do you think?' he asks.

In fact, I myself had a fling with a Dutch painter out in Mallorca, but it was nothing serious. This meant it was a strange time. I found the imagery in Peter's work more and more sexualized, and even violent, compared to his earlier humour, which, although rapier-sharp, had always come from a benign place. Dudley was also drawn into this. Their images were changing too. They both had fashionably long hair and tight suits and Peter was increasingly narcissistic.

The end of the summer: we all returned to Mallorca together. Peter was keen to view the progress on La Sort and to have a bit of a break. As usually happened, he relaxed within days and I even got him doing a little gardening, planting out some lemon trees – quite a significant moment in our relationship. He was very impressed with the work that had been done. The thick farm walls ensured that the house kept the warmth in winter but also modified the heat in summer. I'd had a round window knocked through in the main bathroom, like a porthole, through which one could view the backdrop of the mountains from the shower. The plan was to move in for Christmas. The workmen needed deadlines, but there was still a lot to complete in the next three months. After harvesting the almonds it was time to prune the almond and fig trees, so I enlisted the help of the old farming couple, who were only too delighted to show me the ropes. Peter was glad to leave the gardening at this juncture, the appeal for him being aesthetic rather than practical, but we had made inroads.

Our girls had been proud to show their daddy their Spanish vocabulary and how they collected snails to have races up the patio walls. I had been shown by Sir Philip Dunn's retainers, Ramon and Maria, how to prepare snails, considered a real treat by the poor of the island. I don't think I could do it today, but then I was trying to become a native. First gather your snails, put them in a dry place in a circle of salt, which they will not cross. Feed them with flour to clean out the alimentary canal for three days. Then comes the horrible part: they must be dropped into hot water and cooked, releasing a good deal of foam and slime. Finally they are washed and cooked in a piquant tomato sauce. Not a dish I was likely to serve Peter, but a good one to fall back on in hard times.

Now I had to start gathering furniture. Laura Eastwood took me out to a fascinating place in the countryside where old Mallorcans had collected remnants of interiors of churches: pulpits, carvings, pews, griffins etc. It was quite surreal and had in fact been used as a location in the film *The Magus*, so eccentric was the setting. I came across wonderful carved panels to incorporate into the fireplace surrounds, as well as old Mallorcan oak chests and a wonderful dresser; all very cheap. Another antiques yard yielded sofas which I had re-covered. The local blacksmith created a balcony in wrought iron for the 'Romeo and Juliet' bedroom French windows. The pigsty had become a laundry and shower room and there was a huge area outside, discreetly beshrubbed, for the washing lines. I still feel to this day that nothing is more lovely than sun-dried laundry and I rejoiced then in my laundry-hanging area.

Sometimes I would spot a hoopoe, a wonderful crested bird, which I thought was nesting in one of the old fig trees. I took it to be a good omen. Whatever the week, there was always a fiesta to be celebrated, with dancing in the plaza, fireworks and special food. The children danced about wearing flamenco dresses and joining in the fun. Most children were seldom in bed before 10.00 p.m. and Lucy and Daisy were no exception, although they did have an afternoon siesta.

Now it was autumn and the *setas*, pungent forest mush-rooms, were sought in the mountains, each family jealously guarding their secret territories. Cooked with pork and rice, their earthy perfume hung in the air in Calle Cruces during that time. Next came the *matanca* – the killing of the family porker. Lucy and Daisy were unwittingly caught up in this dramatic ritual when it was performed by Juana's son and family. They have never forgotten it and it may well have contributed to Daisy's decision to become a vegetarian. By midday the pig had been dispatched and turned into trotters, fat belly, *sobrasada* (sausage), loin, salted hams and rashers. It is an honest thing, in my opinion, if you are going to eat meat, to fatten your own animal with good scraps, kill it efficiently and deal with the whole animal so as to provide food for much of the winter. But it is not so easy to kill a pig.

The winter evenings were special. We lit a fire and told stories, roasted chestnuts and had visitors from our little version of Coronation Street, who came to share a glass of wine. The smell of woodsmoke rising above the rooftops always reminds me of that particular winter. I even managed to make Christmas puddings and incorporated some of our own figs, dried in the wood oven on the farm and sprinkled with anis. Lucy and Daisy stirred the mixture and made wishes before we put some silver pesetas in for good luck. It was so exciting to see everything coming together: the doors on their hinges, oiled with that mixture of turpentine and oil that gives Mallorcan houses their characteristic smell. The tiles and cobbled floor in the main room were buffed and water was flowing through the taps. Until now, buckets pulled up from the well had been our only supply. Pale pink shutters were hung, and the *parale* for the vines to grow up over the patio was finished. Now we started to plant the garden. Traditionally, three trees guarded the house: a palm, a pomegranate and a *lledoner*, or hackberry. At the back, where it might be possible to create more irrigation, we planted some fruit trees: oranges, apricots, plums and loquats.

In December the furniture started to arrive. Lucy and Daisy loved their traditional Mallorcan beds, with barley-sugar posts, painted white. We wanted to establish the place properly as a home before Peter came to join us for Christmas. By then we hoped the newness would have worn off. Sally, our former au pair, had come to help with the final stages. I could hardly believe how very beautiful but simple and solid the whole build had turned out. What a fantastic learning process, to have had this opportunity to direct such a work, and it had only cost £10,000 in total to buy and renovate! I wish now I had done up a few more while there were plenty of abandoned old farmhouses around, but it's too late for regrets.

The End of the Run . . .

In the run-up to Christmas, presents were made or bought and wrapped, and decorations fashioned from pine branches, ivy and red ribbons. A goose from a neighbour's farm had been reserved and everywhere there were bowls of clementines, oranges, walnuts and chestnuts. At last the day arrived to go and meet Peter at the airport. Would he be pleased? Excited? Impressed? The plane was delayed, but eventually it arrived and suddenly there was Peter, looking rather gaunt. Yes, there was something different about him, though one was accustomed to seeing his chameleon-like changes. I couldn't quite work it out; there seemed to be a reluctance for eye contact. He knew that I was very quick to read him, so the charm beam was turned up to cover whatever it was I had intuited. Lucy and Daisy danced around, pulling at his coat, demanding to be picked up and we were distracted. We bundled into the car and drove through the dying afternoon sun to enter the welcoming and newly christened driveway. 'WELCOME DADDY' proclaimed a gaily-coloured sign made by us all and pinned to the front door. Peter looked rather misty-eyed.

I showed my husband around with such pride and delight. He was undoubtedly very pleased and impressed, but I sensed an inner struggle. Now was not the time, however, for any confrontation. After supper together, and time spent around the fire, Peter helped with bathing the girls and – a rare event – offered to read them a bedtime story while I cleared up the kitchen. The dream picture of a family together . . . I felt my defences lowering.

There was silence, only the sound of wind blowing in the bamboos behind the house. Peter came down and sat by the fire. 'Wendy, I have something to tell you. I have fallen in love with Judy Huxtable.'

Happy Christmas! I felt completely numb; this wasn't the movie scene I had written. Many thoughts and images chased themselves in quick succession through my mind. Judy Huxtable I knew to be the blonde icon who – bewilderingly to some of us – had married Sean Kenny, the stage designer, a charming man who liked the drink too much.

Judy had been a debutante and was now appearing in films. She always caused a stir when she appeared at the theatre and I had often seen her at The Establishment, though had hardly ever spoken to her. She seemed incredibly unapproachable; all she had to do was stand and ooze sexuality. She drove a Jaguar. She was everything I wasn't. Although I knew that Peter had had many sexual adventures, this disclosure was in another league.

All sorts of voices shouted at me from inside, some telling me it was my fault for leaving a handsome man alone, others arguing it could not be true. I was silent for so long I thought I would explode. Then I ran out of the great front door, down the driveway, as far away as I could get and did some primal screaming.

> We are the mirror as well as the face in it.
> We are tasting the taste this minute of eternity.
> We are pain and what cures pain.
> Both

SO FAREWELL THEN

> You would rather throw stones at a mirror?
> I am your mirror, and here are your stones.   *Rumi*

All those years loving, laughing, quarrelling, moving away, moving towards, building, birthing, mirthing – in one moment they seemed to be trickling away through the cracks between my fingers. I could not stop it. And yet different voices spoke their truths to me ('I am his wife: Judy is a married woman'). No, we had sold our birthright; we had given in to our longings and our desires. In common with our generation we had started to break taboos which had bound our culture for eons, tearing at the hypocrisy that had given men freedoms, but not their women.

How could Peter and I find our way back to rationality, to friendship, to shared responsibilities? In the fury of my own fear and insecurity, I saw only abandonment. We were both deeply afraid of being left. As these thoughts whirled through my mind, Peter came out to find me under a fig tree and tried to embrace me, but I was rigid. All I could say, like an automaton, was: 'We had better get divorced then.' 'Look, Wendy, it's not like that. I'm not wanting a divorce. I just need time. It's probably just the fantasy of a lonely husband.'

Perhaps it wasn't the end of the road, but I was shaken and don't remember too much about our first Christmas in that new home on the Island of Forgetfulness. Lethe helped a little and the wine flowed prodigiously. The children seemed unaware of a parental rift, seeing only the magic: Father Christmas and his host of reindeers had come down our vast chimney, eaten all the chopped carrots and left two shiny tricycles, so Lucy and Daisy were off, practising down the drive. I do remember that Tom and Laura Eastwood invited us for Christmas lunch and I had promised to bring the puddings and the goose, cooked in the local baker's oven. Soon Tom and Peter

were doing versions of his upper-class Sir Arthur Streeb-
Greebling accent and I temporarily let go of my worries as
wine took the edge off the pain.

Was Peter expecting me to grant him the licence he had so
violently objected to and so physically curtailed in my relationship with Simon? It seemed so. Could I find it in my heart
to be that magnanimous? Judy was a completely unknown
quantity. It was strange that we had been so often in close
proximity to each other in The Establishment and yet I never
remembered having a conversation with her. She was known
as 'The Untouchable Huxtable' and for me it was hard to get
beyond her projected image. I have the impression she preferred the company of men, though she did have a girlfriend
who was also a friend of mine and Peter's: the actress Gaye
Brown. Naturally, she found herself in an uncomfortable
position. 'I was too young,' Gaye tells me. 'I didn't know how
to handle it with Judy or with the fact that I was your friend
and his friend and her friend.'

Peter and I talked about a strategy for the future, but it was
difficult. All sorts of plans had already been made, such as a
prospective visit from Peter's parents in the spring. They had
booked their tickets and were looking forward to the holiday.
I wanted to get on with planting the garden, which I knew
would keep me sane; plants and children are the best reminders
of new life. But when Peter returned to London my heart was
very heavy. No decision had been taken. Only time would tell.
I felt insecure and was becoming ever more estranged from our
London way of life and less inclined to return, although I knew
that household matters barely ticked along without me. Peter
disliked paying bills and in my absence the utilities might be
cut off.

Meanwhile, the almond blossom came out, first like a bridal
veil, and then, as it fell, like confetti strewn across the island.

It was the festival of Sant Antoni and we were taken by Maria and Ramon to Sa Pobla to celebrate this fire festival in the midst of winter. Children dressed as little demons and bicycles festooned with exploding fireworks raced through the plaza. Old ladies with immaculate hairdos and camel-hair coats sang blue songs about women and donkeys to the accompaniment of the *ximbomba*, a primitive drum that is jerked into voice by strokes from a suggestive bamboo cane, wrapped in damp cabbage leaves. I can still see the crowd falling about with laughter as a journalist tried to record their songs for posterity.

Each street had built up a themed bonfire with the prunings of olive, carob and almond. We ate pies made of eels from the island's Albufeira wetlands, with spinach, pine nuts and raisins (a recipe of Moorish origin). Sitting cosily around a table draped with a heavy cloth, our toes warmed by a brazier of coals beneath, it was a companionable scene. There was nothing secretive or underhand about this lusty, honest and cathartic marking of mid-winter. Children were introduced to the idea of sexuality without shame because it was all linked to life – country life, full of the abundant forces of reproduction. (Indeed, Lucy and Daisy were transfixed one morning, I remember, as Ramon's great bull mounted the cow in the farmyard.)

The day after the festival, Sunday, as the smell of woodsmoke lay over the town, the townspeople brought out their pets, from rabbits to prancing stallions, each to be sprinkled with holy water by the priest. All in all, it had been a fitting punctuation to the long dark nights of winter and helped, for a while, to shift something dark within my soul.

Our friend the boxer Terry Downes arrived with his wife Barbara and their children. They were negotiating to buy an apartment in Puerto Pollensa and were a comforting presence, full of cheerful cockney humour and good sense. I enjoyed observing them as a family. Their children seemed secure within their prescribed boundaries and I noticed each parent backed the other up. Children are so good at noticing chinks in the armour of continuity between parents and learn at an early age to play one off against the other. As a parent often alone with my children, I had to be both authority figure and comforter.

My moods swung dramatically at this time. I would wake up some days numb and despairing. Mallorca was a place of extremes. The intense light and shadow played games with one's emotions. Daisy would later say to me, 'You know, Mummy, when I'm here I always feel that something utterly marvellous and magic is going to happen, or the opposite, something unimaginably horrible.' It was like that. I understood why the English appear so imperturbably phlegmatic, with their temperament born of the English weather.

With spring, the twisted old trunks of vine and fig sprouted tiny translucent green hands, reaching for the sun. What a virgin green! And there was the hoopoe back pecking in our field with his long beak, golden crest and golden eye. New life pushed through and my Dutch painter, Jan, who had no illusions about a future with me, provided comfort. We'd walk on the beach with his dog. I also spent time with an eccentric next-door neighbour, Watson Ritchie, a Scottish aristocrat whose career as a distinguished RAF pilot had been abruptly curtailed when he got his commanding officer's wife pregnant. He left, I imagine, in some disgrace and pitched up in Pollensa. He played the bagpipes and his little terrier, Sparkie, howled along in tune with him. Wattie started to make some stunning sculptures, mostly of his ex-mistress and child, in Madonna-like studies. He was good company up until 7.00 p.m., when the wine kicked in. I liked him and felt sorry for him, but when drunk his language belonged only in the officers' mess.

Peter and the girls in La Sort

Without a telephone, contact with Peter was difficult. He wrote to us more than was customary, but nothing was ever said that could have been used in court against him, as one might say. I was heartened he had made the effort, though. He was to come out at the end of April and stay till mid-May for Lucy's birthday, when his parents would also come for their week's visit. This might prove something of an ordeal. I certainly don't think Peter had mentioned Judy to his family at this point.

I don't know how we managed it, but there are happy photographs from the week with Peter's parents. I made a huge effort for Lucy's birthday party and the bakery did us proud with a large chocolate cake with tiny Mallorcan windmills on it. Lucy and Daisy wore their flamenco dresses and twirled as a local played the castanets. Margaret and Alec were enchanted and, like their son, relaxed in that warm and expansive Mediterranean climate. Once home Margaret wrote charmingly to say that it had been 'the most marvellous holiday' they had ever had, so we obviously hid our troubles with skill.

Soon after this visit from Peter and his parents I began to have severe pains in my left knee. Over the next couple of weeks it grew steadily worse. The medical care on the island was not great so I went back to London, by then in a wheelchair, with the little girls. Luckily, Sally, our former au pair, was able to come and give a hand and Judy Scott-Fox moved in too. What a wonderful friend she was. She had the most diplomatic of natures and was able to handle my confidences wisely. It was only in Church Row that the full impact of living alone with Peter had became apparent, so having Jude temporarily back in the fold was comforting. The knee did not improve, so I was eventually admitted to a clinic where I received excruciating injections of steroids. Finally, I went back to Church Row for a further month's convalescence.

Lucy and Daisy attended their former kindergarten for a few weeks. They were such sociable and adaptable children. But, as usual, Daisy's asthma became worse in London and we could not go anywhere without her Ventolin puffer. My knee did begin to improve, however. The condition was given a fancy name, which I don't remember, and a cast was made which was designed to keep the leg in shape while I was resting. This would put a stop to any frolics for me, for sure.

It was hard to know where Peter was most of the time, but once I was more mobile I came across accounts from a taxi firm, detailing constant trips to Judy's address near Ladbroke Grove. When confronted, Peter denied it, despite the evidence.

I was incensed more, I think, by him taking me for a fool than by the deed itself.

It seemed a dark time altogether: the war in Vietnam continued to overshadow the American Dream, and then came the assassinations of Martin Luther King and, in the second half of 1968, of Robert Kennedy. In South Africa the actions of Dr Verwoerd and Tom Mboya added to the mounting confusion of the late sixties. I also felt a great unease about the way modern technology affected nearly every aspect of life. Human beings were bent on overcoming every obstacle in life, determined to produce a comfortable future for all those in the West. What was also being generated, however, was a nervous restlessness that would prove hard to satisfy.

In spite of my misgivings about technology, I did not refuse when, in July 1969, I was given the opportunity of watching the moon landing in a TV studio with David Frost. In the event, I was so busy chatting up one of the scientists involved with this historic event that I nearly missed the key moment on screen. I do, though, have an abiding image from that day of our tiny, blue bauble suspended in the great cosmos – the only one of its kind. That scientist later gave me a chunk of rock, supposedly from the moon itself. It is probably up in the loft now.

I flew back to Mallorca to sit and ponder the turbulence both in the world and in my life, cradled in the roots of one of the millennium-old olive trees in our fields. Sitting there I could feel the pulsing of nature, reliable and durable as I watched old Juan plough the field rhythmically with his mule, before stopping for a chat and offering me some of his *sobrasada*. I felt healed by the contact with the outdoors, with the sun and the star-studded night skies.

The year 1969–70 hiccupped along, marked by visits from Peter, announcing that he was about to give up Judy, and by

my visiting Hampstead and witnessing first-hand that this was
by no means the case. I still have a scrap of a letter in which
I accuse him of hiding taxi receipts and accounts with car
companies. I also take him to task over an occasion when he
locked himself in the loo in order to dispose of more evidence
before 'pulling the chain and walking out nonchalantly'. There
were quarrels, inevitably. Caroline Silver, who stayed with us
during this period, observed the tension and the rows. 'One
day when Wendy was out I had my only personal conversation
with Peter. He had been pacing about the house looking distressed. He said he was very behind in his work and had scripts
to write, but the ideas wouldn't come. He seemed at his wits'
end, and said, "I try and I try, but I can't think of anything
funny any more."'

I decided to start divorce proceedings; the marriage seemed
irretrievable. On the one hand, it felt right to end the chaos;
on the other, it was devastating to think of life without Peter.
Eleven incredibly eventful years – an aeon, when you're only
twenty-nine. Who was I if I wasn't Mrs Peter Cook? So much
of my personality and creativity were wrapped up with Peter
and this was part of the problem, as it so often is with couples.
Peter was so magnetic; it was entirely possible to be subsumed
by his intense personality. Dudley was to find this so, too, in
spite of his own strengths. Inside me, a little flame was in
danger of being extinguished, yet something in me, albeit
unconsciously, was fighting to protect it. Lines from Germaine
Greer's *The Whole Woman* sum up how I viewed the battle:

> In *The Female Eunuch* I argued that every girl child is conceived
> as a whole woman, but from the time of her birth to her death
> she is progressively disabled. A woman's first duty to herself
> is to survive this process, then to recognise it, then to take
> measures to defend herself against it.

Peter and Dudley had started a new *Not Only ... But Also*, returning to the BBC after their commercial outing with ATV. They were on a tight schedule, so there were no more relaxed brainstorming sessions in Peter's study, with an unending supply of coffee and home-made biscuits from me. Instead, they sat in an office at Television Centre and dictated straight onto a tape which was handed to a secretary for speedy transcription. There was seldom time for editing and proper rehearsing of the scripts and yet some of it retained the old magic. I liked the cod documentary 'The Life of Emma Bargo' (or Greta Garbo) chronicling her career from her earliest role in films such as *Three Thousand Girls Jump into the Sea*. Peter apparently enjoyed dressing up as Garbo: 'I looked incredibly beautiful – I fancied myself rotten! Thought I looked rather better than she did!' he said.

In one of the first sketches of the series Dudley plays a libidinous piano tuner visiting the house of a Latin teacher, played by Peter. The piano tuner seems to know a great deal more about the Latin teacher's wife than he does himself. The promiscuous wife, instead of visiting her sick mother, is imagined to be walking the streets wearing thigh-length boots, microskirt, see-through blouse and an Indian headband. Dudley suggests 'She might have gone out of the door, crossed the road and fallen under a West Indian'. Well! The description certainly fitted my dress code at the time, as perhaps it might for many a young woman then, but I was getting paranoid. Going to see these new programmes being recorded was not much fun. I wondered what Peter would do for material once I wasn't so prominent in his life. Of course, it was funny to most people, but I became sadder and sadder.

Back in Pollensa the summer crowds had gone and the island breathed a thankful sigh. I had become friendly with Terry Gilliam, a designer for *Mad* magazine who was beginning his

association with the Monty Python gang. He also was recovering from a broken relationship with my old housemate
of Cambridge days, Glenys Roberts, and was very cut up
about it, so we were able to listen to and comfort each other.
(And, no, we did not have an affair.) It was good for him to
be around Lucy and Daisy, who were full of mischief. We all
managed to laugh quite a bit during the weeks of his visit.

I wrote to Peter around this time in a spirit of, if not reconciliation, at least of understanding. It was an epic attempt
to stop us thinking the worst of each other.

'We are like two people groping in the dark blinded by our
own particular sadnesses and afraid or unwilling to see,
accept or understand the other's most powerful needs in life,'
I wrote.

> You are suspicious of my motives and obviously, seen from
> your side of the fence, you may have had in the past reason to
> be . . . you see one thing: that you have been wronged, and
> although, I think, in the quieter, more humble moments of your
> self-examination you are not totally unaware of the lacks in
> your make-up, nevertheless you stick indomitably to your
> position, afraid that if any of the cracks are shown you will be
> destroyed . . . I see them and know them well, and you know
> that I know, but will not lower your defences for fear of being
> overthrown.

I go on to tell him that I am still prepared to fight on his side;
I also admit I have a tendency 'to go about things like a bull
at a gate'. After bemoaning the misery of dealing with each
other through lawyers, each 'relating to us the results of their
tiny tournaments', I remind him of the strong connection we
once had and even now sometimes made again:

I remember the week that I was in London, we were both in the kitchen, I was at the stove and we were in the midst of one of our bitter arguments and you said something, I can't quite remember what it was, though I will, which made us hysterical with laughter . . . and just shows how easy it is to flip the coin . . . that all the venom can be turned into one sentence of understanding, one that crystallizes all that is ludicrous in humanity . . . and there we are watching ourselves . . . I saw something very special in you, a long time ago, although it would have appeared at many times that you didn't want or care for me, I obviously thought you were worth hanging on for, you must know that I am a great 'sticker' . . .

I had an idea of the strain of the competitive nature of his work, although I had fallen right out of love with the celebrity world.

All those friends that emerged out of the same ripe chrysalis, or rode with you on your band-wagon, look at them: some appear to be lost, some are finding themselves, some are 'down', it would appear forever . . . some are down but possibly only dormant and planning to overthrow you. There are always new people coming up, the turnover is fantastically large, as you know, and keeping your foot in the door is obviously a nerve-wracking business, despite your almost arrogant self-confidence, I know that you worry how it will all end, and though you may make a very good beach photographer, it would seem better to be a little provident for the future.

In the end, I ask him to fund our lives in Mallorca and to keep the place as a bolt hole for us all. I was concerned too that the girls had nothing in their names. 'At all events, it's time we grew up . . . the time you spend with us should be our time. In

London, you belong to your audience, Saturday's football, Sunday's newspapers. I want to help you with your work, and would like you to help me with mine.'

As far as I know, my long letter had little or no effect, but it seemed the girls, as children will, were also still hoping for a reconciliation. Daisy remembers they forged Valentine's cards from Peter to me in an effort to soften our hearts. 'There are these two people who you just love and you don't get it when you are a kid,' she says now. 'You don't get it that they can't live together.'

One bright, winter afternoon I drove my open-roofed Triumph to Pollensa, with Lucy and Daisy in the back. I was distracted, I admit, trying to figure out the meaning of some legal letter Peter had sent me about our separation, when I struck a car that was stationary in the middle of the road. The owner had jumped out to pick up something he'd dropped. It was a mighty wallop and my car was a write-off. The steering wheel broke away on my chest and my head was cut by the sun screen. I felt myself hurled out of my body and little cameos of my life started flashing by in quick succession. I was able to look down and see myself slumped forward in the car, the two girls in the back. One of them started to cry and immediately I felt myself pulled back into my body. There were people around, the nuns from the Red Cross were taking care of the children and a doctor was stitching my head wound. I was fairly woozy. 'I've given you twelve stitches,' I remember him telling me, proudly. I was bruised, but nothing was broken. Margarita came to look after us. Lucy and Daisy were miraculously unharmed, just a little shocked and that was all.

This experience, of the kind now referred to as 'near-death', gave me a renewed appreciation of other levels of existence and, at the same time, made me realize I had become rather inattentive in my daily life. I should pull myself together ready for the challenges ahead. My wrecked car had been towed away before the police arrived and as a result details of the accident were hard to unravel. I did not feel strong enough to deal with it, so, after a few days recovering, I made plans to return to England for an open-ended period. Margarita and her husband Pepe, for whom I had found jobs in London, travelled ahead with Lucy and Daisy and their own new baby daughter.

Peter had not come to my side after the accident; learning that no one had died, he felt obliged to continue filming the final programme of *Not Only ... But Also*. HMS *Ark Royal* was being used for the opening sequence and the title of the show was painted on its decks – a job that took the crew three days. The last few frames saw a pair of tailor's dummies dressed as Dud and Pete being catapulted, along with their upright piano, from the aircraft carrier's take-off ramp. When I arrived at 17 Church Row I found an ominously short typed note from Peter, who was still at sea, welcoming me back and blankly expressing the hope I was not feeling too bad.

The stunt itself had a tragic ending, however, because one of the *Ark Royal*'s jets crashed into the sea shortly afterwards at the same point. Both pilots were killed and the wreckage of the plane became entangled with that of the piano. So when Peter arrived home on the Monday he was showing signs of the impact of all this. Too many accidents. I was still a little fragile too, so we gave each other some space and focused on our children.

In the final scenes of the *Not Only ... But Also* series, Dudley's character speaks a few lines at a middle-class party, as a group of well-dressed diners are discussing children's education, their au pairs, etc. He then reveals that he and his wife, Verity, have an extremely honest, but open relationship. It works, he claims, because while she knows he is having the odd affair, she also knows full well that he would never get deeply involved with any mistress. Then comes the bleak pay-off: 'I mean, I've never got involved with her!' Dudley's words jumped out at me. I think this was the last televising of *Not Only* I ever attended. It certainly left some pretty hurtful impressions.

I had no audience with whom to cathartically work out my marital problems, just a few trusty friends. Harriet, whose own marriage to Nick Garland had now come to a sad end, had somehow begun to recover and became a tremendous source of good counsel. Caroline Silver, also going through the beginnings of divorce proceedings from Nathan, was a stoic and humorous friend too. She recommended horse-riding as a good therapy. In Mallorca I had done some riding and my fear of the animal galloping off, out of control, certainly served to knock away any thoughts other than that of survival – so in that sense it provided a therapy.

Goodbye Again

After a short time in the guest room in Church Row, Peter announced he was moving in with Judy. He hadn't really wanted a divorce, he stated, but felt I was forcing his hand and so this was what he was going to do. There was no going back. I felt totally numb and unable to apprehend the enormity of the situation. We were both so ill equipped to salvage anything of our marriage: for my part, I couldn't pretend everything was fine and go on with half a marriage, and now, with another person involved, all Peter's incentive had disappeared too. He had no inclination to seek professional advice, apart from informally from Sidney Gottlieb, who by now was probably wary of being anything other than a sympathetic friend. And it was Peter's friendship, more than anything, that Sidney wanted to keep.

The next weeks and months are a blur. I felt mostly like a zombie, taking valium and other antidepressants. Strange cocktails of drugs were prescribed then without any real understanding of how they might affect the individual. Neither had I given up drinking wine at home in the evening. With no farm to run or physical outdoor work to help me maintain my equilibrium, I really felt lost. Peter was insisting that the girls and I should stay in London and he started to drop in, quite erratically, which was disturbing for all of us.

We had to establish some agreements about visits and this, as is frequently the case, is where the lawyers finally really got their hands on the situation and things got worse. One initiates a process in despair, or anger, or frustration and, lo and behold, things are magnified out of all proportion.

In the middle of one night at this time I was suddenly awoken by the most terrible pain in my gut. I writhed around and was soon screaming. Margarita from Mallorca, who was staying with us until her new job began, ran in to see what was up. An emergency doctor came and immediately called for an ambulance. I was rushed off to the Royal Free Hospital with suspected gallstones. In the early morning I was operated on, leaving me with a scar reminiscent of a postmortem incision – as my own doctor exclaimed later. Gallstones: the stones of sorrow.

For a month I was in a ward full of howling women, all of them in pain. It was an experience that really made me reflect on things. Lucy and Daisy were brought to visit me and couldn't understand why I was away so long. Peter seldom came; he disliked hospitals and I think it made him feel guilty seeing me so helpless. Eventually I was sent home, although home it would not be for long now – the place had to be sold. Peter and Judy had bought a cottage in Highgate, opposite the ponds. Peter was uncharacteristically trying a spot of DIY on it and would come over to take items from Church Row. The first thing to go was the Tiffany lamp, valuable and easy to move. I was really hurt by that, since it had been a present to me, but I was too weak to do anything. The lamp seemed immaterial anyway compared to everything else we were losing. I was urged to look for a house and tried to work up some enthusiasm, but everything I found was considered unsuitable. I found it upsetting too, showing prospective buyers around our beautiful home. It was a gem, though, and soon a couple made an attractive offer.

With no alternative home for us agreed upon, Peter decided he and Judy would move out of Kenwood Cottage and I should move in there with the girls. The house was kept firmly in his name and my bank account and any other accounts were frozen in this period, which was incredibly humiliating, as Peter arbitrarily made me an allowance of £200 a month. He was clearly frightened I might run up huge accounts at Liberty or John Lewis. It was a dark time, as all these moves were made without consultation and I had to start selling things. First thing to go was my Georgian silver tea service; other antiques followed.

I looked for solace in classical music and opera, through Patsy Anderson, our original mother's help from Jamaica. She had by now married Stephen Preston, her baroque flautist who played with Trevor Pinnock and Anthony Pleeth in a chamber trio. There was a brief 'musical interlude' with Tony Pleeth, when we went to the wonderful open-air concerts at Kenwood House. I had missed sharing music, something neglected in my time with Peter, although on a couple of occasions there had been a trade-off when I accompanied him to see Spurs play and he came with me to see some Verdi. (He said he'd enjoyed it, but opera never took root with him. As for me and football? A nonstarter.)

The farm in Mallorca had to be let out as Peter was insisting the girls be educated in London; Lucy was now six and Daisy five. This was a big wrench for me and I fought his controlling hand. I engaged a bulldog of a lawyer, a lady with a double-barrelled name, whom Caroline Silver was also using. My visits to her office in Blackfriars were surreal, but I believed she was a 'toughie' and would be strong on women's rights. So far my treatment appeared to be anything but equitable.

I alternated between feeling totally wounded and disem-powered to feeling great surges of warrior strength, fuelled by

The unparalleled Robert Graves.

a sense of injustice. It appeared Peter held all the cards in terms of finance, public prestige and authority – and Church Row too. I partially owned the little Mallorcan farmhouse, but because of Spanish law the land was cut up into parcels and Peter had his share of that as well.

The day came when we had to pack up our life at Church Row, leaving the plants, but taking the Wendy house and the cat. It was a strange feeling to be moving into Peter and Judy's 'love nest', but it was all that was on offer so we made the best of it. If one was to be imprisoned in London there could not have been a more rural setting than across the road from Highgate Ponds, where ducks and geese provided a comforting cacophony and Hampstead Heath stretched out beyond. But it was not my beloved Mallorca.

Peter's visits were erratic once again and in this sticky run-up to the divorce I tried to formalize them. In response I began to receive lawyers' letters strongly suggesting Peter would be trying for custody of the girls. It was inferred that because I had been a patient of Sidney Gottlieb I was too unstable to be a good parent. Well, this was just the kind of thing that could well push someone into mental instability. What it did do was make me aware of the different realities we all perceive. Living with Peter for me had meant living with a whole pack of different 'loonies' – from Sir Arthur Streeb-Greebling to E. L. Wisty and all the other myriad characters that jostled for attention inside him. All good fun up to a point, but now that there was a whiff of gunpowder in the air it was the authoritative, public school, Cambridge-educated Peter Edward Cook (formerly destined for the Foreign Office) who appeared front of stage and this was a figure you didn't want to muck around with. He was the very convincing character I had seen pulled out in the past for any dealings with police officers or lawyers.

This legal threat filled me with the fury of a tigress whose cubs are endangered. Peter had taken so much, but not the children! I became paranoid that one day after a visit he would not return them. Now I have a little perspective on what was happening. Only in 2005 I learned from an article about Judy Huxtable that she had become pregnant by Peter during this time and chose to have an abortion. There were complications and the result was that she was unable to bear children. Today I can feel compassion towards her as a woman, but then I felt completely terrified by their joint attitude. Here were two people, both performers, both from comfortable middle-class backgrounds, both privately educated and both swaddled against any physical hardship. They really did have a lot in common. Their house, I had noted when we arrived, had been liberally fitted out with mirrors. It seemed they needed to admire themselves.

I couldn't help my antipathy towards Judy. I felt her to be as secretive as Peter. She never offered to state her position, as far as I can remember, so she remained an unknown quantity. In the absence of other information, in my mind this elfin blonde became something of a malevolent Tinkerbell to my Wendy.

> I don't know whether the idea came suddenly to Tink, or whether she had planned it on the way, but she at once popped out of the hat and began to lure Wendy to her destruction.
>
> Tink was not all bad: or rather, she was all bad just now, but on the other hand, sometimes she was all good. Fairies have to be one thing or the other, because being so small they unfortunately have room for one feeling only at a time. They are however allowed to change, only it must be a complete change. At present, she was full of jealousy of Wendy and hated her with the fierce hatred of a very woman. *Peter Pan and Wendy*

Of course, often it suits a man to keep the women in his life at a suspicious distance from each other. Gaye Brown, who tried to maintain a friendship with both of us, felt we were complete opposites. 'The interesting thing is that what Judy offered was the antithesis of what you had to offer, which was this home and solidity,' she says, adding that I provided a firm foundation for Peter's life; the promise of food on the table: 'I never felt that with Judy.'

For my part, I never stopped caring about Peter. I still loved him in a kind of way. I just didn't like him very much and we certainly didn't speak the same language at this juncture. By no means am I saying I feel no responsibility for things going so badly wrong. It had been such a creative partnership, but it didn't have the maturity to evolve, to ride through the confusing and permissive developments in our world.

On the day of the divorce hearing Caroline Silver, who had herself been divorced only three weeks earlier, accompanied me to the Old Bailey. She advised me to sit in on a few cases beforehand, to prepare myself. By her own admission this turned out to be not such a good idea. For a start, the court was packed with reporters waiting for the 'celebrity divorce' case to come up. Then we had to sit through the conclusion to ludicrous proceedings between an Italian and his wife of twelve years who had never consummated their marriage. Caroline takes up the story: 'The second case was even more peculiar: a semiliterate old Irishwoman was divorcing an eighty-one-year-old one-legged man for physical cruelty. She sat before the crowded court, bewildered and inarticulate, and the kindly judge took pity on her.

'"Don't worry yourself about all this, Mrs Reilly," he said to her gently, handing her a piece of paper. "All you need to do is just read through this statement and tell me if everything in it is true."

'Mrs Reilly fumbled for her reading glasses. She stared at the paper for a very long time. "Mrs Reilly," said the judge eventually, "are there any words in that statement that you don't understand?"

'"Oi don't know what 'sodomy' means," confessed Mrs Reilly. "Is it the one with the mouth?"'

Caroline reminds me that we both stuffed our gloves into our mouths and looked away from each other. After this comic interlude, it was quite hard for me to seem careworn and weepy when I got into the dock.

Having pinned a lot of hope on the ability of my double-barrelled lawyer to secure a fair deal in court, I was unnerved to learn that she was to field one of her younger solicitors that day. He was thrashed by Peter's lawyer, who conjured up a picture of an artiste practically on the breadline. I was awarded the farm in Mallorca (which could never be totally mine anyway), £200 a month and the custody of the children with reasonable access for Peter, who was in Australia, touring with Dudley in *Behind the Fridge*. I went home with Caroline, took off my wedding ring and had a bit of a wake with several friends and some champagne.

It would be some time before I oriented myself in my new situation. First of all, it was necessary to increase my income; £50 a week even then was not a fortune. So I took in a lodger and let one of the rooms. Harriet saved me from idle gloom by inviting me to volunteer for her team at Task Force, an organization which assisted the elderly with the help of groups of school children. I also worked one day a week at Sesame, a whole food shop and café in Primrose Hill.

Lucy and Daisy were given places at Gospel Oak Primary School, a school with a good reputation, where the headmaster, a Mr Lendon, was inspired by Rudolf Steiner's progressive ideas on education, so there was lots of drama, music and painting. The girls settled in well and walked to school over the heath on fine days.

Peter and Judy bought a mews house that almost backed onto our old home in Church Row, in Perrins Walk. Peter had gone off to New York, where he apparently amused himself with Lee Radziwill. Judy was later to discover that she had to share him with the women who seemed to find him irresistible. By then his boundaries had become very indistinct. He was taking amphetamines as well as drinking heavily and was certainly very skinny.

Working with the elderly in north London put things into perspective. There were old people sleeping on newspapers and living in such squalor that I couldn't believe this was a welfare state. I wanted to solve everyone's problems, but realized I had to prioritize, or burn out. I enjoyed driving the green Task Force van around Camden and was impressed by the teenaged school kids. We would have decorating parties, giving clients' flats a new coat of paint, or walk their dogs. This work lifted me out of self-pity, although deep down I was affected by the cruel behaviour of Peter, who seemed to want to punish me as much as possible. I tried not to be distracted by what he and Judy were up to, but when the children went for a visit it was hard not to feel resentful when they returned with some new and expensive piece of clothing I could ill afford. They were always overindulged on their visits, but I'm glad to say it didn't turn their heads.

I felt imprisoned in London and found that, although we now lived in a less polluted area and were going on with the yoga, Daisy's asthma attacks continued to be serious. I had to orchestrate playtime with her little friends, for, beyond a certain decibel level of excitement, she would start 'heaving' and I would have to quieten her. It was such a hard thing to live with and has made me forever aware of the quality of a breath – hers, mine and other people's. It is a good indicator of stress.

With relief I then learned that Harriet had taken a wooden cabin in the middle of the Forest of Dean, Gloucestershire, and that we could go for weekends. Down there we were to build fires, cook, knit, chat and go for long walks by the river, collecting wood. On the weekends we didn't travel to the Forest of Dean, I would often go to Cambridge to stay with Ros Myers, my old art school friend. She had taken up with a Dr John Smith, a scientist researching into blood. High up in university scientific circles, he had many friends in Cambridge and there were usually outrageous parties to go to, often in the house of Francis Crick, whose ground-breaking work on DNA, with James Watson, had set him apart from other mortals. It was interesting to witness such a brilliant man behaving in such a puerile manner at social gatherings, for example often looking up the au pair's skirt. Some say this is what happens to real geniuses, who are often a little unbalanced. All the same, I found it fascinating to be in the company of these top scientific minds. I have always remembered Francis Crick commenting at one party, 'Just watch people in any social group; within ten minutes they will have shaken down into their sociological groupings.' Perhaps he saw them simply as strands of DNA, constantly patterning and forming shapes and contours. Several of these clever men shared an attraction to pretty, 'arty' women who would not tax their minds with questions about their work. However, I tended to break the rule and try to extract information from them.

The healing process threw me towards music and musicians too. I found an unusual church in Bloomsbury where the organist was a highly extrovert ex-Oxford man, Professor Ian Hall, a Guyanan with a pronounced accent, who regularly had tea with the Queen Mother. He offered a warm fellowship to those in need and I fell in love with him for a while. The church attracted many young students, much debate and music. Lucy and Daisy seemed to like going, so I met and made friends there with many decent, caring people. Once again I found myself ricocheting at high speed between the irreverent and the reverent. While the ritual and familiarity of the services gave me some security after the years of iconoclasm, I did have problems with concepts such as 'being only worthy of crumbs from the Lord's table' or 'crawling on one's belly like a worm', so far away were these from my understanding of Christ's teachings. The younger group of clergy (a youthful Richard Harries, the current Bishop of Oxford, was among them) were working with new developments for the laity. I was also meeting people who had espoused the thinking of Gurdjieff, the Greek-Armenian mystic, and of Krishnamurti: I found these ideas challenging.

Daisy's asthma was not improving, so in desperation I saw a specialist who gave allergy tests. The results indicated that she was allergic to a myriad things, the most dramatic being cats – indeed, any animals – house mites and many other things. The advice was to get rid of the cat and all soft furnishings, replacing them with plastic that could be sponged down daily. I was furious with the impracticality of this prescription; even if I were to do this in our own home, how could I sterilize every environment she might find herself in elsewhere? At this point I wanted some input from Peter, but it turned out he was far away with Dudley on the last stages of the US tour of *Beyond the Fridge*, retitled *Good Evening*. I have since learned that he wrote a letter to his parents at this point, telling them about the beautiful new house he had bought for Judy and himself and asking them not to let me know (having pleaded penury at the divorce hearing). He indicated too that he thought Daisy's latest medical report was just hysteria on my part. This was difficult, but as often happens when things get dismal, a door to something new opened for me.

Someone I had met in a pottery class told me about a rather special place in north Scotland called Findhorn, the ecological project known for its healthy lifestyle. I made plans to visit that Easter of 1975. I set off with the girls in our VW Beetle with all sorts of goodies for the journey. Lucy was now ten and very capable: she was an excellent map reader. We broke our journey in the Lake District and then went on, passing through the Cairngorms, sprinkled with snow. It felt as if we were going to the moon, as the landscape became more barren and rocky. Finally we reached the village of Findhorn, in a softer landscape on an estuary warmed by the Gulf Stream. Stepping into the Findhorn community was like stepping into a warm bath.

The people there had a balanced life of work, play and meditation, the effect of which showed in the smiling faces and the enormous respect they showed each other. The whole project had embraced vegetarianism; the food was utterly delicious, consisting largely of masses of colourful salads with a Californian influence, sprouted seeds and tofu which we had never had before. The variety and colour gave the best possible advertisement for the wide possibilities within a vegetarian diet. The children were invited to join in the meditation sessions in a room filled with flowers around a central candle and an almost palpable atmosphere of peace. This may all sound very New Age – the butt of many a jest – but in those early days it offered a real antidote to the escalating madness of the consumer society. To sit in a comfortable silence with people you didn't know, not being preached at or to, was a new experience – one where all the clamouring, conflicting noises in your head could abate and a more authentic voice could eventually be heard, coming from a different place.

I became aware of colours around people, and began to feel a resurgence of the sensitivities of my childhood. They had been banished in adult life, but here no one was judging. I met up with a man from San Francisco called Paul Hawken (now a well-known environmentalist) who told me he had been an asthma sufferer but had cured it with a macrobiotic diet. He had studied with Michio and Aveline Kushi, macrobiotic pioneers, and he put me in contact with a macrobiotic group in London.

Daisy was free of asthma during our visit. She and Lucy befriended the six children of a family called Marberg, who were also visiting. These children were all so creative and independent that I found myself enquiring of their mother, American painter Sarah Lee, where they were educated. They attended a Steiner school in Sussex, she told me as I prepared for the long journey back to London. My heart was lighter; I had some new ideas about how to help Daisy's condition that would benefit all of us.

Back in London, it didn't take long for Daisy and a best friend to make a pact. They had seen lovely little lambs frisking about the fields and came to me one day with grave expressions on their faces, announcing forcefully, 'We have become vegetarians.' After two weeks of vegetarian fare, I realized there was more to it than cheese soufflés and omelettes, so I signed up for classes with Aveline Kushi and spent the next four years studying and practising this traditional Japanese macrobiotic way of cooking, eating and living. Each meal was like a carefully constructed sculpture. Cutting vegetables was a contemplative act; everything was done slowly, with great attentiveness and pleasure. It didn't altogether stop me from making honey and cream custard tarts at Sesame, but at home dairy produce was pretty much omitted, as were sugar and all the addictive things like coffee and alcohol (though I did enjoy sake – rice wine).

This new approach to eating made me see what a prison we had created for ourselves in the West, with our obsession with rational thinking. The study of yin and yang allowed for diversity, and a world full of paradox for the imaginative mind: a mind that doesn't seek to control. At this time I also read the Mullah Nasruddin stories to Lucy and Daisy, who loved them. They are humorous Sufi stories where the Mullah is Sancho Panza to Nasruddin's Don Quixote, both aspects of the same being, always playing tricks upon each other. I meditated with a Japanese Zen teacher too and the depressions that descended upon me cyclically seemed to vanish.

Our new circle of friends clearly made Peter feel threatened. I would have spent longer at Findhorn but Peter put a legal block on it, having unearthed as much salacious press as he could on the subject. Although this avenue was closed down to me, another path became visible as we started to visit the Marberg family in Forest Row, Sussex. Here I called in on the Michael Hall Steiner School and was impressed. The school was in a wonderful setting only thirty miles from London and offered a great deal of what I was looking for. It was also backed up by a spiritual philosophy that reached out beyond education into many practical spheres of life: agriculture, architecture, medicine and many other disciplines. Surely Peter could not object to this as an environment for his daughters?

Nevertheless, I had to force the issue, with the help of medical back-up, and make a case for putting the girls into Michael Hall School. After considerable resistance, Peter reluctantly acceded. After all, he was mostly out of the country at this point – in the USA and Australia – so he did not have a good record of regular paternal visits. What children need more than anything is consistency.

At their school interviews Lucy and Daisy were asked to make a drawing for their prospective class teacher. I think they both drew a family who lived in a teapot – a story I had made up in Mallorca and which they loved. The teachers apparently deduce a lot from a child's drawings and my girls' work seemed to have been appreciated. They were offered places to start in September, so I would need to find a house near the school. In the next few months I came up with three possibilities and set about getting surveyors' reports.

While this was done we arranged to drive to Mallorca to spend the summer at the farm, which would need attention as things grew so quickly. (I already had an arrangement with the builder for him to look after the land in return for a half-share of the produce.) We stopped on the way in Chartres and spent hours in the wonderful cathedral, marvelling at the stained-glass windows. I watched Daisy taking in the colour with a great intensity. I suspect the visit had a formative effect on her later work as a painter.

We spent the first weeks of the holidays cleaning out the house and reclaiming the garden, getting rid of rats' nests, hornets' nests and all manner of hitherto unknown creatures. We even found scorpions. Lucy and Daisy were by now excellent swimmers and adored being in the sea. At night we sat under the vines, now heavy with ripening grapes, aware of the stars and the fact that we too were in a constant dance around the hemispheres.

One evening in August the post boy came down our drive on his Lambretta with a telegram. My heart sank: I knew it was bad news. My father had collapsed with pneumonia and my mother wanted me to return. His condition was deteriorating fast, so we flew to Gatwick the next morning. My sister was already at my parents' house in Duloe, so when I arrived we took it in turns to go to the hospital and relieve my mother, who was quite shocked as the GP had told her my father just had a nasty 'flu. A smoker all his life, he had started each day with a terrible bout of coughing. He now had lung cancer as well as pneumonia.

I was horrified to see my handsome father with his face all sunken in and wearing an oxygen mask. The prognosis was bad: it would be a matter of days. I sat for hours by his bed hoping that he would come to and recognize me. Then, quite suddenly, he opened his eyes and said, 'Wendy?' I squeezed his hand. He momentarily stared at the nurse passing by with some medicines and said, 'Ask that barmaid if we can have a drink' (presumably he thought he was in an unusual public house). Then he squeezed my hand as though trying to pass on any residual strength he might have. And that was it; he left. I cried.

My secret dream had been to look after him in his dotage, while discussing philosophical matters and sharing books. He had been reading works by Gurdjieff and his fellow mystic Ouspensky when he died – a self-educated man, he was always a seeker.

Loss had compounded loss, just when I was rediscovering a joy in life. I'd lost a parent – my father, with whom I had been in closer sympathy than my mother, was gone. Nevertheless, it seemed the strength he had put into that final squeeze of my hand left a lasting imprint. Lucy and Daisy and I stayed on with my mother. She was stoical, still drove a car and managed the large garden. My father was seventy-five when he died and she continued to live until she was ninety-six. My sister went back to Birmingham, where she now lived with a new husband and two daughters.

There was no time to return to Mallorca that summer and we continued negotiations to buy a house near the school in Forest Row. As Peter was still abroad, arrangements were held up and it looked as though my plan was being sabotaged again. However, strangely, I was aided now by Peter's former neighbour and teenage pal from Uplyme, Jenifer Platt, by then, Jenifer Donaldson. Our paths had crossed once more at Sesame, where she was also cooking, and it emerged that our destinies too were following similar lines. Jenifer had been living in Forest Row and her children had been pupils at Michael Hall. Her wealthy stockbroker husband was now seeking custody of their adopted children and so she needed to return to London and sell her house in Forest Row. We had run into each other again at a propitious moment it seemed and, as time was running out before the start of term, an obvious and practical solution presented itself. We would swap houses! And that is what we did; at first as a temporary measure. Through his solicitors Peter had agreed to the girls starting at Michael Hall, but he had not given written instructions to proceed on a house purchase. This left me with little choice. We moved into Jenifer's house and Jenifer moved into ours, thereby also gaining a huge papier-mâché elephant that lived in the garage – part of the Highgate and Kentish Town carnival apparatus.

By a cat's whisker the girls made the start of the new term and they loved it. For the next seven years, come rain or shine, even if they were not feeling 100 per cent, they wanted to go to school. The immediate result, however, was an angry tirade from Peter, who went to visit Jenifer at the cottage on his return to Britain.

'My memory is that he was very different from the young man I had known who was doing something amazing in London,' she says now. 'He was rather overweight and puce with anger. His face got redder and redder as he talked to me. "How dare you collude with Wendy about this!" he said. It was very puzzling because there was this rebellious young man, who had cocked a snook at the whole of the Establishment, and suddenly he was personifying the Establishment.'

Goodbye Again

I had forced Peter's hand, and, despite the animosity it produced, he had to allow that I was in earnest. He bought the sturdy Victorian house in Chapel Lane, Forest Row, where we lived for the next ten years – ours only for the duration of the children's education. The £200-a-month allowance continued without increase. I was bewildered at the number of obstacles he continued to place in my path; I had imagined that now he was with Judy and married, things would be different because love makes you happy and happiness makes you generous. A simplistic hope – it was clearly more complex. To leap from one long-term relationship into a fresh relationship never leaves you entirely free. On my side, it was to be seven years before I entered into another long-term relationship. There were a few romantic interludes; each helping me regain a self-confidence that had been badly bruised.

It was so good to get away from London. We were on the edge of the Ashdown Forest and it stretched for miles, right over to Pooh Bear country and Pooh Bridge. Talking to some of the teachers at the school I began to realize that Steiner pedagogy was built on more profound principles than I had thought. Both Jonathan Miller and Nick Garland had spent some of their education in one of these schools, that I knew, and although they were a little dismissive of it in later years, they were two of the most successful polymaths I have ever met. The cultivation of artistic intelligence and the imagination that this school offered was my primary concern. With good imagination one can withstand adversity.

I could see that if I was to support the education of our daughters I would need to understand more of the philosophy behind it. There, in our very village, was the movement's adult training centre, Emerson College, and I signed on for a part-time foundation course. Twenty different nationalities were represented on the course. Steiner's theories, known as anthroposophy, turned out to be a fascinating synthesis of the main elements of the great religions, but essentially a new kind of Christian consciousness. Anthroposophic education is about developing the whole human being. Science is studied in an artistic way and art, in turn, can be treated as a scientific discipline. Pupils were taught in an experiential manner so they retained what they learned, rather than just cramming for examinations.

For my own part, it was wonderful to be singing in a choir again, to be helping make costumes for the annual Shakespeare production and preparing weekend meals with marvellous produce from the college's biodynamic farm. We got rid of the television: there was so much to do!

I became engaged with thoughts of Goethe the scientist, less well known than Peter's literary hero, the author of *Faust*, the poet and philosopher. I studied Goethean observation with John Davy, the vice principal of the college. I had such respect for this man, who had been the *Observer*'s science correspondent for fifteen years. I once saw him take the stand in a conference after a contribution by Uri Geller: 'Well,' he said, 'it's all very well being amazed at someone's capacity to bend spoons, but how many of us realize what a miracle it is for plants to strive towards the sun, or for the human being to maintain an upright posture?' His thinking struck a chord with me. Yes, it was the unnoticed daily miracles of nature that interested me. Having been a cook for so long I was well aware of the many exchanges and alchemical processes that happen in the kitchen. I had now found a research area that might provide me with some answers.

I was drawn (as ever!) to the college's kitchen in 1976 and I stayed for five years, helping to run it, at the same time studying nutrition with Dr Gerhardt Schmidt. So this later became my life's work, in schools, clinics and a medical practice with schizophrenic patients in Hawaii. Working with fresh biodynamic produce I was able to witness the often profound effects of well-grown and well-prepared food. My experiences while entertaining with Peter had been a good grounding, but now it was taken to another level – where food is seen as primal medicine.

One Easter, while the girls were holidaying in Cornwall with Peter at the Gottliebs', I went on an art trip with some students from Emerson College to Italy. We sang in many churches and chapels. On this trip were two attractive young men, identical twins and both training to be priests. They were from South Africa and their names were Denis and Alan Hopking. Sitting together on the back seat of the bus we laughed a lot together during the journey, but also had some pretty deep conversations. Their voices were nearly identical and they both appeared to be shy, due, I guessed, to the onerous prospect of becoming priests, but they had also developed a means of silent communication with each other that replaced any small talk.

When we returned to Forest Row I found myself in a theological study group with them. Although Alan was perhaps the more handsome, I found myself being attracted to Denis, the eldest by two minutes. He seemed to have an inner authority, was incredibly masculine with a wonderful frame, but at the same time very sensitive. They had both spent their previous seven years in monasteries as celibates, and both were now ready to change that state. Having done everything together for the first twenty-eight years of their lives, now appeared to be the time to discover that they were in fact individuals.

After three months of friendship and study, Denis and I started a relationship. In time he moved in with us in Chapel Lane and the children grew to love him very much. Our household became a centre of activity. Denis and I shared our lives for fourteen years with no infidelities. We respected each other and shared the same values, and lived among others who supported those values. The culmination was a shared project on a mountain farm in north Mallorca – but that is another story.

Meanwhile, the girls grew strong and independent. Daisy's asthma more or less disappeared. They were both talented artistically, Lucy drawn towards crafts and Daisy to fine art. Peter's visits were sporadic. Daisy recalls him coming down to see the odd school play. 'Friends were quite interested in meeting him,' she says, 'but it was quite an alternative school and half the teachers there were foreign, so he wasn't anyone to them.'

Often he would appear looking rather unkempt and conversation was stilted. The ashtrays were always overflowing, his teeth and fingers yellow and orange with nicotine. I found it heartbreaking to see him deteriorate so. Yet his armour was still in place – not a chink through which one could glimpse anything.

The girls, unbeknown to me, had found a way of smuggling copies of *Derek & Clive* in for their circle of classmates. How they managed to keep it quiet I shall never know. I found out much later on, when they shared it with me, probably at Lucy's twenty-first when a good many confessions came out: the first kiss and the time Lucy ate some magic mushrooms growing in the very grounds of the school. She said, 'Don't you remember, Mum, I came home from school unwell and you put me to bed. When you came into my room later your head looked like a goldfish bowl! But you never found out.' The girls and I were really close friends, but clearly certain things were not picked up by my beady eye.

Adolescence is a stage dreaded by most parents. In Waldorf schools, part of the Rudolf Steiner system, the education is usually quite age-specific and key points in a young person's life are accompanied by what might be considered a modern-day rite of passage. In Lucy and Daisy's school, as in others, teenagers whose hormones and souls are often in a state of turbulence tend to wear dark clothes – black and navy – out of choice, which seems to point to what they need. So, in Waldorf Schools, rather than pretty coloured paints they get lumps of Portland stone to carve, clay to pit themselves against and charcoal. They are taken white-water rafting, climbing over Hadrian's Wall, on long treks, and shown how other people's working lives provide the things they take for granted. This gives them a perspective, showing them freedom does not come without responsibility.

I had few problems with Lucy and Daisy's adolescent years. I had found a good and safe place for them to grow up, among caring people who had little interest in the cult of the celebrity. People hardly ever asked me about my life with Peter Cook, so I could be myself, untrammelled by association. But in no way did life stop in 1971 when I divorced – it became more and more exciting.

I had found a more practical, meaningful way to live. Here was a spiritual road map which allowed me to make sense of the events in my life, yet, it was firmly based on exploring new thoughts about fundamental things like agriculture, education, architecture and medicine. I couldn't help concluding that part of what ultimately left Peter, this brilliant genius, so bereft was his inability to deal with physical tasks. His hands had never been educated. Now Judy had moved out (the second of his partners to seek solace in the countryside), leaving Peter alone and at the mercy of his demons.

Alcohol may temporarily take away the pain, but it releases a monster within that takes over, leaving the original person unrecognizable. Sometimes when he was drunk, Peter could be sweet and docile and funny, but he could also be angry and violent. The strange thing is, I seldom remember him being drunk in all our years together; he just could not bear to be out of control in those days. I visited him with the girls a couple of times in Perrins Walk. He was living almost like a tramp, knee-deep in unpaid bills, empty vodka bottles and cigarette stubs. How had this come to be? Surely something or someone could help, I used to wonder. How did his parents and sisters feel about this?

His sister Elizabeth views it as the downside of his effortless talent. 'It was all achieved so easily. Maybe it was a bit like Dudley and his musical gift: Peter didn't particularly know how he was doing what he did. Because what he did was so easy for him, it wasn't a matter of working. What you don't work at, well, it is hard to know that you are doing it.'

Of course, Peter did remain capable of connecting with some people and Suzy Kendall, divorced from Dudley in 1972, but still living around the corner from Peter, remembers there was plenty of surviving affection between our ex-husbands. After his two divorces Peter used to call around quite often, as did Dudley when he was in the country, accepting the role of godfather to Suzy's daughter, Elodie. 'Peter was always nice about Dudley, and vice versa,' she says. 'When Dudley did his solo benefit show at the Albert Hall, he gave us a box and we all went. Peter, who you know could be a bit caustic about people, turned around to us and said: "I just have so much admiration for Dudley. I could never have carried the whole of the Albert Hall myself."' When Dudley visited, Peter would come and see him, Suzy says. 'Contrary to what people say, they remained good friends.'

In time, after the girls had both taken cordon bleu cookery courses which have stood them in good stead for the rest of their lives, Lucy became a trained aromatherapist. She was born with healing hands and has been able to cure my headaches since the age of three. Now she lived in London with her American partner. Daisy had set up house with a school sweetheart, Simon Hardy, and, besides teaching English as a Foreign Language, had started to work seriously on her own painting. Lucy was in Swiss Cottage and often shopped in Hampstead. How much she would have loved to have been able to drop in and have a cup of coffee with her dad. There were even times when she bumped into him in Hampstead and he would make excuses or apparently be too busy to invite her in.

More than once she parked herself on his doorstep, knowing he was inside drinking himself to death, and pleading to be let in. She was desperately sad about it. Daisy would invite him to dinner; he would agree to come only to ring up at the last minute to say he wasn't well. It seemed he was too ashamed for them to see him as he had become. But they both loved him as their father, no matter what, and longed to be with him, at least from time to time. Occasionally he was able to show he cared, for instance making the long journey down to Devon to celebrate twenty-one-year-old Lucy's new job. 'I was working in the one-starred Michelin restaurant the Carved Angel and he actually came down to visit me,' she says, 'which was unheard of. He drove down. He was a terrible driver, he couldn't drive to save his life, but he was dead proud. Because Daisy had also trained for a while in cordon bleu, he always had a fantasy of opening a restaurant with us, but it never happened.'

The girls managed their grief quietly and steadfastly, sometimes confiding in me, but they knew it made me upset and frustrated to see the man I still cared about in apparent free fall.

Jonathan Miller suspects Peter's relationship with alcohol was almost a modish accessory at first, a badge of class. This wasn't the case with Dudley, he says. 'For Peter it was upper-class drunkenness. It was totally different for Dudley. Dudley was afflicted with being afflicted. He had this club foot. He was very small. And working class. He was very, very worried about being working class and coming from Dagenham, but at the same time he was this astounding musical talent. He wasn't a drunk, but he was very promiscuous for the simple reason that he was fantastically attractive. There wasn't a single model of the Kate Moss kind who wasn't in his trailer. He had this charm, this puckish charm.

'Peter was very different. He had what in fact certain public school boys have, an armour of decorum and of repression and, I suspect, also not quite knowing whether he was gay or not.'

By this point Peter and I were living in different worlds with different values. I felt helpless and I imagine Judy must have too. I still ponder on this downward spiral into alcoholism, while accepting it is a complex pathology. We grapple to understand how someone who, on the surface, has had the benefits of a good public school and a top university could become such a prisoner of addiction. The truth is, it can happen to anyone. The imposed self-discipline of early years in a public school, the cold showers and rigorous time-tabling may provide a thin veneer of conformity, but underneath can lie a teeming world of conflict, desires and ambition. Peter's emotional life was something of a mystery to him, only glimpsed haphazardly in the characters he created, much as he might have captured random figures on film in his days as a beach photographer. Certainly, his understanding of women was often utterly confused, but he was undoubtedly needy.

Eleanor Bron, who, late in Peter's life, was working again on a planned stage show with him, recognized this about Peter: 'We hadn't seen each other for many years because I was never that comfortable with him and I think he was not always comfortable with me, or women generally. He used to come and talk to me, though, because I think he wanted someone to talk to. He was one of these public school chaps who needed women, but didn't really like them very much. Somehow he had climbed over this hurdle and we were able to have a conversation.'

Peter picked Eleanor up in a car and immediately adopted a silly, cod middle-European accent which they both kept up for some time. However, she says, she sensed a change in him, something she put down to the therapy he said he was having. He was disciplined, too, it seems when it came to the work.

'It was very interesting to see that, whereas everybody thought he was spooling out in an undisciplined way, his first preoccupation was to improvise with the aim of then settling it and writing it all down, and then, when we had it solid, he would be able to go off and do his thing . . . and to be sure of being able to land. I thought, "What Peter needs is someone to talk to". And it must have happened with Dudley.'

Peter's biographer, the late television producer Harry Thompson, told me before he died in 2005 that he was not so convinced there was a resurgence of Peter's powers going on: 'I wasn't aware of any recovery. I wouldn't say I knew him well, but I wouldn't say most of the people who were around him at the end knew him properly at all.'

Jean Hart occasionally bumped into him in Hampstead and they passed time together in a tea shop. Peter even suggested they should don hats if they were going to do this often. 'It was quite embarrassing,' says Jean, 'because a lot of the ladies there obviously knew who he was, but very studiously pretended they didn't know and so they would talk very loudly, so we didn't think they were listening. How it went was all dependent on how much he had had to drink. Sometimes he was very, very drunk and I didn't really enjoy that. He quite liked cream cakes, which I found odd, but that might have been the alcohol.'

Eventually Peter did ask for help and joined AA groups, where I believe, predictably, he had everyone in stitches and avoided the exacting work of self-scrutiny. Strangely enough, I met someone later who had been part of one of these groups and I did hear a little, although understandably the participants were sworn to confidentiality. As the years passed, friends shared with me Peter's increasing emotionality, his new ability to shed tears in public and to talk more readily about personal matters. It may well have been true that he changed. While we were still in the process of parting, I received a letter from him that was quite candid about the closeness he felt to the ailing Alec, his father, who was recovering from a stroke, as he helped him to undress.

Right until the end he had a good history of responding to emergencies with decisiveness and authority (as he had done that day when we were stranded in Athens). His sister Elizabeth remembers his calm tones when he had to call her back from a holiday in Africa because their mother was ill, for example. 'He was really fantastic. He did everything he could not to alarm me, because he knew how impotent I would feel.'

Similarly, when my own father was taken to hospital and my mother given a wrong diagnosis, it was Peter who intervened and complained forcibly to the medical staff. Usually something got done, such was his commanding nature. Yet left to his own devices, he seemed to be uncoiling fast.

Roger Law came across Peter at a party at around this time and asked him how he was earning a living. He told Roger he was doing commercials and was on edge that night because he was waiting to hear back about one campaign that would mean he would not have to do anything else for a year. This was a sad contrast to the human dynamo Roger had known at Cambridge.

There was a last-ditch attempt too to bring the *Beyond the Fringe* team back together at least once socially, as Alan Bennett recalls: 'Dudley's wife, Brogan Lane, had a notion we should all get together. So we went up to a Hampstead restaurant in about 1988, Dudley and Jonathan and me. And then Peter rang from Hillingdon to say he couldn't get there. He just wasn't particularly bothered.'

For Christopher Booker an earlier incident sticks out as an indication of how Peter was living. In 1979 Peter had offered to tape a television programme that Christopher was making for him. A few months later they both tried to find the relevant tape in Peter's collection: 'There were three or four hundred videos,' says Christopher. 'We watched blank screens. Buzz and crackles and nothing. We tried for about forty minutes and found nothing. It was a very good image of what had happened to him.'

The other Christopher – Christopher Logue – had pulled back from friendship in reaction to the heavy drinking, he says: 'Very uncharitably, I couldn't put up with his drunkenness. I should have been much more kind and patient. I was selfish about it. People are boring when they are drunk. And also I would have Peter in the car sometimes and he would be drunk and I would be driving along and just afraid of what was going to happen to us. He could be uncontrollable.'

Despite his addiction, friends and admirers still loved him for his flashes of brilliance. One of the most frequently quoted examples of his mordant wit in later life is the response he gave to David Frost's unexpected telephone invitation to go to dinner with Prince Andrew and Fergie; Peter paused dramatically, noisily thumbed through his diary, and then said, 'I see I am watching telly that evening.' This line catches the free-spirited, anti-sycophantic streak in Peter: I loved that too.

Soon the girls and I started to hear about Lin Chong, the Chinese woman he had met at one of Victor Lownes' house parties. First she was tidying up his house, and next his life. One day, Peter uncharacteristically asked me out to dinner in his local Italian restaurant to meet Lin. It was the only time I met her. Nevertheless, I could instantly feel her intentions towards Peter; it was as though she had put up a barbed wire fence around him. She didn't say much, but Peter was more animated than I had seen him for a while, so I thought this might be a good thing.

Lucy and Daisy were happy for their father to begin with: it looked as though they might be included a bit more. But on the occasions they visited, Lin appeared jealous of the signs of affection Peter showed them. There were several angry out-bursts. Harriet remembers taking Daisy over to see Peter one afternoon. 'After about half an hour, the awkwardness was being got over,' she recalls. 'Then we heard this extraordinary noise of all the china being swept off the shelf in the kitchen onto the floor below. Lin had come back and was furious we were there. So we got ourselves together and left.'

This kind of thing was devastating for the girls, so utterly starved had they been of their father's presence. They tolerated this rather precarious situation as the only way to be with him from time to time.

Daisy and Simon had done a fair amount of travel to exotic destinations through Simon's work as a BBC news journalist – to Indonesia, Africa and Korea. Returning from a trip to South America in 1994, she broke the news that, after eight years together, she and Simon had decided to get married. I was really pleased. Daisy glowed at the thought that one of her long-term ambitions would be realized: both parents would be present on her special day. She and Simon, the son of the local doctor, would be married in September in our village church and she would be given away by her father. We took over our friend Rose's old rectory and the night before her hair was fixed in rag-ringlets as I read to her, by candlelight, from her childhood favourite, *The Little Prince*. In the corner an ivory-white satin bridal gown hung, with a lace veil cascading down beside it.

Not far away, inside a posh hotel in the Ashdown Forest, the bridegroom and his brother were entertaining Peter. The next day – like my own wedding day in New York – was squally with sunny bursts. Daisy looked radiant and mischievous, with one little ringlet dangling down her forehead. The rest of the family gathered at the Hardys' house and were decorated with nosegays. I wore a yellow rose pinned onto my corn-coloured wild silk dress.

We made our way to the church and sat in nervous anticipation at the front, handkerchiefs at the ready. Peter arrived with Daisy under a protective umbrella (no press had got wind of this occasion). As the organ played, father and daughter appeared, he looking smart in a grey suit. My heart was fluttering – many emotions jostled with each other, but the predominant one was love, love for our beautiful daughter and for handsome and dashing Simon. The fruit of my life and Peter's life was on display on this day: swords were sheathed and good memories prevailed.

The service had many of us in tears. Later, as we were standing by the register, Peter, speechless with emotion, gave me a look which seemed to say, 'Well done! You've done a good job with them!' Pure pride shone in our eyes: we were surrounded by wonderful friends. The reception afterwards was in a lovely country pub and Peter attempted his special brand of dancing. By now his frame was quite large, though, and he decided it was safer to sit down. Such an important event in our lives – and the last time I saw Peter.

Epilogue

Monday 9 January 1995 was a bright and sunny morning in Campanet, Mallorca. I was about to put on my watch when I noticed it had stopped. 'That's odd,' I thought. I had only recently had a new battery put in. A friend was there when the telephone rang. It was Lucy to tell me that Peter had died, just around the time my watch stopped. He had suffered a haemorrhage brought on by liver disease.

I knew he was ill, but was unprepared and felt much like Dudley, who, on learning of Peter's death, said, 'The fucker's gone! There's a hole in the universe!'

We were not the only ones to feel this, because whatever else might have been on the news that night was banished; eulogies and sketches filled the TV screen over the following days. No matter that Peter had been largely unemployed during the preceding fifteen years, the accolades poured in and really haven't stopped. Despite his tearing so much down, he had occupied a special place in many people's hearts. The character of that universal armchair philosopher, E. L. Wisty, in particular, seems to have chimed with the public: it recognized some sort of lonely archetype.

Peter, a man, I think, of irreducible complexity, had from his first months and years pushed at his boundaries, constantly looking for resistance. Eventually he met some – certainly in me. I sensed our relationship would lead to mutual destruction and opted out, perhaps prematurely. But in revisiting our youth and marriage I now feel such sadness at how self-centred we both were, part of an increasingly egotistical culture in which boredom – particularly in Peter's case – was a perennial threat. We lived in a battleground of the sexes: in previous times men and women had their circumscribed roles; for us, it was no longer the case. Although I never burned my bra, I did sympathize with the cause. Nowadays Peter would not have been able to cut me off with so little financial support after twelve years of cohabitation, never mind marriage. And when I witness the relationships my daughters enjoy with their partners, where childcare and chores are shared, I wonder whether our marriage would have stood a better chance of survival if there had been more sharing.

My first reaction on hearing of the death was to book a flight to be with my daughters. Upon arrival I rang Lucy and Daisy. Lucy was very grave on the phone. Apart from the loss, they had been told I would not be welcome at the funeral – Lin's decree. I felt numb. Judy was also banished. Not only was Lin trying to own him in life, but now he had gone she still seemed to want to possess him.

I felt like Elizabeth Cook's Achilles: 'The arrow went into his breast, where it continues to bleed, a steady agonising leak of blood . . . It feels as if the arrow is still embedded.'

The last thing I wanted to do was to worsen the situation for my daughters, but part of me wished they had stood up for my right to attend the funeral. I contacted a wise old friend, Diana Girdwood, and together we created our own service for Peter, which was a help to me. One has to find ways to grieve, an activity that our culture seems to find embarrassing. At a later date a star-studded memorial was staged at the very church Peter and I had often attended. Of course, I wasn't invited and neither was Judy. Even our daughters would have been excluded, but for some pressure applied by friends.

Ten years on, the tributes still pile in. No one can compare with Peter. Harry Thompson had an acute appreciation of his subject's gifts, and his torments. He told me before he died that Peter had what all great comics have, 'a pathological need' to be the centre of attention. 'If they weren't funny, they would be doing something else,' he said. 'They would be riding a motorcycle over the edge of a mountain or something. They just want to be looked at.'

Our old friend Tariq Ali still carries the strong impression that Peter could have been almost anything he wanted to be. 'I was too young to think, though, "Is something haunting him?" I didn't want to know,' he says now. 'Clearly he was a very tormented guy on many levels.'

Today I often wonder, had Peter had the choice between a stable, balanced life, or the roller-coaster ride he took, which path he might have chosen. If he had opted for calm and peace the world would have been deprived of a jewel, but there might have been fewer broken hearts around.

Index

Index

Index

Index

Index

HarperCollins*Publishers* would like to thank the following for providing written material and photographs and for permission to reproduce copyright material.

While every effort has been made to trace the owners of copyright material reproduced herein, the publishers would like to apologise for any omissions and will be pleased to incorporate missing acknowledgements in any future correspondence.

Text credits

Peter Pan © 1937 Great Ormond Street Hospital for Children Extracts from *Peter Pan and Wendy* by J M Barrie reproduced with kind permission of Great Ormond Street Hospital for Children

The Whole Woman by Germaine Greer © Germaine Greer (Anchor)

Achilles by Elizabeth Cook © Elizabeth Cook (Methuen)

The Divided Self by R D Laing © RD Laing (Penguin)

Goodbye to All That by Robert Graves © Robert Graves (Carcanet)

Picture credits

p.252 © PA/Empics: p. 295 © The Kobal Collection, London: page 318 © Topfoto

Plate section one: page 3; top, bottom right and bottom left © John Bulmer: page 4; photographs © Ian Flemming; article © Varsity Publications, Cambridge: page 5; top, middle and bottom © John Bulmer: page 6; top © Christopher Angeloglou; bottom © Peter Goodlife: page 7 © Popperfoto

Plate section two: page 1; © Lewis Morley Archive / National Portrait Gallery, London

Plate section three: page 1; © Mirrorpix: page 6; bottom © Mirrorpix

All other photographs are from the author's personal collection.

C3723

WEAVERS REST HOME